THE NEW MIDDLE AGES

BONNIE WHEELER, *Series Editor*

The New Middle Ages is a series dedicated to pluridisciplinary studies of medieval cultures, with particular emphasis on recuperating women's history and on feminist and gender analyses. This peer-reviewed series includes both scholarly monographs and essay collections.

PUBLISHED BY PALGRAVE:

Women in the Medieval Islamic World: Power, Patronage, and Piety
 edited by Gavin R. G. Hambly

The Ethics of Nature in the Middle Ages: On Boccaccio's Poetaphysics
 by Gregory B. Stone

Presence and Presentation: Women in the Chinese Literati Tradition
 edited by Sherry J. Mou

The Lost Love Letters of Heloise and Abelard: Perceptions of Dialogue in Twelfth-Century France
 by Constant J. Mews

Understanding Scholastic Thought with Foucault
 by Philipp W. Rosemann

For Her Good Estate: The Life of Elizabeth de Burgh
 by Frances A. Underhill

Constructions of Widowhood and Virginity in the Middle Ages
 edited by Cindy L. Carlson and Angela Jane Weisl

Motherhood and Mothering in Anglo-Saxon England
 by Mary Dockray-Miller

Listening to Heloise: The Voice of a Twelfth-Century Woman
 edited by Bonnie Wheeler

The Postcolonial Middle Ages
 edited by Jeffrey Jerome Cohen

Chaucer's Pardoner *and Gender Theory: Bodies of Discourse*
 by Robert S. Sturges

Crossing the Bridge: Comparative Essays on Medieval European and Heian Japanese Women Writers
 edited by Barbara Stevenson and Cynthia Ho

Engaging Words: The Culture of Reading in the Later Middle Ages
 by Laurel Amtower

Robes and Honor: The Medieval World of Investiture
 edited by Stewart Gordon

Representing Rape in Medieval and Early Modern Literature
 edited by Elizabeth Robertson and Christine M. Rose

Same Sex Love and Desire among Women in the Middle Ages
 edited by Francesca Canadé Sautman and Pamela Sheingorn

Sight and Embodiment in the Middle Ages: Ocular Desires
 by Suzannah Biernoff

Listen, Daughter: The Speculum Virginum *and the Formation of Religious Women in the Middle Ages*
 edited by Constant J. Mews

Science, the Singular, and the Question of Theology
 by Richard A. Lee, Jr.

Gender in Debate from the Early Middle Ages to the Renaissance
 edited by Thelma S. Fenster and Clare A. Lees

Malory's Morte D'Arthur: *Remaking Arthurian Tradition*
 by Catherine Batt

MARGARET PASTON'S PIETY

Joel T. Rosenthal

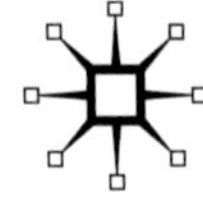

MARGARET PASTON'S PIETY
Copyright © Joel T. Rosenthal, 2010.

First published in 2010 by
PALGRAVE MACMILLAN®
in the United States—a division of St. Martin's Press LLC,
175 Fifth Avenue, New York, NY 10010.

Where this book is distributed in the UK, Europe and the rest of the world,
this is by Palgrave Macmillan, a division of Macmillan Publishers Limited,
registered in England, company number 785998, of Houndmills,
Basingstoke, Hampshire RG21 6XS.

Palgrave Macmillan is the global academic imprint of the above companies
and has companies and representatives throughout the world.

Palgrave® and Macmillan® are registered trademarks in the United States,
the United Kingdom, Europe and other countries.

ISBN: 978–0–230–62207–4

Library of Congress Cataloging-in-Publication Data

Rosenthal, Joel Thomas, 1934–
    Margaret Paston's piety / Joel T. Rosenthal.
      p. cm.—(The new Middle Ages)
    ISBN 978–0–230–62207–4 (alk. paper)
     1. Paston, Margaret, 1423–1484. 2. Paston, Margaret, 1423–1484—
Religion. 3. Paston, Margaret, 1423–1484—Literary art. 4. Gentry—
England—Biography. 5. England—Social life and
customs—1066–1485—Sources. 6. Letter writing—History—
To 1500—Sources. 7. Paston, Margaret, 1423–1484—Correspondence.
8. Paston family—Correspondence. I. Paston letters. II. Title.

DA247.P27R67 2010
942.04092—dc22   2010001969
[B]

A catalogue record of the book is available from the British Library.

Design by Newgen Imaging Systems (P) Ltd., Chennai, India.

First edition: August 2010

10 9 8 7 6 5 4 3 2 1

Printed in the United States of America.

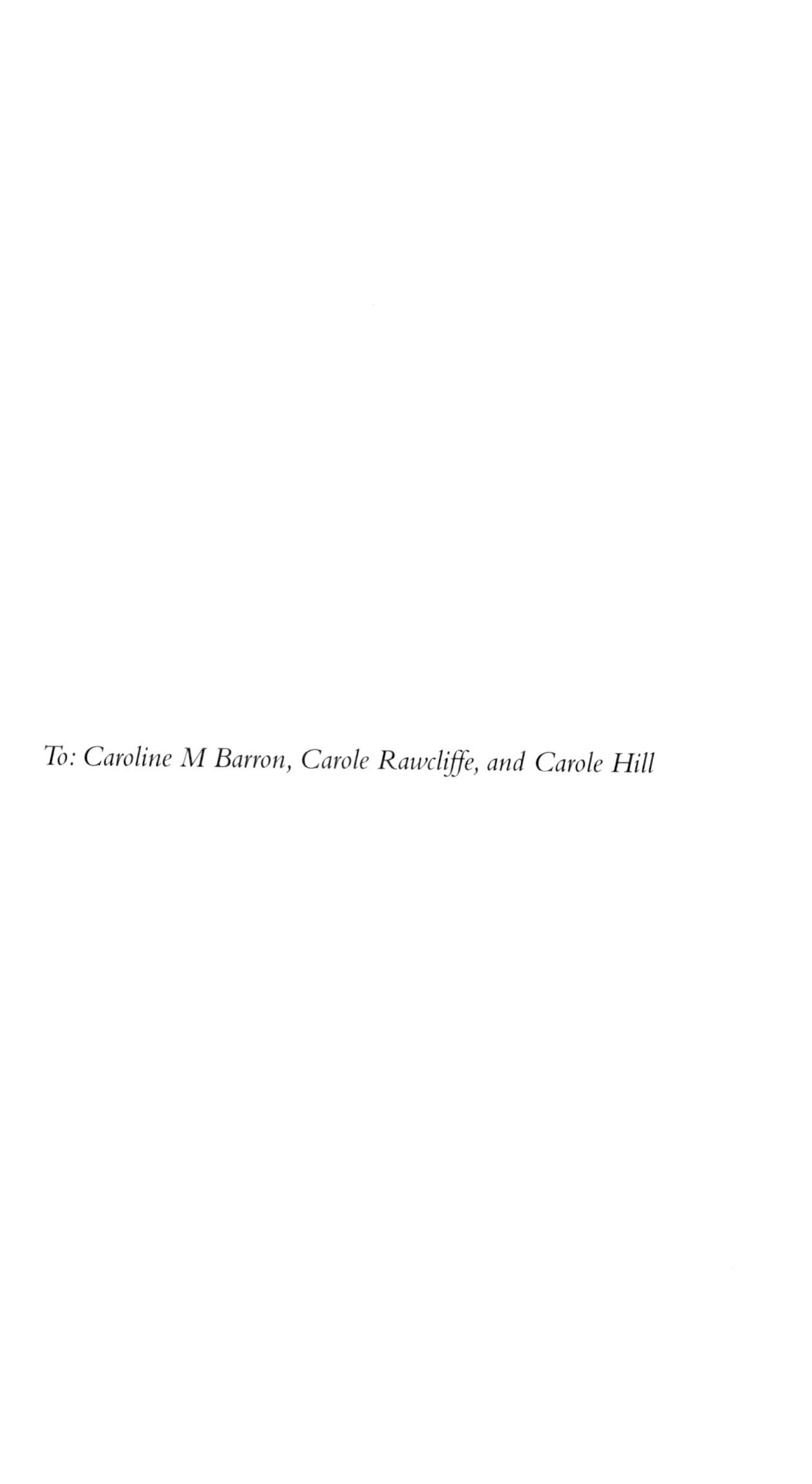

To: Caroline M Barron, Carole Rawcliffe, and Carole Hill

CONTENTS

TABLES

ILLUSTRATIONS

Maps

Figures

PREFACE

A long look at the religious life and practice of Margaret Paston, matriarch of the Pastons through much of the middle of the fifteenth century, can be characterized as an exercise in trying to learn more and more about less and less. This is a case study, a close reading, of sources that offer us the unusual opportunity to see how conventional religious conviction, expression, and behavior were integrated into the long, busy, and complicated life of a pious laywoman. What has drawn me to Margaret Paston is the premise that while she carried her spirituality with her at all times and in all circumstances, she never became a woman of enthusiasm; never given to mystical visions or inner revelations, let alone waves of revulsion against the life she was leading. In fact she almost never talked about her faith *per se*. She was a worldly figure—heiress, wife, mother, widow, and one who does not seem to have had any ambivalence (let alone any guilt or remorse) about either her sexuality or her rather lofty economic and social status. And since it behooves a social historian to look for what we can learn and reconstruct about daily—if not quite ordinary—life, Margaret Paston steps forward, an unwitting but informative subject for our inquiry.

Margaret Paston has drawn my interest over the course of many years. An interest in women's lives, in the religion of the late medieval laity, in family structure and intrafamilial interaction, and in the nature of epistolary expression have all come together in this study as I have worked my way through her letters and her will. Though she has hardly been neglected by historians (albeit her role as an author has been slighted), little effort has been made to gauge the extent to which Margaret Paston can stand on her own. We mostly know her as a vital link in the chain of the Paston family enterprise and correspondence, and we think of her in this setting. However, I try to work in these essays to separate her from the others and to see how much individualization we can extract from (or impose upon) her own words.

I first learned about the Paston letters and the family that produced them when H. Stanley Bennett came to the University of Chicago as a visiting professor in the late 1950s. Though the family's letters and papers had been edited and published by John Fenn (starting in 1787, and he got knighted for his efforts), and then by James Gairdner in the late nineteenth century, and most recently (and definitively) by Norman Davis in the 1970s, and have been well explicated by Colin Richmond and Helen Castor in recent years, it was Bennett who really put the Pastons into the agenda of social history with his marvelous *The England of the Pastons: Studies in an Age of Transition* (1922 for its first edition). When he came to Chicago Bennett had recently completed his little volume *Six Medieval Men and Women* (1955), much in the model of his friend Eileen Power's classic *Medieval People* (1924 for its first edition) and in Bennett's deceptively learned collection of biographical essays he had chapters on both Sir John Fastolf and Margaret Paston. In his seminar, as we read and discussed the letters, he made the Pastons—John III and his love match, the fierce mothering of Agnes and Margaret, the amiable John II, and the others—into distinct people with personalities and eccentricities. If I have followed in his footsteps and have been able to add to our picture of Margaret Paston, I like to think that I absorbed something from his lectures and seminar, and I pay tribute here to the guidance and the enthusiasm that he shared so long ago.

As prefaces are wont to say, books seem to be a long time coming and many friends and colleagues have been supportive and sympathetic. I want to indicate a debt to Roger Virgoe, an old friend with whom—long before I expected to write about them myself—I discussed ways of focusing on the Pastons. Questions about the family that we mulled over in Robin DuBoulay's seminar in London, when I was a graduate student, are among the issues I have tried to address in these essays. And every historian owes a debt to the institutions within which he (and she) has been able to work. The Institute of Historical Research of the University of London and the New York Public Library have been my main historiographical hunting grounds, with help for manuscripts from the British Library, the Bodleian at Oxford, and the Spencer Collection of the New York Public.

Over the years colleagues have invited me to air bits of this work at conferences and seminars at Leeds, Cambridge, San Francisco, Chicago, and London. Gail McMurray Gibson had enough faith in my treatment of the family letters to invite me to write about them for the *Oxford Encyclopedia of British Literature*. Naomi Braun Rosenthal has been casual about my long-term affair with Margaret Paston, assuming that in due course it would prove to be just a passing infatuation. Many thanks to Bonnie Wheeler, editor of the "New Middle Ages" series, as well as to the in-house and always helpful editors ensconced in the Flatiron Building and to the anonymous reader who advised me on how to tighten and focus my comments. Special thanks to N. W. Benson and C. M. Benson for their cheerful tolerance of the inconvenience caused them when I came to London "to look things up." And regarding those friends to whom I dedicate this volume; in various combinations and at numerous times they have discussed Margaret Paston with me, read earlier versions of this work, encouraged me to finish it, and—neither last nor least—have taken me on tours of churches and pubs in Norwich and through the lonely and often bitterly cold countryside of rural Norfolk, all in an effort to help me run down what is left of "what did Margaret see."

ABBREVIATIONS

Blomefield—Francis Blomefield (and Charles Parkin), *An Essay towards the Topography of the County of Norfolk* (11 vols., London, 1805–10).

Cely—Alison Hanham, ed., *The Cely Letters and Papers, 1472–1485,* EETS, o.s. 273 (1975).

EETS—Early English Text Society

Gairdner—James Gairdner, ed., *The Paston Letters, 1422–1590 A.D.* (3 vols., Westminster: Constable, 1895).

NA—Norfolk Archaeological Society

ODNB—*Oxford Dictionary of National Biography* (Oxford: Oxford University Press, 2004).

Plumpton—Joan Kirby, ed., *The Plumpton Letters and Papers,* Camden Society, fifth series, 8 (1990).

Stonor—Christine Carpenter, ed., *Kingsford's Stonor Letters and Papers, 1290–1483* (Cambridge: Cambridge University Press, 1996).

VCH—Victoria County History

References to Norman Davis's edition of the Paston letters are simply given by volume and the number of the letter or paper (for example: I, 230).

CHAPTER 1

READING THE RELIGIOUS LIFE OF MARGARET PASTON

This inquiry into lay or popular religion in the fifteenth century is a brief on behalf of Margaret Mautby Paston. If we wish to reconstruct the religious life of the late medieval English laity, whether female or male, it is hard to do much better than to follow in her footsteps, footsteps she has left by way of her 100-plus extant letters and her long and elaborate will of 1482.[1] These documents, set and read in the context of the Paston family letters and papers, provide an epistolary or literary pathway into a territory of religious expression and conviction that stretches in time from Margaret's earliest letters, written as a newlywed and newcomer to the Paston family enterprise in the early 1440s, through her final missives of the late 1470s and her will, written two years before her death in November 1484. In adopting this approach we are in effect signing on for the long march; case studies are not easily constructed for medieval women and men.[2] Accordingly, I recognize from the start that the journey is going to be one that lacks those high points of spiritual drama and personal revelation that others of Margaret's day and world sometimes provide. If the choice I am making in this study is between siding with the tortoise or with the hare, there is no question but that I come down, quite firmly, on behalf of the former.

★   ★   ★

Margaret Mautby was born in the early or mid-1420s, the heiress of an East Anglian gentry family of reasonable wealth, good connections, and a minor but legitimate claim to descent from the nobility. In the early 1440s she was introduced to her prospective bridegroom, John Paston, eldest son and heir of Judge William Paston, a local boy who had made good by virtue of the law and the many lucrative and useful connections to which it had led. Margaret and John found each other to be appropriate partners, as we judge from the letter her prospective mother-in-law Agnes Paston sent to William, and the young couple entered into a marriage that lasted until John died, a man in middle age, in 1466.[3] This marriage was a real step up for the Paston heir: a "coup," in the words of one student of the letters, or "a very good match for the son of a professional lawyer," as another reader has characterized it—and the advantage for the Pastons lay as much, perhaps, in Margaret's family connections (particularly with Sir John Fastolf) as it was for her substantial dowry.[4] During the course of their years together Margaret bore at least seven children (five boys, two girls), and she invariably stood as the reliable and dutiful bulwark of Paston family fortunes and enterprises. These had often taken a dire turn—as when Lord Moleyns drove them out of Gresham, or when John's claim to be heir of Sir John Fastolf opened years of legal contention and violence, or when the duke of Norfolk drove them out of Caister, or when Hellesden was sacked by the duke of Suffolk's men, or when John was outlawed and imprisoned. After John's death in 1466 Margaret had difficult relations with her two eldest sons, John II (d. 1479) and John III (d. 1504), and in the mid-1470s she "retired" to her natal family's old manorial headquarters at Mautby. It was there at Mautby that she came to the end of her long days, making her will in 1482 and dying in 1484, and requesting burial in the chantry in the new south aisle of the parish church of St Peter and St Paul at Mautby that she was now subsidizing with her testamentary benefactions.

Though we have no specific information about why the Paston letters and papers of the fifteenth century were preserved, it seems not unlikely that Margaret—the stay-at-home clearinghouse and communications director of and for family affairs—had some considerable hand in the decision—whether made in a deliberative fashion or just as a matter of convenience or inadvertence—to keep letters and drafts of letters as well as various other kinds of business papers that might be of value, especially in that never-ending world of litigation that occupied so much of the collective or extended family's time and energy.[5] Her role as the dutiful, reliable, loyal (with an occasional quibble), and efficient wife to her patriarchal husband has been noted—and usually accorded a complimentary assessment—by virtually all students of the Pastons and their letters and of the late medieval gentry in general. James Gairdner refers to her as "a most devoted wife…a woman not only of great force of character but of truly affectionate nature." Colin Richmond gives her the accolade of being "God's Englishwoman," and Roger Virgoe added some compliments for the way she gained confidence in her judgment and stayed her

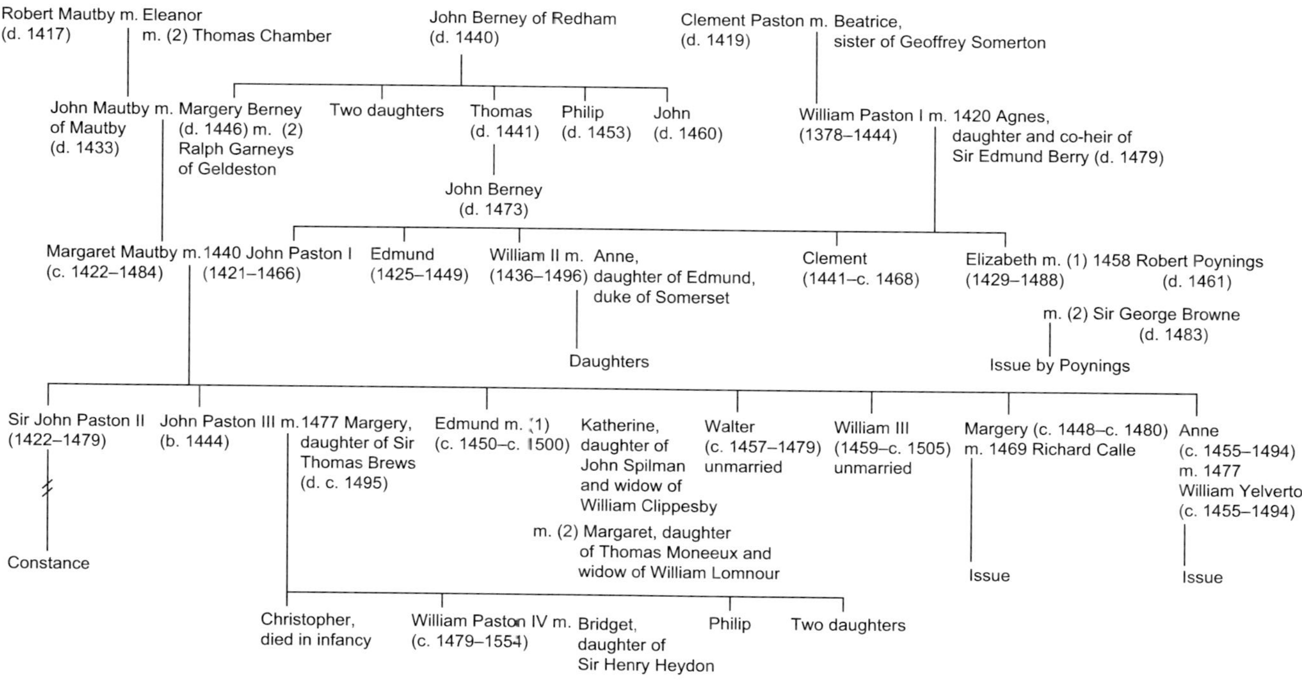

The Paston Family
Robert Mautby m. Eleanor
(d. 1417)   m. (2) Thomas Chamber
John Berney of Redham
(d. 1440)
Clement Paston m. Beatrice,
sister of Geoffrey Somerton
(d. 1419)
John Mautby m. Margery Berney
of Mautby   (d. 1446) m. (2)
(d. 1433)   Ralph Garneys
of Geldeston
Two daughters
Thomas
(d. 1441)
Philip
(d. 1453)
John
(d. 1460)
William Paston I m. 1420 Agnes,
(1378–1444)   daughter and co-heir of
Sir Edmund Berry (d. 1479)
John Berney
(d. 1473)
Margaret Mautby m. 1440 John Paston I
(c. 1422–1484)   (1421–1466)
Edmund
(1425–1449)
William II m. Anne,
(1436–1496) daughter of Edmund,
duke of Somerset
Clement
(1441–c. 1468)
Elizabeth m. (1) 1458 Robert Poynings
(1429–1488)   (d. 1461)
m. (2) Sir George Browne
(d. 1483)
Daughters
Issue by Poynings
Sir John Paston II
(1422–1479)
John Paston III m. 1477 Margery,
(b. 1444)   daughter of Sir
Thomas Brews
(d. c. 1495)
Edmund m. (1)
(c. 1450–c. 1500)
Katherine,
daughter of
John Spilman
and widow of
William Clippesby
m. (2) Margaret, daughter
of Thomas Moneeux and
widow of William Lomnour
Walter
(c. 1457–1479)
unmarried
William III
(1459–c. 1505)
unmarried
Margery (c. 1448–c. 1480)
m. 1469 Richard Calle
Anne
(c. 1455–1494)
m. 1477
William Yelverton
(c. 1455–1494)
Constance
Christopher,
died in infancy
William Paston IV m. Bridget,
(c. 1479–1554)   daughter of
Sir Henry Heydon
Philip
Two daughters
Issue
Issue

ground to give John I advice, even when she knew he was not likely to welcome what she was saying.[6]

Though she has come in for her share of kudos, there are two aspects of Margaret Mautby Paston's long and active life that have tended to be slighted. One has to do with her unrecognized and unheralded status as a writer, a woman who produced a great deal of English prose (all in the form of letters that were dictated to a variety of scribes, including several of her sons). The other touches her religious life: her identity as a conventional, pious, sober (and feminine) representative of late medieval lay religion. By any standard we can apply she was a pious woman, typical of her day and always well within the boundaries of orthodox expression and behavior. Therefore, that her life and letters open a lid on a woman's spirituality makes her an inviting, if reticent, object of inquiry, as it makes the relative neglect of this side of her life even more surprising. Her immense value and importance as a case study of the typical, the ordinary, has been eclipsed by other religious figures of her day, women of flamboyant but atypical religiosity. It is Margery Kempe and Julian of Norwich who have drawn so much scholarly (and even popular) interest, and they do so because they are strikingly atypical, and the mystic and the weeping breast-beater certainly differed from their contemporaries in some obvious and arresting ways. However, in the analysis I offer below my hypothesis or my unwavering opinion is that Margaret Paston was conventional in virtually every respect, and that it is this persona that makes her such an important and attractive centerpiece for a case study of spiritual life as part of daily life.[7]

As a writer of English prose, an author, Margaret Paston has been sadly and rather strangely overlooked. Though the language of her letters has been examined in great (and sympathetic) detail by Norman Davis, as he worked toward his monumental edition of the Paston letters, the value and interest of Margaret's corpus of 104 letters, beyond what they tell about family enterprises of all sorts, does not seem to have attracted much interest.[8] Reference volumes and surveys of British authors, whether looking at women writers or at medieval authors both male and female, give her little or no mention when they list the prominent writers of the day, though Norman Davis points out that we have the significant total of some 60,000 words as she dictated them, from mouth to paper.[9] Though vindicating her role or rescuing this side of Margaret Paston as a writer of English prose is hardly my main purpose here, a word on her behalf does not seem amiss. Given that I am about to subject much of what she wrote to a close examination—for its wording, for her reliance on and frequent use of casual and stock phrases of pious intent, or her heavy use of such throwaway references as the saint's day on which a letter was written, as well as for more obvious pointers to religious life—a tribute to the ease with which she turned to letter writing as a reliable and significant form of communication seems appropriate. If she was primarily the rock at the home base who kept the itinerant members of the Paston world abreast of their own and other people's affairs, we should remember that she did so through the medium of well-articulated English prose as it was put to paper, time after time, year after year, letter after letter. She was a champion of epistolary expression, both in terms of the quantity of extant material and of the variety of topics touched upon. She stands out, among all the other men and women we encounter in the various collections of fifteenth-century family letters, for her long-term activity over the decades and for the many windows her letters open, sometimes by design and sometimes almost by inadvertence, coincidence, or mere chance. As Colin Richmond says, "she wrote at any time"—at all hours, from all the places at which we can trace her over the years.[10]

Of special concern in the essays that follow is what Margaret Paston tells us—or allows us to know—about her spiritual life. That she is a valuable source for an assessment of lay religiosity by itself poses an interesting challenge, for virtually nowhere in all her writings, with the exception of a few clauses in her will and one tale of a pilgrimage to Walsingham or an injunction to attend mass and to accept God's will, does she focus on spiritual concerns. There are numerous related areas of activity that touch upon the Church as an institution more than as the center of a belief system, and in her references to such matters we do learn a fair amount, over the years, about Margaret's secular dealing with various clerics, about her interest in maintaining a license for her private chapel, about filling the ecclesiastical livings over which the family had control, and about other such aspects of worldly interaction and negotiation between the laity and the Church and its personnel. But nothing at all in her letters about internal spirituality, nothing about private devotions (beyond the existence of that chapel), and, until the end and her will, nothing about her concern for her soul, either in this world or in that to come. As we shall see, she was eager to invoke God's blessing for her near and dear, but this is pretty thin material on which to probe deeper convictions. She was laconic about private matters, if always dutiful and orthodox. But as an indication of the inextricable mesh of what we term the secular and the spiritual, in the body of her letters she sheds much light on the religious convictions and practices of an unexceptional woman in the century before the coming of the Reformation, which would make decisions about faith into a contested chapter of the public agenda.

Much of what I have to say in introducing Margaret Paston takes the peculiar form of discussing what she was not. There are many areas of interest touching lay religion in the fifteenth century that we explore for indications of devotion, commitment, articulation, erudition, individuality, and enthusiasm. In most of these areas Margaret Paston gives us a negative return; she is "the county not heard from" *par excellence*. We may not learn much about possible or sporadic descents into valleys of despair and anomie at times when life must have seemed pretty bleak, but we know even less about any interest on her part about climbing the peaks. Some of this may be due to gaps in the letters, as in that period around the death of John I, but some certainly seems to be that it is her style—her choice of what she was given to talking about and not talking about.

One line of approach, and one that opens on to a somewhat more positive note, at least in terms of a methodology that helps frame our inquiry, is to set what we can learn about Margaret's spiritual life into the context of a family study, one that deals with her as one of the Pastons and one that sees the Pastons in an aggregate fashion. They were a small but definable social unit bounded by time and kinship boundaries. The family approach for social history has often proved to be a useful and attractive line of scholarly presentation, and there are numerous families of Margaret's world that have left enough information about their spiritual lives and dealings with the Church to be worth explicating in this fashion.[11] The drawback, of course, is that aggregating the data we have about a family as a unit or micro social universe diffuses the light from any beam we might hope to turn on a given individual, if and when we are fortunate enough to have sufficient information about that one person. As an approach to a study of this particular family, "the religion of the Pastons" has been treated a number of times. Clear and incisive chapters in H. S. Bennett's pathbreaking study combine a close reading of the Paston letters with instructive generalizations about late medieval religious life of the gentry.[12] Papers that focused on the family's religious life by David Knowles, written many years ago, and by Gillian Pritchard, offered more recently, have covered familiar ground and in doing so have offered many insights. In Colin Richmond's long treatment of the Pastons, especially in his third volume, he offers assessments of their spirituality and looks at some of them (especially Margaret and John II) in considerable detail.[13] But an assumption of and a problem with such a family-in-aggregate approach is that it tends to look for, and therefore to focus on, common behavioral patterns within the bonded social universe under analysis. In grouping together the members of the family we tend to take what we know about the more visible members and impose their behavior upon others who have less to say for themselves. In some of what follows I will work to separate Margaret from the pack, though my level of success varies with different realms of activity and the different modes of expression we encounter.

An inquiry into the religious life of a given family like the Pastons, when they are considered as a social unit or defined universe, is a subset or a segment of more general inquiry into the religious life and practices of the late medieval gentry. This is an area of scholarly investigation that has been conducted in recent years with some degree of heat.[14] Whether or not those who have contributed to the discussion (or debate) are always willing to acknowledge that they write with an eye on the coming of the Reformation, our awareness of what would come to pass in the early sixteenth century does seem to color their reading of the material and the conclusions they draw from their reading. Questions about the privatization of religious practice—private chapels, individual prayers, reading one's own book of hours, segregated pews in church, a growing emphasis on a personal dialogue with Christ by way of a greater concentration on his physical suffering and the roles of his own family members—have all been raised. Some scholars argue that the "old religion" remained vital into if not through Henrician times, accepting the idea that the Reformation in England was indeed an act of the state, rather than of faith and believers.[15] Others have held that by the fifteenth century the privatization and laicization of religious expression and worship had weakened the old structure of the Church and the egalitarian theories of Christianity that had prevailed and supported it over the centuries, thereby making both the faith itself and its institutional guardians more susceptible to changes imposed from above. Seams were being strained, if not actually ripped open, in what was supposedly the seamless garment of Christ's Church—or so some have argued.

But wherever the compass needle in this discussion comes to rest, such debates do look back at the fifteenth century and try to read its tea leaves as a guide to the future. While this may be a challenging enterprise it is not the best way to assess the spiritual world of Margaret Paston. She knew not Luther and had no inkling of what would become "the king's great business" at the time of her grandchildren and their children. Moreover, and certainly more relevant for an assessment of fifteenth-century spirituality, there are virtually no indications in the Paston letters that the great schism of the fourteenth century or the conciliar movement of the fifteenth or the new papal concern for making Rome the center of renaissance art and worship had any effect on religion as people in England treated it as part of daily life. If the fall of Constantinople in 1453 seems to have gone unnoticed—or at least unmentioned—we can hardly expect any great interest in the disputes among the schoolmen of Paris or the temporary victories of Hus's followers in far-off Bohemia. Rather, taking Margaret Paston on her own terms—not those of a larger Christendom, and not those formulated with an eye on changes yet to come, and not those shaped by autobiographical outpourings—is what we have to do. I talk below about the importance of avoiding the temptation of grading her for her levels of spirituality or behavior, whatever comparative yardstick we might choose. Was Margaret's one known pilgrimage to Walsingham deserving of a low mark because it was not followed up on a regular basis? She may have lost standing in the eyes of those with a stake in the enterprise, such as innkeepers or sellers of pilgrim badges; it is unlikely that her own view of self, as a spiritual creature, suffered. She seems to have rested in the confidence that what she did was what she should do, in this area, and neither guilt nor doubt nor misgivings about the past have much of a presence in her conscience or her psyche as we can follow her through her letters. She may have had woeful views about the state of worldly affairs in the England of the Wars of the Roses, especially in an East Anglia so dominated by the king's overmighty subjects, and she may have doubted the wisdom of some of her husband's more daring or problematic enterprises, but we do not hear many second thoughts about her basic choices in life.

Because there are problems about trying to situate Margaret within some mold of collective behavior, we might take a quick look at some other relevant categories of activity and see if they are of much help when it comes to assessing lay religiosity. This is a search for the appropriate contextualization of an individualized investigation; we already know better than to expect a great deal of success. Margaret Paston was a woman of some social importance and considerable affluence and she lived her entire life in East Anglia. This means that she spent her days amidst a world, or a society, that could boast of an exceptional level of lay activity in matters of faith and the Church, especially on the part of educated, devout, and well-placed women. Does Margaret fit in among a group of well-known and well-documented contemporaries to any significant degree?[16] In comparative terms—that is, when we highlight those of Margaret's contemporaries or near contemporaries who had the highest profiles, or the loudest voices, or the most eccentric expressions of spirituality, or the strongest urge to put it down in writing, or the greatest interest in being patrons of authors and scribe—we find the Margaret invariably comes up short. In fact, she does not even enter the contest. There are three veins of contemporary activity that open wide windows upon the rich world of faith, patronage, and internalized spirituality that flourished in Norfolk and Suffolk in her day, and all of these are well treated in current scholarly inquiry. Furthermore, this is without taking into account the lively and popular or democratic world of the drama cycles or the pageants of towns and guilds.

One line of activity (and scholarly investigation) tracks such highly individualized lines of behavior as those charted by the two most famous and vocally prominent spiritual women of late medieval England: the world as lived and described by Julian of Norwich and by Margery Kempe.[17] But whatever these famous contemporaries could recount about their visions and callings, and whatever their tales tell us about the difficult but permissible extremes of personal religion, not much help for us. For Margaret Paston there were no visions, no personal conversations with Jesus, and/or other saintly and heavenly figures. Neither—and this seems worth asserting in view of much recent scholarship that focuses on the appeal of virgin saints and a life marked by some measure of withdrawal—does Margaret ever seem to have any doubts or misgivings about marriage, pregnancy and motherhood, or sexuality, whatever the state of relations with her menfolk and whatever the dangers and pains of childbearing.[18] In her will she left a reasonable scattering of money to the anchorites of Norwich, to those who had left the world and who lived on alms and air. But in life, as revealed by all those letters, there were no indications that Margaret found such lives and the message of those who lived them attractive, at least not beyond singling out some of them as suitable recipients of a testamentary bequest in return for their prayers. Women who chose to step out of the mainstream may have been admirable, or objects of charity, or valuable for their help in negotiating the pains of purgatory, but Margaret certainly did not see them as role models, either for herself or for her daughters. She married young, stayed in the world, and had no patience for her own daughters who delayed their own leap into the conjugal bed.

If neither a mystic nor an obsessive breast-beater, what do we find when we set Margaret alongside those impressive circles of female patrons of devotional literature? Here too the communities of Norfolk and Suffolk (and Essex and Cambridgeshire) were rich in the names of women who figure very prominently in the prefaces and dedicatory passages in the hagiography and devotional writing of the day.[19] We need only think of those women to whom Osbern Bokenham dedicated his saints' lives: the life of Mary Magdelan to Isabel Bouchier, Countess of Eu, or the life of St Katherine to Katherine Howard, or the life of St Elizabeth to Elizabeth de Vere, countess of Oxford, or the life of St Agatha to Agatha Flegge, to name just some of those given a place of honor in his work, and if Bokenham and "his women" are the most prominent in this world, they are hardly the only ones we could single out. But this, we might say, was not Margaret Paston's scene.

A third vein of women's devotional activity is made up of those who were involved in circles of pious reading. Though no hard numbers can be offered, we now accept a high degree of literacy for fifteenth-century women of substance; certainly for reading (in at least one language), though probably not as much for writing in one's own hand. This fits with what we know about the widespread ownership and popularity of books, and in feminine circles this means the probability of books of hours and of other devotional and liturgical texts in the cupboards of most laywomen of reasonable status and wealth. And though the sources are probably slanted to tell more about the use and ownership of spiritual rather than of secular texts, they have much to say regarding women as book owners, as people who transmitted books in their wills and as *inter vivos* gifts, and as lenders and borrowers of such items.[20] But here again, Margaret Paston offers us about as little as possible; she perhaps just stops just this side of giving us nothing at all. We shall see that a few books are mentioned in her will, though we know that she was aware of books being circulated among her children, of the books that John II inquired about buying from the estate of her chaplain John Gloys, and of books that her son Walter needed as he went up to Oxford. But mostly she is quiet, though her knowledge of the saints and their days (as we shall see below) argues for a book of hours and perhaps even for a copy of *The Golden Legend*. And in that private chapel that was so important to her there surely were other devotional texts, or so we like to think. But she is not given to talking about her private life, even in letters to her husband, and she leaves us free—if we choose to follow this route—to speculate about other books and more books.[21]

★ ★ ★

Whether we think in terms of comparison or elimination, the procedure of holding Margaret Paston and what she tells us about her spiritual life against the cloth cut by more vocal, or more articulate, or more generous, or more introspective contemporaries is one that fails to give us many returns. The limits of both our materials and the tools with which we can approach them are only too apparent. As we try to mine the Paston letters, we are very aware of the harsh fact that what we have in them is what we have, an existential circle of lost letters (and missing people) from which we cannot escape. Whether the extant letters represent a minor fraction or a major fraction of what they wrote and received is beyond calculation. As the correspondence has been preserved and transmitted there are blocks of time, sections of life, and even some members of the inner family circle that remain dark. Furthermore, because of the pragmatic factors behind the writing (let alone the preservation) of the letters, so many aspects of daily life that were either taken for granted or deemed not relevant or appropriate for epistolary communication just go unmentioned. And beyond those letters and papers that were squirreled away for future generations, we have almost nothing about the Pastons. They are only really knowable as far as their letters take us; no household books, no ministers' accounts or manorial records, no parallel family letters from some of those Norfolk gentry families with whom they did business, no wills from others wherein they might have been named as beneficiaries or executors or witnesses.[22] So even though we know more about the Pastons than we do about the other fifteenth-century families whose letters have been preserved, our knowledge is a trade-off of more information about those topics on which they chose to write as against almost nothing at all on those they ignored and on those that would depend on such sources as household books or manorial records.[23]

All these caveats and disclaimers take us back to where we started, to a recognition that an assessment of Margaret Paston's spiritual life and style of religious expression rests almost completely on what she herself said in her letters and that she almost never said much for the explicit purpose of discussing faith as a personal or internal matter. She inserts a line here and there to help us to unravel her dealings with a priest or a chaplain, or about attending church and perhaps taking the sacrament, or touching her awareness of the truth of life as being lived in the midst of death, fully in accord with the divine plan. In her will she talks of and leaves bequests to godchildren; nothing along this line about spiritual kinship was noted during her long life, at least not until the very end. She expresses many pieties, and on occasion she does so with a splash of English prose that shows her to be an accomplished wordsmith. But in most of her 100 letters there are few if any flights of fancy, let alone of long passages of personal revelation. An occasional saw to the effect of "men cut large thongys here of othere mens lethere" (I, 190) or "And fore Goddys loue, remembyreyt rythe welle and takeyt pacyently, and thanke God of hys vysitacyon" is about as philosophical as she allows herself to be about life and fate. It is this very lack of explicit focus, this taking-for-granted approach, that seems to express or encapsulate her basic belief system—its convictions, its personnel, and its potential for personal solace—that makes her such an ideal case study: a typical woman of her class, culture, and time.

CHAPTER 2

MARGARET PASTON'S CALENDAR AND
HER SAINTS

This inquiry into Margaret Paston's religious life begins by following her lead as she reaches out to the saints. That late medieval religion rested heavily on the cult of the saints is a proposition from which there is virtually no dissent. The saints, along with the Holy Family and the depiction of Jesus as a man who suffered and died, rather than as a remote and judgmental divinity, were very much the material from which the cloth of late medieval popular piety was cut. The roll call of saints who were honored and invoked included figures from virtually every category of Christian history and tradition: female and male, local and universal, recent and historical, biblical and/or mythical; we shall see below that many more were male than female. But these saints and countless others, either individually or in any and all sorts of aggregations and combinations, figured heavily in the way people linked their own lives and fates to what they hoped was an ascent of the ladder of redemptive spirituality. The saints in heaven were also near at hand for worldly needs and emergencies; a storm at sea, deserved or undeserved imprisonment, the death of someone near and dear, fertility to be sought (or to be avoided), childbirth, and other such fates and turns of fortune's wheel. To note a saint's day, if only as a passive participant or observer of a church service, was an easy way to establish or reestablish a link with the holy man or woman of the moment.[1]

However, despite all the generalizations about the roll and popularity of these ubiquitous saints, case studies of lay piety that illuminate a known individual's own hagiographic focus or personal cast list are not easy to find. In our search for such a case study to illuminate the way in which a specific and a known historical figure stationed herself in regard to the annual cycle of feasts and fasts and the holy figures enshrined and evoked by that cycle, Margaret Paston comes to our rescue. She offers a personalized and quite individualized example of a laywoman's knowledge of and deference to the saints. She enables us to dot some of the i's and cross some of the t's of conventional piety as we tell of it and as it was acknowledged on a daily basis. Furthermore, she does this, not in any special moment of crisis or of spiritual epiphany, but rather bit by bit—saint's day by saint's day—over the years, as she notes those days in her letters. The saints and saints' days she refers to are mentioned by way of casual or practical references in letter writing, not as devout treatises and disquisitions on faith and intercession. Therefore I offer Margaret Paston's knowledge of the saints as an example of how references to and awareness of the saints, and of their special days, were smoothly woven into the tapestry of daily life as it unrolls before us by way of the mundane, secular, and ephemeral agenda of family letters.

★   ★   ★

A striking characteristic of Margaret Paston's 100 letters is that not only do almost all of them carry a date—which by itself is a bit unusual for the family letters of the fifteenth century—but that virtually all of those that are dated are dated by the ecclesiastical calendar. For the early months of the year, beginning in February, the moveable feasts that revolve around Easter but that actually run from Shrove Tuesday through Trinity Sunday are generally in the ascendant. But then, come summer and autumn (and occasionally before that, when she was so moved) it is the fixed saints' days that provide her basic and customary points of reference for dating her letters.[2]

This phenomenon of Margaret's dating letters in this fashion is a basic fact of the Paston letters. Each of her letters (with only 13 exceptions of various sorts, out of 104 documents) contains this particular detail, usually inserted toward the end of the letter and expressed in the most matter-of-fact faction: "Wretyn at Geldiston on the Wedynisday nexte after Sent Thomas" (I, 127), to give a typical example. A discussion of her epistolary practice in this regard, and of the dates she chose to note, is our entry point for an exploration of her spiritual life. Though the dating style of letters is admittedly a narrow wedge with which to open up a world of lay piety or popular religion—however we choose to label it—it does offer an entrée into what is, in so many other ways, a closed world. It seems appropriate to use the saints and their days as our wedge.

Because no one else from any of the fifteenth-century letter-writing families, Paston or otherwise, has left a pattern of letter dating that even approaches Margaret's in terms of the proportion of dated letters, let alone for those dated by a consistent use of ecclesiastical dates, it seems to follow that her practice in this regard should be read as an expression of deliberate choice. The challenge, of course, is how to follow her lead and how to decode her style and her choices. As we will see, there are few surprises among Margaret Paston's choice of saints, few departures from the high road of long-established lay piety and of well-known figures. But if this was conventional behavior, reflective of conventional knowledge of the ecclesiastical calendar and its familiar and long-accepted list of heroes and heroines, we can still ask why no one else, among the many fifteenth-century family letter writers, used ecclesiastical dating as often or as consistently. Nothing particularly esoteric or idiosyncratic in Margaret's style; "Wretyn at Norwyche on Seyne Gregorys Day" (12 March: I, 136); laconic, basic, and her own standard style.

Anyone else of her world could presumably have walked this same path, had she or he wished to; these were well-known saints, well-known feasts. But quite clearly no one else chose to do so. While most of those who have left a modest number of letters in the Paston collection did use ecclesiastical dates at times, no one else used them as frequently. This distinction between Margaret and all the others bespeaks a singularity on her part. Indeed, in one context Margaret's usage could be considered as the norm and the relative nonuse of saints' days the peculiar practice. In some legal proceedings the saint's day was "almost invariably" the method used, and there were even cases literally thrown out of court because of a failure on the part of one party to conform to this style.[3]

Because Margaret dated so many of her letters by the ecclesiastical calendar she gives us a database that points to various favorites, saints chosen from many different categories of Christian history and saints with a variety of attractive points and attributes. Beyond the appeal saints could offer, thanks to specialized powers or attributes—Roche for the plague, Margaret for childbirth, Giles for protection against sterility, Christopher for protection against sudden death and for travelers, Hubert for success in the hunt, and so forth—there may have been other hierarchies, other frames of reference. We can think in terms of a saint's proximity to the historical Christ, or to a saint's widespread veneration and popularity throughout Christendom, or of the call of local shrines and cults, as well as of all sorts of personal factors (such as birth or christening dates) that might govern individual preferences. The dating style of Margaret Paston's letters allows us to reconstruct a calendar—an abbreviated version of the fuller and more elaborate one that was an integral part of her book of hours, her primer. For this reconstruction I will cobble together all the saints' days she mentions in her letters as they stretch across the span of her long letter-writing career. Her dating practices seem to shed light on the way that basic religious data (a particular saint's day), noted no doubt on the calendar in her book of hours (missing; gone without trace) were integrated into such daily routines as in the dating of her letters. The insights and implications we can draw from this reconstruction of her calendar are transmitted to us by someone with no pronounced claim to personal or mystical links with those saints. Her conventional religion revolved around a basic knowledge of many of the major and minor players of the faith, rather than from any self-proclaimed privilege of direct conversation with some select group of celestial celebrities.[4]

We have a considerable amount of material informing us of instructions given to the laity of Margaret's world concerning the proper ways to absorb and practice their faith; domestic and household prayers, the proper instruction of children, the responsibility of the lord and lady for the morals of servants and dependents, the patriarchal family as the microcosm of Church and society, an inculcation of the necessity of hearing mass and receiving the sacraments, and much more along these lines. However, we know a good deal less about how these normative proscriptions were actually converted into practice, especially within the home.[5] So too with the cult of the saints: many choices, and many reasons to choose, and much preaching and teaching about their importance. But beyond this it turns out that we have a very limited amount of specific information to guide us about choices and favorites.

Margaret Paston's choices of saints (or rather, of saints' days) will be set out as a reconstructed calendar year, a "virtual reality" year, running from January through December and drawing on the entire corpus or chronological span of her letters. From her first letter, probably written in 1441 (I, 124) through one to her eldest son John II in May 1478 (I, 22) she almost always stuck to her guns in her dating style. She dated that letter of 1441: "wretyn at Norweche on Trenyté Sunne-day," and her last one concluded in much the same way: "Wretyn at Mawteby the day after Seynt Austyn in May, the xviij yere of Kyng Edward the iiijte." A look at those many saintly figures whose feast days she notes is further confirmation of the assertion about her conventional tastes (and perhaps of her knowledge). She was an unlikely candidate for the front ranks of those who flocked to the new cults and the new liturgical feasts that caught the public fancy.[6] Her path of piety ran the route, with but few exceptions, of the well-known and oft-invoked saints of the Church—a mainline approach to the mysteries of a late medieval religiosity that Colin Richmond has aptly termed as "saintocratic Christianity."[7] Given that Margaret lived virtually all her life but a short journey from such renown centers of piety and pilgrimage as Bury St Edmunds or Walsingham or Bromholm, she was about as insensitive or indifferent to the chauvinism of local cults and saints as she was to novelty. However, we cannot choose to hold her up as a case study in conventional piety and then chastise her because she was not more adventurous, more sensitive to new currents that blew in the wind. There are no end of ways in which a literate women of Margaret's upbringing and status would have come to know her saints, let alone to choose her favorites. Wherever she turned—in church, in her private reading and devotions, in attending baptisms or weddings, in gazing at the external or internal ornamentations of church or cathedral, or in looking at the familiar and personal objects of her own chapel—she was confronted by saints. Lollards, of course, might find this a false focus, though they had been muted pretty effectively in East Anglia by Margaret's adult years.[8] Others of an orthodox but rather puritanical inclination may have found the contemporary focus on the saints a bit excessive. But for most, it would seem, the hagiographical emphasis of lay religiosity was seamlessly woven into ideology and practice, into the aural and oral and visual, into the private as well as the liturgical, into the internalized and the contemplative.[9]

The attempt to re-create at least a portion of Margaret Paston's calendar is to gain a glimpse at how she meshed secular business with the cycle of the Christian year. Her actual calendar—the artifact, the physical object that she would consult—would almost certainly have been a basic and integral part of her book of hours.[10] That she had a book of hours—or more than one such book—seems pretty much beyond dispute. The book of hours was the most widely produced, distributed, and used book of lay religious reading and counsel in the fifteenth century, with women even more eager consumers, and presumably readers, than their mentolk. Given that the Pastons had had their own domestic chapel as far back as the days of William I (who died in 1444, shortly after Margaret entered the family), and given that Margaret herself went to considerable efforts late in life to keep her own chapel at Mautby, it is unthinkable that she was not properly trained and equipped for private prayers and devotions, perhaps both on her own and with her chaplain.[11]

Before we come to consider her saints we can offer a bit more regarding Margaret's letter dating.[12] This aspect of her letters, perhaps along with her last will, stands as the most individualized pointer she leaves us. What can we deduce from the bald fact that virtually all her letters are dated by the ecclesiastic calendar, whereas none of her contemporaries followed this practice with anything approaching her consistency? When a letter writer dated a letter by a saint's day he or she is reminding us of how a secular world was calibrated with the revolving wheel of ecclesiastical fasts and feasts. Those saintly intercessors, citizens of heaven now as they had been of earth before, could be thought of as standing 24-hour

watch: guides and protectors, spiritual doorkeepers, hotlines for advice
to the bewildered, comfort for the wary and the weary. The dating of
the letter is certainly small beer when we consider all the critical and/
or useful information each Paston letter was meant to convey. Amidst
the many Paston letters, with their news of deaths and battles, sieges and
lawsuits, marital prospects and negotiations, and so much else, the dating
tag does not seem of great moment—at least not beyond its practical value
for slotting the letter into its chronological niche and for an indication of
how fresh was the news it carried from sender to recipient. The dating
clause usually comes toward the end, as though the problems of writing
might string out the process and the dating, like the sealing and folding,
was best dealt with when all else was in now, finally, in place: "And the
blyssyd Tryntye haue yow in jys kepyng and send how god sped in all
yowyr materys, and send the victory of all yowyr enmyis. Wretyn in hast
on Sowlemas Daye. By yowyrs M.P." (I, 163) in closing a letter of 60 lines
to John I in early November 1461.

Was the dating actually Margaret's own touch? Because her letters
were dictated, we cannot disprove the possibility that the dating style
may have been left to the scribe, a sort of "you can close now" gray
area, to be dealt with after the serious business had been taken care of.
However, I do not think this is the case, and any and every test I can put
to the data argues for this practice as Margaret's own distinctive style,
despite the ubiquitous scribe who actually put pen to paper.[13] No factor
other than Margaret herself, dictating her many letters over the decades,
emerges as the key variable. If we compare her usage with that of the
Paston men, as well as with other Paston women, we see how different,
or distinctive, she was (as in Table 2.1). In their dated letters the Paston
men were about evenly divided in their use of a secular or an ecclesiastical date: 78 of 176 dated letters in the former style (or 44 percent of the
group), 98 letters (or 56 percent of the group) in the latter. Apart from any
religious significance in this, the circumstances of their letter writing,
often outside the family and writing to recipients of a different class or
status, may have made the less personal and more "business-like" secular
date seem the one to choose. The women, on the other hand, were more
likely to be writing from home, in the relative comfort of the manor
house, and a personal touch might be expressed in terms of an ecclesiastical reference, as to the church calendar. But even granted the possibility
of this gendered distinction, Margaret Paston stands out in terms of her
adherence to ecclesiastical dating. Her reliance on this style is leaps and
bounds beyond of anyone else's.

Table 2.1 certainly bears out that dating a letter, *per se,* was hardly a
requisite step in epistolary construction. Of the 349 letters as printed in

Norman Davis's edition of the Paston letters, 17 percent (59 of the 349) are undated (and if we exclude Margaret the undated letters compose 21 percent of the total: one in every five). Obviously, each and every letter writer was free to choose whether or not to bother with the date. Though for most of the Pastons dating may not have been all that significant—and we see that they fell back on the various styles in a haphazard fashion, including the option of no date—for Margaret there was a clear path that she chose early in her letter-writing style and stuck to throughout.

A few more reflections. Of Margaret's 104 documents, seven were dated in what I refer to as "existential dating"; they were written when they were written. We see this in such as "Wretyn at Norwyche on the

Table 2.1   Dating Styles of the Paston Letter Writers

Letter Writer	No. of Letters	Secular Dating	Ecclesiastical Dating	Undated	More than One Style	Existential Dating[a]	Letters w/ Eccl. Dating (%)
William I	8	3	1	4	—	—	12.5
Agnes	13	3	9	1	—	—	69
John I	27	4	15	7	—	1	56
Edmund I*	2	1	1	—	—	—	—
William II	20	10	5	5	—	—	25
Clement*	7	2	5	—	—	—	—
Elizabeth Poynings*	—	1	1	—	—	—	—
MARGARET	104	4	86	6	1	7	83
John II	70	36	20	9	2	3	38
John III	70	16	28	18	—	8	59
Edmund II*	9	1	4	4	—	—	—
Walter*	3	—	2	—	1	—	—
William III*	9	5	2	2	—	—	—
Margery (Brewes)	6	2	2	2	—	—	—
William IV*	1	—	—	1	—	—	—
Total	349[b]	88 (25%)[c]	181 (52%)	59 (17%)	4 (1%)	19 (5%)	

*Too few letters to be analyzed in terms of percentage.
[a]"Existential dating" is explained on pp. 19–20.
[b]Letters and drafts of letters only in this tally. The number of miscellaneous documents, respectively, for each person as listed in the table: 4 (for William I), and then 9, 17, 0, 13, 5, 2, 3 (for Margaret), 16, 8, 2, and 1; nothing for William II, Margery, or William IV.
[c]Percentage of total letters.

wedenys-day nexst after thett ye partyd hens" (I, 128), or "Writyn in hast, the same day that ye departyd hens" (I, 159), or "Wretyn in hast on Satyrday" (I, 187).[14] Other letter writers, Pastons and non-Pastons, also went this route on the odd occasion; John II and John III, among others, fell back on it from time to time.[15] Furthermore, it is likely that in many cases what we have as an undated letter had been dated, perhaps by word of mouth, or by the courier, or in accompanying materials, or in some envelope or wrapping that has long since vanished. The courier might indicate upon arrival when he had left Norwich or London, which would usually slot the letter within a day or two. If we keep in mind the need-to-know nature of the letters, set like beads on a necklace, "Wretyn the sonday next after your departing" (I, 186) clearly sufficed, little help though it is to us. An extra touch like "at xj of the clok in the nyth the same day I departyd from yow" (I, 170), or "Wretyn on Sent Gyles evyn at ix of the belle at nyght" (I, 202), for that extra splash of precision.

Was Margaret's reliance on ecclesiastical dates, rather than on the secular (Roman) calendar, a feminine practice, a species of the genus, "women are more devout than men?" Table 2.1 offered some limited support for the idea of a gendered dating style, and we have speculated on why this might have been the case, though once we move beyond Margaret, the numbers are small and it is hard to push the argument very far. Her mother-in-law Agnes is a healthy second in the use of ecclesiastical dating: 41 percent of her letters and 69 percent of the dated ones are in this category. But here we are playing with small numbers. Since Agnes's total output only ran to 13 (extant) letters they offer a flimsy platform on which to build an edifice of spiritual sensitivity. Moreover, Margaret's two oldest sons—her principal correspondents after the death of John I in 1466—used ecclesiastical dates on numerous occasions. While their record does not rival that of their mother or grandmother, it is strong enough to cast doubt on the idea that gender alone was a critical variable. For John II, the percentage of letters with ecclesiastic dating was 27 percent of all documents, 38 percent of his dated letters; for his brother it was 35 percent and 59 percent, respectively. So while gender may be linked to a propensity for ecclesiastical dating, it hardly carries the day.

Margaret herself resorted to secular dating in her letters so infrequently that her occasional "lapses" are too few to allow for much analysis. Though I cannot disprove that the dating tag might have been left for her scribe to take care of, as the date itself was not a contested matter regardless of style, any test I can put to the matter seems to argue in favor of Margaret's own touch.[16] In some instances we can follow a particular scribe in letters penned for Margaret and some other letter writer, and the variations in dating style between the two make it unlikely that the scribe made the choice. The few secular dates Margaret uses pose a minor mystery, though since there are but four such dates they hardly alter the main flow of the current. They all are in letters to John I. The first, written by Richard Calle, was from May 1462 (I, 171). The other three were penned by John Wykes between 10 and 20 May 1465; the middle letter was dated 18 May.[17] In no other way do these letters differ from their fellows. Nor can we simply attribute the distinction to Wykes, since in addition to these letters of May 1465 he penned others at Margaret's dictation and all were dated by the ecclesiastical calendar.[18]

The obvious and rather belabored conclusion to all this just seems to be that it was Margaret Paston who chose to date her letters by references to the ecclesiastical calendar. Her singularity of usage stands out even more if we compare it with what we find in the other fifteenth-century letter collections and with letters written to the Pastons. Of the 33 letters written by members of the Stonor family, 13 had secular dating, 12 ecclesiastical; an even divide, and not many letters. The Celys were men of business, or at least they are in their surviving correspondence, and of their 168 letters, only 6 took note of the Church's calendar. For the Plumptons it was but 10 in the ecclesiastical style, out of 46 letters.[19]

Nor do we expect the prevailing winds to shift when we turn to letters written to the Pastons; the same variations. Of course, not only were these letters written by a large number of correspondents, which means we are lumping together all sorts of styles and preferences, but also they cover a wide range of enterprises with different recipients over the course of many decades. The ten letters with existential dating addressed to John I show that such dating was not confined to the family, whether it was a matter of convenience or whether it bespoke some special familiarity and contact between the parties. What is also striking about the data of Table 2.2 is the high proportion of letters with ecclesiastical dating sent to John I; 90 such, compared to 118 with secular dating. But John I received his letters from so many different letter writers that we cannot draw any useful conclusion from this.

There are some correspondents who, over the years, wrote a fair number of letters to various Pastons. How did they—those who did regular business with and for the family—fit our various categories or styles? Table 2.3 sets this out. Richard Calle, Margaret's bailiff (and then her unwanted son-in-law) stands out here, even more than any of the clerics such as Friar Brackley.[20] However, a look at the record of Sir John Fastolf reminds us of the limits of this kind of analysis. Whatever Sir John's spiritual commitments, his epistolary business with John Paston was business and little else; the secular dating seems the appropriate style of such transactions. Of Fastolf's letters to John I, 23 come with secular

Table 2.2   Dating Styles in Letters to the Pastons

Paston Recipient	Secular Dating	Ecclesiastical Dating	Undated	"Existential"	Total
William I	4	7	2	—	13
Agnes	1	1	1	—	3
John I	118	90	50	10	268
Edmund I	—	1	—	—	1
William II	—	—	11	—	11
MARGARET	6	6	15	3	30
John II	17	18	10	2	47
John III	43	10	18	—	71
Edmund II	1	—	—	—	1
William III	2	2	3	—	7
Margery Brewes	—	—	1	—	1
William IV	5	—	—	—	5
Total	197 (43%)	135 (29%)	111 (24%)	15 (3%)	458
Received by the Paston Women	7	7	17	3	34

Table 2.3   Dating Styles in the Letters of "Regular" Correspondents to the Pastons (8 or More Letters)

Correspondent	Secular Dating	Ecclesiastical Dating	Undated	Existential Dating	Total Letters
Friar Brackley	—	5	8	1	14
Richard Calle	3	16	5	2	26
Thomas Denys	4	2	2	1	9
Sir John Fastolf	23	6	1	1	31
James Gresham	2	12	3	1	18
12 Earl Oxford	9	—	—	—	9
13 Earl Oxford	18	—	1	—	19
Thomas Playter	1	2	9	—	12
John Russe	2	1	5	—	8
Thomas, lord Scales	11	—	—	—	11
Total	73 (46%)	44 (28%)	34 (22%)	6 (4%)	157 (100%)

dates, a mere 6 noted the ecclesiastical calendar. Those peers of the realm who wrote to the Pastons, communicating as they were with their social inferiors, found secular dating appropriate for the peremptory style of their business. At the same time, their salutation and closing did conform to the customary language of courtesy and fraternity.[21] How about the clerics? Twenty-eight letters came to Paston recipients from regular correspondents who were men of the cloth; 10 were dated by the secular calendar, 11 by the ecclesiastical, 6 were undated, and 1 from Friar Brackley carried an existential date. So no matter how we try to analyze or isolate Margaret Paston's dating, or in whatever company or context we set her, her predilection for ecclesiastical dating shines through.

★   ★   ★

If we return to Margaret's saints' days and the days of moveable ecclesiastical feasts, what sort of yearlong trail does she blaze for us? The ecclesiastical dates that she used in her letters are the building blocks from which I offer this (partial) reconstruction of her calendar (Table 2.4), compiled on a monthly basis to give us a 12-month if fictive year. The fixed saints' days and the movable feasts (and fasts) are distinguished, thereby highlighting the dominance of the latter category in the early months of the year, the reemergence of the saints and their feasts in summer, autumn, and early winter. While only the fixed dates of the saints would have

Table 2.4   Margaret Paston's Ecclesiastical Dates in Her Letters, Month by Month through the Year

January[a]

Day of the Month	Fixed Dates	Moveable Dates	Margaret's Letter(s)[b]
6	Twelfth Night		#165 (1462)
13	St Hilary		#220 (1473)
21	St Agnes		#169 (1462), #172 (1463)
25	Conversion of St Paul		#150 (1454)

[a] The ecclesiastical dates in January as used by other letter writers, including those found in the Plumpton, Cely, and Stonor letters (and for each succeeding month): Jan. 6: Edmund Paston (#298, 1480); Jan. 13: John I (#70 & #71, 1465); Jan. 15, Feast of St Marius: Agnes Plumpton (#172, 1503: "Sent Maury Day"); Jan. 21: John III (#338, 1470); Jan. 25: William II (#88, 1460).
[b] Davis's numbering and the year.

February

Day of Month	Fixed Dates	Moveable Dates	Margaret's Letter(s)
2	Purification of the BVM		#145 (1453), #151 (1454), #221 & #222 (1475)
5	St Agatha, V & M—"Sent Agas"		#215 (1472)
14	St Valentine		#131 (1449)
24	St Mattias the Apostle		#137 (1479)
28		Friday Next After Pulver Wesnesday	#132 (1449)

Other Letter Writers:
Feb. 2: Agnes Paston (#14, 1445), John III (#325 & #326, 1467), Edmund II (#399, 1481), William Stonor (#136, 1474); Feb. 14: John II (#301, 1476), Robert Plumpton (#185, 1504); Feb. 15, Ash Wednesday: Clement Paston (#118, 1464: "Hasse Wednysday"); Feb. 17, First Tuesday of Lent: John III (#267, 1467); Feb. 18, Pulver Wednesday: Agnes (#19, 1450); Feb. 24: William III (#407,1479: "Seynt Mathy the Apostyll").

March

Day of Month	Fixed Dates	Moveable Dates	Margaret's Letter(s)
1		Second Sunday of Lent	#158 (1446)
5		Mid-Lent Sunday	#223 (1475)
12	Gregory the Pope	Mid-Lent Sunday	#136 (1450, St Gregory); #200 (1465, for "Myd-lent Sonday")
15		First Monday of Lent	#138 (1451)
30		Mid-Lent Sunday ("Tuesday next Be-fore Mydlente Sonday")	#139 (1451)

Other Letter Writers:
March 1: William I (#4, 1426); March 8, "first Monday of Cleene Lent": John III (#360, 1473); March 12: Agnes (#20, 1450: St Gregory), Clement Paston (#120, 1466: St Gregory); March 21, "Saint Benedict Day": William Plumpton (#176, 1503); March 25, Annunciation: John III (#361, 1473), Thomas Stonor (#205, 1478), Elizabeth Stonor (#239, 1478), William Cely (#212, 1484); March 29, "thys Wednysday in Eastern week": John III (#364, 1475); March 31, "iiij Sonday of Lent": John I (#49, 1454).

April

Day of Month	Fixed Dates	Moveable Dates	Margaret's Letter(s)
2		Palm Sunday	#133 (1449)
3		"Eastern Munday"	#201 (1469)
8		Monday After "Palme Sonday"	#178 (1465)
23	St George		#143 (1452), #146 (1453)

Other Letter Writers:

April 9, Good Friday: Richard Cely (#47, 1479); April 16, Good "Fryday": John II (#275, 1473); April 17, "Deus qui errantibus": Agnes (#13, 1440: third Sunday after Easter, named from the first word of the collect); April 23: John I (#42 & #43, 1452), Clement Paston (#119, 1464), William Stonor (#127, 1473: "Seyne Jorgeys day"); April 25, Mark, Evangelist: Agnes Plumpton (#190, 1504).

May

Day of Month	Fixed Dates	Moveable Dates	Margaret's Letter(s)
3	Invention of the Cross		#135 (1449), #179 (1465)
6		Thursday Before "assencyon"	#176 (1464)
19		Trinity Sunday	#129 (1448)
23		Tuesday Next After Trinity Sunday	#224 (1478)
26	Augustine of England		#228 (1478)
27		Monday Next After Ascencion	#183 (1465)
31	Petronella, V		#216 (1472)

Other Letter Writers:

May 13, "Wednesdaye in Wyghtsonweek": John II (#311, 1478); May 14, Thursday before Whitsunday: William Stonor (#122, 1472); May 16, "Whyteson eue": Edmund II Paston (#395, 1472); May 19, St Dunstan: Walter Paston (#402, 1476); May 22, Saturday after Ascension: Walter Paston (#403, 1479); May 25, Thursday in Whitweek: John Cely (#88, 1480), Richard Cely (#169, 1482); May 27, "Mondaye next Holy Thurrysdaye the Assencion": John II (#299, 1476).

June

Day of Month	Fixed Dates	Moveable Dates	Margaret's Letter(s)
3		Ascension Day	#140 (1451)
11	St Barnabas	Corpus Christi	#177 (1464: St Barn.), #184 (1465: Corpus), #226 (1477: St. Barn.)
24	Midsummer		#185 (1465)
29	Peter & Paul		#141 (1451)

Other Letter Writers:

June 2, Sunday next after Trinity Sunday: John III (#322, 1464); June 22, Friday next after Corpus: John III (#342, 1470); June 23, St Audrey: John II (#307, 1477); June 24: John I (#55, 1460), William II (#81, 1452: Midsummer), Clement Paston (#115, 1461: St John Baptist), John III (#343, 1470: John the Baptist); June 29: John I (#73, 1465), Edmund Paston (#79, 1447), John II (#300, 1476), John III (#378, 1477), Walter Paston (#404, 1479).

July

Day of Month	Fixed Dates	Moveable Dates	Margaret's Letter(s)
7	Translation of St Thomas of England		#127 (1444), #142 (1451), #160 (1461), #188 (1465), #206 (1470)
11		Relic Sunday	#199 (1467)
15		"Relike Sonday"	#161 (14617), #207 (1470)
20	St Margaret		#162 (1461)

Other Letter Writers:

July 12, "Relike Sonday": John I (#58, 1461); July 20: John I (#45, 1452), Agnes (#26, 1453; John III (#330, 1468); July 22, Mary Magdalen: John III (#348, 1471 & #362, 1474); July 25, Apostle James: John I (#52, 1455), John III (#363, 1474); July 26, Anne mother of the Virgin: Richard Cely (#121, 1481: "Sent Tanys Day").

August

Day of Month	Fixed Dates	Moveable Dates	Margaret's Letter(s)
1	Lammas Day		#189 (1465)
10	St Lawrence		#225 (1475), #227 (1477)
15	Assumption of the Virgin		#190 (1465)

Other Letter Writers:

Aug. 1: John I (#59, 1461; #75 & #76, 1465); Aug. 10: William II (#85, 1458), John II (#256, 1470); Aug. 24, Apostle Bartholomew: Clement Paston (#116, 1461), John II (#231, 1461 & #312, 1478); Aug. 29, Decollation of John the Baptist: John II (#301, 1476).

Day of Month	Fixed Dates	Moveable Dates	Margaret's Letter(s)
1	Giles, Abbot		#202 (1469)
14	Holy Rood		#204 (1469)
29	Michaelmas		#126 (1443), #192 & #193 (1465), #205 (1469)

Other Letter Writers:
Sept. 8, Nativity of the Virgin: William II (#84, 1454); Sept. 14: John II (#243 & #244, 1469; #263, 1471), John III (#323, 1465); Sept. 29: John II (#235, 1465, & #264, 1471).

October

Day of Month	Fixed Dates	Moveable Dates	Margaret's Letter(s)
13	Translation of Edward, King & Confessor		#148 (1453)
18	Luke the Evangelist		#154 (1460); #194 (1465); #217 (1472)
28	Simon and Jude		#155 (1460); #196 (465); #198 (1466); #208 (1470)

Other Letter Writers:
Oct. 8, St Faith, V & M: John III (#324, 1465 & #335, 1469); Oct. 13: John III (#345, 1470), William II (#101, 1748), Thomas Stonor (#91, 1468); Oct. 16, Michael in Monte Tombe: John III (#355, 1472); Oct. 28: John II (#315, 1479), John III (#349, 1471; #366, 1475), Jane Stonor (#106, 1470), Edmund Stonor (#155, 1470).

November

Day of Month	Fixed Date	Moveable Date	Margaret's Letter(s)
2	Soulmas		#163 (1461)
6	Leonard Abbot		#144 (1451), #209 (1471)
11	St Martin of Tours		#174 (1463), #210 (1470)
16	Edmund, Archbishop and Confessor		#164 & #165 (1461), #175 (1463), #211 (1471)
23	St Clement		#219 (1472)
25	Catherine, V & M		#156 (1460), #218 (1472)
30	St Andrew, Apostle		#157 (1460), #166 (1461), #212 & #213 (1471)

Other Letter Writers:
Nov. 1, All Hallows: Agnes (#23, 1451), John III (#319, 1462), William III (#406, 1478), Margery Paston (#417 & #418, 1481), Thomas Stonor (#46, 1424); Nov. 6: John II (#281, 1473), John III (#381, 1479); Nov. 11: John III (#318, 1476); Nov. 14, Translation of St Erkenwald: John II (#258, 1470); Nov. 16: Agnes (#24, 1451), Edmund II (#395, 1471); Nov. 23: John II (#271, 1472), Richard Cely (#111, 1486); Nov. 25: John III (#356, 1472), Agnes Plumpton (#170, 1502); Nov. 30: Agnes (#29, 1461).

December

Day of Month	Fixed Date	Moveable Date	Margaret's Letter(s)
21	Thomas, the Apostle		#125 (1441)
24	Christmas Eve		#153 (1459)
29	Thomas, Archbishop and Martyr		#164 (1461)

Other Letter Writers:
Dec. 8, Conception of Our Lady: John III (#320, 1462); Dec. 21: Agnes Plumpton (#171, 1502); Dec. 24: William Stonor (#296, 1481).

been in Margaret's calendar, some sort of Easter table, supplemented by information from her priest or chaplain, would have kept her abreast of the timing of this year's Lent, Easter, Whitsuntide, and the rest.

As we have constructed it here, a rich albeit a conventional calendar. No surprises, this being the woman whom Colin Richmond has summed up in this fashion: "Margaret's spirituality was neither profound nor adventurous: it was as we have observed of her already, as decently middlebrow and an properly unexciting as fifteenth-century English spiritual life could ever be."[22] We have seen Margaret issue a roll call of saints and holy days quite befitting the outlook and awareness of a conventional lady. She clearly felt free to dip into either of the two wells of sanctity, that of the fixed dates of the saints or that of the moveable feasts of spring and summer. What guided her choices: which saints, which milestones? These questions hold a key to how she wove her own tapestry as she chose from among the many alternative colors and patterns to be found in the crowded ecclesiastical calendar. The first distinction to address is that between the moveable and the fixed dates. Even a fleeting glance at her choices shows that for spring into summer—the holy half of the year—moveable feasts and fasts carry the day with little competition from the saints. The majesty and drama of Good Friday leading to Easter, and the wide circle of related dates that run from Shrove Tuesday though Trinity Sunday, hold pride of place. From Lent through Pentecost and beyond the mnemonic and spiritual power of Christ's death and resurrection was the call that Margaret heeded. The saints would not really come into their own until early summer, though then they would hold pride of place until Lent came once again.

When they did come into their own, their ranks consisted of many more male figures than female; so much for any idea that a woman on Margaret's background and culture can be assumed to have an affinity for holy women over holy men.[23] Though we will return to an analysis of her "team" below, we note that through the course of the 12 months of her fictive year she noted 22 different male figures; some flexibility in the count, as she noted the feast of Peter in Chains (Lammastide) and also that of Peter and Paul, of Simon and Jude together, and a few other such wrinkles. While the total of nine women (included several Marian days) was short of ignoring female figures, it came in a fairly poor second. And as we shall see, the abundance of days throughout the course of the year gave one a fairly free hand when it came to picking and choosing. It would seem that, at the very least, Margaret had no discomfort in naming male saints, they mostly being the familiar, tried-and-true heroes of widespread acceptance.[24]

Table 2.5 shows the choices Margaret made when we separate the two halves or segments of the Christian year. Between February and July moveable feasts prevailed: 17 of them, as against 14 fixed (saints') days, as against 21 to 0 for the saints from August through January. This brings home the powerful hold the Passion had upon the lay imagination, as it had upon the liturgical and sacramental year, on the drama cycles, and on the iconography of church and home. Though Margaret did note such saints days as those of Agatha (5 February), or of Pope Gregory (12 March—and still a figure to conjure with in the English church), or of George (23 April), she ignored the attractions of such familiar figures as Joseph (19 March), Cuthbert (20 March), Philip and James (1 May), or Boniface (5 June), among others who came along in those months. And

Table 2.5 Margaret Paston's Monthly Dating by Fixed Dates and Moveable Feasts

Month	Fixed Dates	Moveable Dates
January	4	—
February	4	1
March	1	5
April	1	3
May	3	4
June	3	2
July	2	2
August	3	—
September	3	—
October	3	—
November	7	—
December	3	—
Total	37	17

yet for all the focus on Easter, the key Sunday itself goes virtually unmentioned. She came close, but it was Easter Monday, not the Easter day itself (I, 201, April 3, 1469). Perhaps, once a year, even Paston business got postponed for a day or two.[25]

Over the years Margaret touched numerous bases in the sacred half of the year. She began her stroll through the sacred months by picking up (in 1440) with "the Fryday nexst after Puver Weddenys day" (I, 132), and then, in one letter or another, working her way through Lent: the second Sunday of Lent, the Mid-Sunday of Lent, Mid-Lent, and the first Monday of Lent. She pretty much stayed with the moveable feasts as she approached the zero point of holy week: Palm Sunday, the Monday after Palm Sunday, and the like. She did come close to Palm Sunday and Good Friday and Easter Sunday, though she never hit them squarely: "Wretyn at Norwyche in hast on the Wednensday nexst be-fore Pam Sonday" (I, 133), or "Wretyn at Caster in Haste the Monday next after Palme Sonday" (I, 178), or, afterward, "Wretyn in haste on Eestern Munday" (I, 201). As April gave way to May and then to June, she continued in this vein: the feast of Ascension (I, 140, 176, 183), and then Trinity Sunday (I, 129, 224), and the Corpus Christi (I, 184), and finally Relic Sunday (I, 161, 198), to ring down the curtain. If we look at her full spread of moveable dates, we find six of her dated letters fall between Ash Wednesday and the days leading up to Palm Sunday, three fall in the week between Palm Sunday and Easter, and five come after Easter.

If Margaret's awareness of the stages whereby Lent led to Easter and then to Whitsuntide and beyond tells us something about her comfort with the time lines of the ritual year, what can we offer regarding those saints whose days she noted? This is more complex. We can think of the great multitude of saints and probe a bit at lay perceptions regarding their historicity, their relative powers, their inclination to intrude and intercede, their special attributes, and their popularity, be it regional and parochial or universal. Would Margaret Paston think of her saints as incorporeal spirits, or as one-time historicized men and women who, because of the sanctity of their lives, were now able to intercede in earthly matters when they chose (or when properly invoked). Or were they abstract icons, each perhaps armed with various attributes and powers?[26] If we turn to artistic depictions of saints we find alternative styles of presentation, and all of them would have been before Margaret Paston had she cared to look. One style is what I think of as the "team picture" approach; ranks and aggregations of saints, posing together with no indication of how this violated or transcended the mundane realities of place and time. We see this at its highest level in Ducio's "Maesta" in Siena, though it was to be seen in countless variations in the England of Margaret's day. Dozens of saints (and perhaps even some Old Testament figures) from across the landscape and the temporal span of Christianity and now all standing in some sort of harmonious arrangement to pay tribute to the Virgin. They indeed did form a heavenly host.[27]

Nothing here goes against accepted teaching or doctrine. However, when we approach saints by way of "their" days, the singularity of each saint is what seems to resonate. Individualized presentations and depictions abounded, as in the St Christopher wall painting at Paston or at Fritton in Suffolk, another of Margaret's churches, or as in many of the windows of St Peter Mancroft in the market square in Norwich. They served to turn the viewer's thoughts to separate hagiographical tales, separate attributes, even separate variations on the common and repetitious fate of martyrdom or miracle.[28] Would Margaret Paston have felt any closer to a saint like Thomas of Canterbury (d. 1170) or St Osmund (d. 1095) because each had been dead for but a few centuries, and a figure who in historical time had lived in a region of Christendom with which she might identify, in contrast to Martin of Tours or Benedict Abbot, long ago and far away? What distinction might she draw between St Edmund, king and martyr and buried just down the road, and saints of the early Mediterranean Christianity like Catherine of Alexandria or Laurence or Sebastian? These are deep waters of "belief," which, like "love," is embedded in a cultural context we cannot recapture with any certainty or confidence. Nor do these considerations take aesthetics into account. Would a "good" depiction of a saint in stone or in a window or in a wall painting have greater impact than a rough-and-rude version of the same figure (or might the opposite be the case)?[29]

This sort of speculation is intriguing if inconclusive. But if we return to Margaret's cast of saints there are other questions to pose. What does her list of saints tell us about her awareness of Church history and its vast pantheon of heroines and heroes, she being an educated and pious laywoman? We can categorize her saints into some basic groupings, as in Table 2.6. Merely to take note of a saint's day does not by itself argue for great sophistication touching church history or doctrine. On the other hand, we should be reluctant to dismiss such a reference as mere lip service, and the liturgy and perhaps a sermon on that day would emphasize some elements of singularity for the saint being named and/or involved. The categorization of saints in Table 2.6 points toward some degree of informed piety regarding the long and wide span of Christian history. Margaret paid homage to an impressive range of men and women: New Testament figures, virgins and martyrs of the early Church, confessors, bishops and abbots of renown, popularly accepted saints of her day, and figures from the medieval or historical church.

Table 2.6 Categories of Saints as Named in Margaret Paston's Letter Dating

Jesus and His Personal and Family Circle[a]	Apostles & Evangelists	English Saints	Universal Saints	Other Fixed Dates
Purification of the Virgin (4)[b]	Conversion of Paul	Augustine of England	Hilary	Soulmas (2 Nov.)
Nativity of John the Baptist (called Midsummer)	Mathias, the Apostle	Thomas of Canterbury: Martyrdom & Translation (5)	Agnes, V & M (2)	Lammastide[c] (Peter in Chains)
Assumption of the Virgin	Barnabas, the Apostle (2)[d]	Translation of Edward, King & Confessor	Agatha, V & M Valentine	Twelfth Night (2)
Christmas Eve	Peter & Paul	Edmund, King and Martyr (4)	Pope Gregory	Invention of the Holy Cross (2)
	Luke, the Evangelist (3)		St George (2)	Exaltation of the Holy Rood
	Simon & Jude, Apostles (4)		Petronella, V	
	Andrew, the Apostle (4)		Margaret, V & M	
	Thomas, the Apostle		Lawrence, Martyr (2)	
			Giles, Abbot	
			Michael, Arch-Angel (3)	
			Leonard, Abbot (2)	
			Martin, Bishop & Confessor (2)	
			Clement	
			Catherine, V & M (2)	

[a] Saints are arranged in the order of their feast days through the year.

[b] The number in parentheses indicates the number of times Margaret noted that saint in the course of her letter-writing career.

[c] For Lammastide (1 August): that term used by the Pastons: Margaret (I, 189): "Wednesday next afore Lammas Daye" and also John I (I, 59, I, 75, & I, 76). No mention of 1 August as the Feast of "Petrus ad vincula," though I have tallied this St Peter, alongside his other feast days, in the list of saints whom Margaret named.

[d] For Barnabas: in I, 177 ("the Fryday next before Sceynt Bernabye") and I, 226 ("Seynt Barnaby is day") the saint's day is used; in I, 184 it is "Tewysday nex be-fore Corpus Cristi."

All in all, she offers a considerable spread across the ages. Many of her saints were from the Holy Family, a group growing in popularity among the laity.[30] In her letters she noted the Feasts of the Purification and of the Assumption of the Virgin, along with Christmas Eve (I, 153: "Wretyn on Crystemes Evyn"), a day that would have honored both Mary and the Christ Child. Her Marian dates reflect her homage to the Virgin—much in keeping with contemporary currents of popular piety. And yet, of the seven days in England associated with the Virgin, she mentions but two or three; hardly a striking indication of veneration and adoration.[31] Other Marian dates are noted by other Pastons: The annunciation (25 March), the feast of St Anne, Mary's mother (26 July), and both the Conception (8 December) and the Nativity of the Virgin (8 September). And while Margaret dated a letter by the Nativity of John the Baptist, it was John II who mentioned the Decollation (I, 301), in addition to two letters from him dated by Mary Magdalen's day (I, 348 and I, 362).

What about those other figures who surrounded and moved with the living Jesus of the New Testament—the apostles and evangelists—the founding fathers of Christianity? Margaret named seven of the apostles, plus Paul, who both shared a day with Peter (29 June: I, 141) and who was also noted on his own for the feast of his Conversion (25 January). Simon and Jude shared a day, as they were wont to do. In addition, Luke the evangelist was noted, and no less than three times (and only by Margaret, among all the letter writers). If we widen the circle and look at the apostles and evangelists whom Margaret slighted but whom others remembered, we can add James and Bartholomew; we can put Mark beside Luke among the evangelists, and we can bring in Matthew, held to be both apostle and evangelist.[32]

The supply of saints from postapostolic times was very large indeed. Table 2.6 makes a distinction between those of English history and those we can think of as being universal, that is, celebrated throughout (western) Christendom.[33] Some of the women and men named by Margaret may seem a bit less familiar, such as Petronella or Leonard, but neither time nor place worked against the enduring and widespread popularity of Agatha or Margaret, both virgins and martyrs, or Lawrence of gridiron fame, or Martin of Tours. Other letter writers from among the Pastons (and from those other families) added the feast days of St Faith and of Michael in Monte Tombe, but given how many other letter writers there are, the aggregation of saints named in any (or all of) the family letters did not run that far beyond those noted by Margaret.[34] English saints make a strong appearance, though they hardly dominate. Augustine of

Canterbury, Edward the Confessor, the local Edmund King and Martyr and, last but hardly least, Thomas of Canterbury and Margaret noted both the translation (7 July) and the death (29 December) of the Archbishop. In fact, the feast of his translation was the date she used five times, more than any other. But against this sign of commitment or allegiance we note that no Paston child or grandchild during Margaret's years in the family ever seems to have been named Thomas.[35]

Just as the calendar came around every 12 months, so Margaret's fondness for her heroines and heroes led to a fair amount of repetition; there are 15 instances of this over the years. The Purification of the Virgin, the feast of Simon and Jude, and that of Edmund king and martyr, were each noted four times, and the translation of Becket, as we said, was oft repeated. There seems no obvious pattern to guide us regarding duplications: St Hilary, St George, Luke the Evangelist (thrice), St Leonard Abbot, among others, and her references to their dates goes from early letters to later ones (I, 154, I, 194, and I, 217). Because the date as given on a letter often was two or three days on either side of the actual feast—as in "the Thursday next after sent Andrew" (I, 166) or "The Fryday next be-fore sent Thomas of Caunter-bery" (I, 206)— other choices of other saints for those intervening days were almost always ready at hand. This argues that the repetition of a particular saint's day probably meant the neglect of someone else who fell within the same two- or three-day outer boundary. While Margaret did not slight her English saints, some such as Hugh of Lincoln or Cuthbert or Dunstan, and various minor figures but with cults and shrines in East Anglia, are only noteworthy by their absence.[36] No mention of William of Norwich, though his shrine still had some minor currency among pilgrims.[37] No signs of interest in St Bridget (Birgita), despite Henry V's outlay in her honor at Syon. Margaret also noted a few fixed dates not associated with an historicized saint. She does take note of such now-popular dates as the Invention of the Holy Cross ("The Fryday nexst after Crowchemesse Day": I, 135) or "Wryten...on Holy Rode Day, etc" (I, 179) and "Wretyn the Tuesday next before Holy Rood Day" (I, 204, for the 12 September), though she mostly struck to old favorites in both name and date.

The world of the Pastons was flooded with hagiographic literature, both new and old, just as it was with artistic and performative pre-sentations focusing on the saints. As the *Golden Legend* was the basic reference book for hagiographic material, we can look to see what guidance it offers regarding Margaret's choices. It is no surprise by now to discover that except for three English saints—Augustine of England, Edward king and confessor, and Edmund king and martyr—all the saints Margaret noted in her letter dating rate a chapter or a tale in *The Golden Legend* (including Thomas of Canterbury). There are also chapters in *The Legend* on the Invention of the Holy Cross and the Exaltation of the Holy Cross—both noted by Margaret.[38] The *Golden Legend* has entries for Peter and Paul but as separate entries, denying them the sort of joint coverage Margaret (and five other Pastons) accorded them for 24 June. She might shorten a reference; "wretyn att Norwyche in hast on the Thursday next after Seynt Peter," leaving Paul in the cold as far as explicit mention guides us (I, 141)—though it was the joint feast day. Such events or milestones as the Purification and the Assumption of the Virgin rated coverage in the *Legend,* as they did in Margaret's dating. Overall this kind of comparison seems to offer yet another indication of how closely Margaret stuck to the main lines of hagiographic focus. Sources that could have offered more diversity, or deviation—had she wanted this to be a characteristic of her calendar—were not hard to find, and minor saints had their own cults in the counties in which she passed her long life.[39]

We have made many references to the calendar that Margaret could have or would have consulted in her book of hours. And while that actual physical calendar and the book that contained it have not been preserved—except by inference or deduction, as we reconstruct it—many comparable calendars have been preserved, offering points of comparison. Such a comparison indicates how many names and days were awaiting a call, though for the most part such a call never came, at least not from Margaret. But if we bring up the months of May and November for a close look, we see this in detail. Table 2.7 unfolds these months as in a standard calendar of the Sarum Use, as they are actually noted in the Wingfield Psalter in the New York Public Library, and in Margaret's letters.[40]

This sort of comparison is further confirmation of what we have been saying; that is, that those days Margaret did note were but a few of those "available" by the light of virtually any calendar she would be likely to have use of. Beyond this wider list of options, her repetitive mention of some favorites reduced her pool of saints chosen even more. Of course, had we more letters, we assume we would have been able to expand the cast list, though whether a less traditional set of saints and feast days would have emerged may seem unlikely. After all, more saints, more dates, and more choices, are easy to pick up if we look around a bit, and presumably Margaret could have done so as well, as she been interested in such a quest. A Rawlinson liturgical manuscript in the Bodleian Library, probably from fifteenth-century East Anglia, gives us a whole set of untapped riches, focusing just on

Table 2.7 Saints' Days Noted in the Sarum Use, in the Wingfield Psalter, and Margaret Paston's Letters

May

Date	Sarum Use	Wingfield Psalter	Margaret Paston
1	Apostles Philip & James	X	—
2	Athanasius, Bishop[a]	—	—
3	Invention of the Holy Cross	X	X
4	—	—	—
5	Translation of Aldhelm[a]	—	—
6	John before the Lateran Gate	X	Moveable Feast
7	John of Beverley	—	—
8	—	—	—
9	Translation of Nicholas[a] and Andrew[b]	—	—
10	Gordian & Epimachus	X	—
11	—	—	—
12	Nereus & Achilleus & Pancras	X	
13	—	—	—
14	—	—	—
15	—	—	—
16	—	—	—
17	—	—	—
18	—	—	—
19	Dunstan, AB & C	X	X
20	Ethelbert, King & Martyr[c]	—	—
21	—	—	—
22	—	—	—
23	—	—	Moveable Feast
24	—	—	—
25	Aldhelm;[a] Urban, Pope & Martyr[c]	Aldhelm	—
26	Augustine of England, AB & C	X	X
27	Petroc, Confessor[c]		Moveable Feast
28	Germanus of Paris, B & C	X	—
29	—	—	—
30	—	—	—
31	Petronilla, V	—	X

Note: Margaret dated letters from the Ascension and from Trinity Sunday in May.

November[41]

Date	Sarum Use	Wingfield Psalter	Margaret Paston
1	All Saints	X	—
2	All Souls; St Eustace[a]	X	X
3	Winifred, V & M	—	—
4	—	—	—
5	—	—	—
6	Leonard, Abbot	X	X
7	Willibrord[a]	—	—
8	4 Crowned Martyrs	X	—
9	Theodore, M	X	—
10	Translation of Wilibrord[a]	—	—
11	Martin, B & C	X	X
12	—	—	—
13	Brice, B & C	X	
14	Translation of Erkenwald[b]	—	—
15	Machute, B & C	X	—
16	Edmund of Abingdon, AB & C	—	X
17	Hugh of Lincoln, B & C	—	—
18	—	—	—
19	Elizabeth of Hungary	Elizabeth, widow	—
20	Edmund, King & Martyr	—	—
21	Columbanus;[a] Rufinus[b]	—	—
22	Cecilia, V & M	X	—
23	—	Clement	X
24	Chrysogonus, Martyr	—	—
25	Katherine of Alexandria, V & M	X	X
26	Linus, Pope and Martyr	—	—
27	—	—	—
28	—	—	—
29	Saturninus, Bishop & Martyr	X	—
30	Andrew, Apostle	X	X

[a] These dates are to be found in the calendar given in *Horae Eboracensis: The Prymer or Hours of the Blessed Virgin Mary*, Surtees Society 59 (1920).

[b] As in the calendar printed in F. E. Eeles, "Part of the Kalendar of a xiiith Century Service Book once in the Church of Writtle," *Transactions of the Essex Archaeological Society* n.s. 25 (1960), 68–79.

[c] As in the calendar printed in J. B. L. Tolhurst, *the Customary of the Cathedral Priory Church of Norwich* (London, 1948): The manuscript is Corpus Christi College, Cambridge 465.

the month of January.[42] Though the manuscript ignores the feast of St Hilary (13 January) that Margaret noted in 1473 (I, 22), its listings are far richer than hers. In fact the manuscript—which is hardly a lavish one in either size or decoration—offers more saints for January than do all the fifteenth-century family letter writers combined. Margaret had four January dates: Twelfth Night (6 January), St Hilary (13 January), St Agnes (21 January), and the Conversion of St Paul (on the 25th). We can expand this a bit by bringing in Agnes Plumpton, who dated a letter by the feast of St Marcellus, pope and martyr (16 January). Beyond those saints named by any and all of our letter writers, the Bodleian manuscript offers a notation of the feast of St Berethus or Brithun on the 9th, of St Sulpicius on the 17th, of St Marius the Abbot, and then of Fabian and Sebastian, as a pair, on the 20th of January.

For an example of some variation as shaped by English geography and regional loyalties, we can turn to the calendar of a York Missal.[43] For that second half of the year—those months devoid of moveable feasts—the Missal has entries for more days than it leaves blank; only five blanks (ferial days) for August, seven for September, and so on through the autumn. While the York calendar notes St. Chad and St. Cuthbert, hardly surprising given its northern orientation, no saint's day that Margaret does note is absent from its list. No Paston letter is dated by the feast of the translation of St Martin of Tours (4 July), though his 11 November feast was noted. Nor do we learn from Margaret of the feast days of St Praxedis, virgin and martyr (21 July), or of St Apollinaris, bishop and martyr (23 July), or of the Seven Sleepers (27 July), or of St Germanus (31 July).[44] Not much popularity, not much by way of cults of dedication or baptismal affiliation. Of course, there is virtually no end to the list of saints; a favorite would get the nod and thereby push rivals whose feasts fell a day or two or even three on either side of her or his day into the shade. When Margaret noted the semiofficial or quasi-national cult of St George (23 April), she did at the casual price of snubbing St Anselm (21 April) and the Translation of St Wilfrid (24 April). Likewise, her mention of St Andrew (30 November) denied St Birinus (3 December) a chance to make the list.

Though the naming of the saints who figured in the construction and expression of Margaret Paston's piety makes them seem like competitors—men and women working at rival stalls, hawking their wares in the marketplace of lay spirituality and salvation—it also gives them a living or dynamic reality. This was a serious feature of medieval religion, enhanced by the doctrine of purgatory and the mendicants' emphasis on a spirituality that could be internalized and assimilated into the lives of secular women and men. The spiritual circles in which Margaret Paston lived saw no end of organized campaigns on behalf of a new or a redis-covered saint, efforts comparable to the lobbying or marketing strategies on behalf of consumer products and political candidates in our day. At various times, and emanating from various sources of power or an orga-nized public voice, there had been a west country lobby (to have Thomas Cantilupe of Hereford canonized: 2 October was his feast day), one for Carmelite favorites, one on behalf of those deemed political martyrs (like Simon de Montfort or Thomas of Lancaster), one for pious monarchs like Edward the Confessor and Henry VI, one for the new liturgical feasts, and so forth. Though All Saints' Day on 1 November guaranteed that all the sacred heroines and heroes had at least a shared moment on center stage, an individualized feast day—noted in the liturgy and perhaps cul-minating in a pilgrimage at the very top of the pyramid of public devo-tion—was the goal of every ecclesiastical lobbyist in Christendom.[45]

This tale could be told at much greater length, though it hardly seems necessary to do so, and the variations in the prayers of a book of hours and the saints listed in its calendar represent an individualization that makes such books of great interest. Variations abound, as in a calendar from these years that reflects usage in Kent. Such a calendar steered its readers to figures like Romanus (30 March) or Ithamar (10 June) or Paulinus (10 October), though as Anglo-Saxon bishops of Rochester it is no wonder their cults had never gone north of the Thames.[46] While we would not expect a Paston to show much interest in the proscribed cult of Richard Scrope, martyred archbishop of York, the Sarum calendar did single out Hugh of Lincoln; Margaret never did so.[47] Nor were many candidates from the well-stocked ranks of East Anglian saints to be found.[48] And if we go in search of serious eccentricity we do much better if we turn to the Scottish court rather than to the epistolary piety of a Norfolk matri-arch. At the court of Scotland we can find a calendar noting the feast day of St Kentigern, which we might expect, but we also have such paro-chial celebrations as a remembrance of Bannockburn (23 June) or Stirling Bridge (11 September), alongside conventional feasts for northern figures like Monan, or William of Perth, or Ninian or Malachy.[49]

★ ★ ★

Having set Margaret Paston so firmly among the ranks of the conven-tional, can we temper the picture—not by redefining her, but rather by showing the world around her to be just about as conventional in expres-sions of piety, even if many of its denizens were not necessarily as dedi-cated as she seems to have been? A walk down virtually any street or lane in fifteenth-century Norwich meant passing parish church after parish

church. To whom were these churches dedicated? A city that could boast
of over three dozen churches in Margaret's day provides a broad screen
on which to project a fair number of saints. Furthermore, in contrast to
unlikely saints we find in an exotic calendar such as that of the hours
of Catherine of Cleves; the world of parish churches and their patron
saints was a familiar part of the townscape.[50] If we turn to the Norwich
churches still standing today and covered in Nikolas Pevsner's *Buildings
of England,* we have dedications to saints who were very much part of
Margaret's world.[51] Covering them in alphabetical order by dedication
(that being how Pevsner lists them), after the parish church of All Saints
we have churches dedicated to Andrew (M = a saint noted by Margaret
in dating a letter), Augustine (presumably of Canterbury, not of Hippo:
M), Benedict, Clement (M), Edmund (M), Etheldred the King, George
(three churches: M), Giles (M), Gregory (M), Helen, James, John the
Baptist (M), John the Evangelist and/or Apostle (two churches), Julian,
Laurence (M), Margaret Virgin and Martyr (M), Martin (two churches:
M), The Virgin Mary (two churches: M), Michael the Archangel (three
churches: M), Peter (four churches: M), St Saviour, Simon and Jude (M),
Stephen, and Swithin. This gives us 25 different patron saints for the
Norwich parishes; Margaret dated a letter by 15 of their feast days.[52] This
does not take into account that she noted some feast days—and therefore
some saints—more than once, just as the people of Norwich felt free to
use the same saint for more than one dedication. So we have what we
can term a 60 percent level of duplication between Margaret's saints and
Norwich dedications. She and the voice of local piety, however it had
been formed, seemed in considerable agreement: stick to the tried and
true.[53] And though most of these churches had been founded and dedicated by the twelfth or thirteenth century, there are no indications that
when they were rebuilt or when parishes were merged there was much
inclination to jettison the old and bring in the new as far as the patron
saint was concerned.

We can also turn to an institution that came into its own closer to
Margaret's day; the guilds of Norfolk and their patron saints. Those patron
saints of the local guilds, as tallied for the late fourteenth century, offer
us a case of "another county heard from" in terms of dedications; little
here by way of either novelty or variety. In 1389 the ten leading ecclesiastical figures, in terms of their patronage of the county's guilds, were
Mary, John the Baptist, the Holy Trinity, Peter, All Saints, Margaret,
John, Corpus Christi, Andrew, and Thomas the Apostle. Though over 20
other figures can be found (including Jesus, the Holy Spirit, and the Holy
Cross), the "top ten" were the patrons of almost two-thirds of the guilds;
Thomas of Canterbury, Catherine, George, and Edmund all appear, but

without any great following, and our roll call of the familiar accommodates this traditional or old-fashioned database as easily as it does that of parish churches.[54] Here too, by the criterion of guild patrons and dedications, Margaret's conventional taste was close to mainstream taste as it was shaped closer to her own time.

We conclude this discussion of names and saints by returning to the Pastons themselves, that family into which Margaret married and to whose enterprises she devoted so much of her life. What baptismal names were used in and chosen by the family; which saints were (or might have been) their personal patrons? In a culture where the given names of John, Richard, William, Thomas, and Robert heavily dominated the onomastic pool, and usually in that order, we find the Pastons were generally content to go with prevailing social (and spiritual) currents.[55] What men's names would Margaret have known (and chosen), either for Pastons already on the ground when she arrived and for those yet to come? First, of course, she was and would continue to be surrounded by men named John: husband and her two eldest sons. William meant her father-in-law, her husband's next brother, and then a grandson. Edmund covered a brother-in-law (d. 1449) and a son. After these conventional choices that were duplicated (or triplicated), we run to single usages: one Walter (a son), one Christopher (grandson, son of John III), one Edward (nephew through marriage, the son of Elizabeth Poynings), one Philip (son of John III, though possibly born after Margaret made her will in 1482), one Robert (son of Edmund, though again possibly born too late). There were two Clements—though as they were her grandfather-in-law, long dead, and a brother-in-law—this may have been too much of a stretch. Finally, one Harry—whom I think to have been a brother-in-law who had died young and who presumably was a Henry, which smacks more of English patriotism than of the heavenly host.[56]

That many of these men carried the name of a popular saint is to be expected. Was there a likely saint of popular currency for whom a Paston male might have been named? And, when the answer is yes—as it usually is—did that saint appear on the calendar of Margaret's letter dating? As popular usage guides us, John seemingly means John the Baptist; Margaret does date a letter by his day. John Paston II dated a letter by 29 August, the date of the Baptist's Decollation, though his mother never did so (though 1 September was noted as the feast of Giles Abbot). Edmund, king and martyr, had his day noted on a letter of 20 November; no letter dated to commemorate his translation (29 April), and none for St Christopher (25 July), though in the form of a large wall painting in the church at Paston he would have been a familiar figure in family circles. Margaret's brother-in-law Clement had his patron saint's day noted in her letter of 23 November (I, 219; also by John II, I, 271). Son Walter seems an unlikely candidate for hagiographic notation, though Farmer says there may have been a local albeit a minor cult. A family tradition, or the whimsy of a godparent, seems a more likely reason for this choice.[57] John III's son Philip may have been born after his grandmother's death, so he is not really a member of the team as we construct it as centering around Margaret. The Apostle Philip does not show at all on the list of Norfolk church dedications, and the feast day he shared with James (1 May) seems to have passed without notice (and 5 March was named as the Feast of the Invention of the Cross).[58] Margaret had had an uncle, Philip (Berney), which may explain this choice, though this seems a long stretch and there are few signs of Paston ties with what remained of Margaret's natal family. Since we know neither the birthdates of Margaret's children nor the identity of their godparents, we get no help from two avenues of naming tradition that we can sometimes turn to. The family's pool of names was small and not much given to extravagant bursts of feeling or fancy—no Humphrey, no Achilles, not even an Osbern—and whether the Paston men felt any special bonds with their patron saints remains a mystery. No letter writer ever added a tag to the dating clause like "today is my patron saint's day and my birthday."

What about the women's names?[59] Margaret's sister-in-law (sister of John I) was an Elizabeth—a familiar saint but not one who drew much focus by way of dedications (nor, judging by the dating of letters, was her feast day of family interest). Margaret's daughters were Anne (and her brother-in-law William II also married an Anne, the high-born Anne Beaufort) and Margery—she of the much-denounced marriage with Richard Calle. Margery was probably a familiar or diminutive of Mary, or perhaps of Margaret. These variations on Mary—and no one carried this simple and evocative name—were hardly rarities; John III married a Margery (Brewes). But as a diminutive or derivative name Margery would carry little hagiographic distinction. Against this, we have St Anne, mother of the Virgin, a towering figure in popular religious expression in fifteenth-century England, and Margaret did note her day (26 July) in a letter, just as she did that of her mother-in-law Agnes (21 January for the feast).[60] Margaret's mother had been a Margaret (Berney) and they shared the saint's day of 20 July, as well as the custom of the same name for parent and (first?) born child. Margaret noted that date in one letter (I, 162: August 18, 1461): "The Saterday nex be-fore Sent Margarete."[61] The women who married into the family offered more diversity: Edmund II married Katherine Clippesby and Clement married Beatrix Somerton.[62] The children of this next generation all stayed near the onomastic home base: Margery Calle's sons were John, William, and Richard, as we learn from their grandmother's will. John II had an illegitimate daughter Constance, though the girl's mother might have made the choice, it being about as exotic as we find. Edmund II's son was Robert, which like Constance, was not of note in the English calendars. As with the men, birthdays and the role of godparents are unknown; no help from that direction.[63]

Time to conclude. I have no inclination to grade Margaret Paston for a level of devotion as defined by either boldness of iteration or by striking behavior. That she knew her saints is hardly in dispute, guided by her calendar as well as by countless other reminders of how the passing of the year was marked. Margaret Paston clearly took the saints seriously—"friends and helpers," as Eamon Duffy sums them up—and if anything Margaret may have paid even more heed to the moveable feasts that marked the climax of the Christian year. What can we deduce from her dating style, touching what we might think of as deeper aspects of lay religiosity? We might say that her links with all those saints and their days is best seen as the top layer of the bedrock of a wholly assimilated faith, one endorsing and utilizing the role and value of intercessory figures, the efficacy and comfort of the treasury of merits, a real (if rarely articulated) fear of purgatory, and confidence in the imminence of those legions of the heavenly host. But on such issues there is little that we can pin down as hard evidence; no paper trail that stands apart from the business-as-usual letters, no personal avowals or explicit declarations, no "Book" of Margaret Paston wherein she tells it all and then goes on to tell it again, no public weeping and wailing. Margaret Paston did as she did, and all we can say with certainly is that the dating style she chose and stuck to over the years must reflect her way of going about her business as the year rolled along, as it does her idea of how to weave mundane affairs into the larger and unchanging backdrop of a transcendental world. She knew her saints and she chose from among them as she wished, as they in the variety of their feast days and attributes passed before her. She always stuck to the tried and true. Beyond that she kept herself to herself and we have to live with her choice.

CHAPTER 3

MARGARET PASTON IN CONTEXT:
THINGS SAID, DONE, AND OWNED

Saints and the moveable feasts of the Christian year seemed a good place to begin, guided as we are by Margaret Paston's own choices on such matters. And yet noting saints' days in the dating clause of her letters can be thought of as Margaret talking to herself. She chose this particular style and we have come to expect her to express herself in this fashion; "Wretyn in hast on Seynt Edmundys Day the kyng" (I, 165). No one else in her world followed her lead, at least not in letter after letter. At the same time there is no reason to think that any of her recipients was put off stride by her style. It was her own touch, her own business; if it did not make the letter better or more useful, it certainly did no harm and seemingly caused no confusion about the date. But an analysis of her dating style only takes us so far. We now turn to other aspects of Margaret Paston's expressions of religiosity. One of these concerns other forms of usage, of speech-into-writing, this still being in the realm of "thing said." Then I will turn to "things done" and then to "things owned" and see what else falls into these realms.

Beyond her epistolary genuflections to the fixed and moveable feasts of the annual cycle, what can we extract from Margaret Paston's letters in our quest for her religious outlook and practice? As we move to other aspects of her letters, to variations on what she said/wrote that also embraced aspects of her world of belief, we see that this line of inquiry—unlike our look at her distinctive use of saints' days—will tend to draw her back toward the crowd, back toward other Pastons and correspondents who spoke in a similar fashion about God's will and the Virgin's intercession and such matters. Accordingly, it is words—ritually uttered expressions, formulaic one-liners, micronarratives, and, in many instances, what I suggest we think of as speech acts. These stand as a key to sentiments and beliefs as well as guides to behavior, to things done by Margaret. And though she remains our central focus, a look at things said and done (and material possessions owned) will draw us back toward some of the other Pastons, we can note the circularity of our construction; the premise that what Margaret says and does is typical and conventional, and that what those hypothetical "typical" and "conventional" people of fifteenth-century England did (and said) is just about what Margaret did and said.

The course of this entire inquiry has a multilayered agenda. One is simply to determine what Margaret Paston said and did. Another is to seek a context in which her words and deeds resonate with what we know about the workings, the cultural values, the socioeconomic realities, the material possessions, and the discourse of fifteenth-century lay or gentry society. We set Margaret off on her own; we bring her back into the family circle; we compare the Pastons with each other. In so doing we make Margaret our bellwether point of reference, our Greenwich meridian of spiritual expression and conviction. There is no sure test as to whether this is fair, proper, anachronistic, a reflection of authorial bias, or right on target. But the past, as we know and are wont to say, is a strange country, and Margaret Paston is a useful if not always a very loquacious guide. We can do much worse than to follow what lead she offers, as we do in this chapter on speech styles, on information about church attendance and priests, and about personal possessions that bespeak people of some substance who took their worship seriously.

★   ★   ★

Words and a manner of speaking. Let us turn once again to Margaret's words—to the way in which she expressed herself. Speech is one of those realms of behavior in which the conventional and the mainstream are mingled with the individualized and the idiosyncratic. Furthermore, these lines between what is common and what is more distinctive can be crossed any number of times and in many directions. In what follows I accept the idea of a strong correlation between the language of the letters and the spoken language, in keeping with the judgment of Norman Davis, particularly regarding the language of Margaret Paston (and Agnes, her mother-in-law.)[1] I begin with a look at Margaret's constant recourse to pious wording and phraseology in her letters. How did she express herself, and what can we offer about her religious views from a close reading of her mode of expression?

Before I come to the substance of this chapter, I want to lay the ghost of the "wreytn...in ryth grete hast" (I, 126) tags because they seem to be a convention of letter writing, having no bearing on either the content of the letter, its style of discourse, or its length. That many of the letters, of Margaret and of virtually everyone else, tell the recipient that the letter had been composed under pressing conditions just seems to have been the way the Pastons set themselves to the task—whether it was the men, writing on their own, or any of them by way of a scribe. This disclaimer (against not having included even more information) was a commonplace, found in a letter of 69 lines, which must have consumed a good deal of time in its composition (I, 154), as in one of 19 lines (I, 206: "wretyn the Fryday next be-fore Sent Thomas of Caunterbery in hast").[2] And it was Margaret herself who threw in that evocative postscript, "paper is dainty" (I, 142), reminding us of the labor and expense involved in writing a letter. Her observation brings home the need to take seriously any and every phrase that was included, every invocation or conventional expression of piety that was rolled off. The presence of all the stock phrases we are about to look at added to the length of a letter; presumably the letter writers considered such "boilerplate" verbiage sufficiently important to be worth the time and effort it took to insert them. Perhaps they were just accepted as being so much a part of normal expression that their omission would have seemed strange.

How did Margaret and her contemporaries express themselves in ways that shed light on their spiritual mindset? Gillian Pritchard and David Knowles both remarked on the pious coloring of so much of the Pastons' language—even when dealing with the most secular or mundane topics on their wide agenda. As Pritchard says, "Religious language, phrases and appeals are a common feature of the Pastons' understanding of religious themes and the universal familiarity of those ideas."[3] Clearly, these modes of expression were simply incorporated into how people spoke and then wrote, even when writing "in hast" and on matters with little that was inherently spiritual or religious. We see, when we look into such matters, that most fifteenth-century family letters were heavily laden with invocations, blessings, and calls for support from God or from others of the Holy Family.[4]

The writer's assumptions of an easy passage between the stock phraseology of piety and deeper spiritual needs and thoughts can be read to reinforce the idea that both the saints and the uncertainties of life were held to be near at hand. Did the pious phraseology of fifteenth-century family letter writers carry more weight, in terms of deeper commitment, than it would today? We assume that it did, though this is certainly hard to pin down; the high incidence of pious invocations and of "god bless" tags points to an affirmative response to our question. The inclination to roll so much of our speech and writing down the familiar or reflexive channels of expression has to be taken into account—for them as for us. Even today people mumble a semiautomatic "god bless" after someone sneezes, a "thank god" for any happy chance or for disaster averted, as in an auto accident that bends the metal but not the bodies. In this casual fashion we mix conventions of speech with those of manners. We "swear to god" when trying to impress others with our seriousness, far though we may be from belief in any god to whom we are swearing. And the occasional "god damn" was strong language of condemnation, or it was until the counterculture of the 1960s pushed it down the pecking order of strong speech.[5]

Reading the Paston letters to decipher the expression of common-place pieties is hardly an exercise of great challenge, though linking these expressions to deeper convictions might be. Pious wording and pious expressions abound, found in most letters and, more often than not, more than once in a given letter. Starting with Margaret, who in this regard is far from idiosyncratic or the most common user of these tags, we can distinguish a number of such modes of expression. We have an abundance of the relatively simple "god bless" or "god be thanked" tags. Virtually throwaway phrases, generously sprinkled throughout the cor-respondence; few letters are without them or some variant thereof. These tags seem to have been a part of ordinary speech. They are the briefest of throw-ins, the top layer of the bedrock foundation of the speaker's faith, though they may not be much help in any effort to get below the surface. We can think of these as invocations, to be found in most of Margaret's letters (and those of almost everyone else). They fall into a couple of categories. There are the short or undirected invocations, merely ask-ing for divine aid and general blessings. Then we move up, in a sense, to the directed or focused invocations in which God and His helpers are given more detailed instructions about how, when and where to aim their arrows to maximize Paston family fortunes. Then there are the blessings bestowed, with their own rules about who could bestow them and upon whom. These come out of and indicate patriarchal or matriarchal status on the part of the blessing-giver. They are distant descendents of the kind of top-down grace that was bestowed or transmitted by the birthright blessings of Isaac and Esau (or Jacob), and in keeping with this model it is fitting that such usages are mostly found in the letters of parent-child exchange.[6] When they do appear it is but once per letter, and in terms of using this form of speech as an expression of spirituality (and matriarchy), Margaret really only comes into her own after the death of John I. The blessing runs along a two-way street, bestowed by the elder and some-times explicitly sought by the younger—a top-down dynamic in speech that mirrors the social hierarchy and the quasi-sacral authority of the old over the young, of parent over (grown) son or daughter. It is a fairly standard opening in a parent-child letter.

Regardless of the style or identity of the letter writer, all these forms of wording and variations of phraseology seem rigidly orthodox—whether they are casual utterances or more introspective and elaborate statements. To take them seriously, they can be read as indications of how the utterance of the right words might activate some mechanism of divine intervention—like Milton's two-handed engine at the door. Calls to God (the father) and the need for His aid and support were constantly on their lips, be they young or old, male or female, master or servant, parent or child. The multiplicity and ubiquity of these stock phrases in most letters gives support to the idea that these men and women thought of their world as one in close contact with the next. We know their thoughts turned in this direction in moments of crisis. But the letters indicate that no business worth explicating through this medium was too insignificant to be sanctified by the use of pious tags of speech.

If we start with the simplest phrases we have a vast stock of "god bless" and "at the reurence of God." These two- or three-word catchphrases are entered in or rather woven through the text of most letters, regardless of author. In regard to such usage Margaret was but typical, outstanding neither for the frequency of her usage nor much by way of idiosyncratic turns of wording or variations from the stock phrasing. She expressed herself much as the others did, as we might expect regarding the conventional, repetitive nature of these utterances. Her "be the grase of god," was basic, though she might enlarge on this in the same letter: "Trust verily in God and leve hym and serve hym, and he wyl not deseve yw" (I, 129).[7] This was to John I, whom we can always assume to have been in need of as much support as he could assemble, and her "the Blyssyd Trinité haue yow in hys kepyng and send vs good tydyngs of yow" was on behalf of her effort to give succor from a distance (I, 168). Her "(I) pray you hertely at the revernce of God that ye be of good comfort" was also unexceptionable, though she went on to talk about the downfall of their enemies (I, 191). As she sums up in another letter to her eldest son, "I trust god xal helpe ryth wele, and I pray God so do in alle owr maters"; and then, at the very end, "God helpe at nede" (I, 203).

Most fifteenth-century letter writers used phrases of this sort, and the other Pastons spoke much as Margaret spoke. John II rolled off his "God haue you in kepyng" as he promised that more news would soon follow, "wyth goddys grace" (I, 241). When there was good news about John III—wounded at Barnet but alive—his older brother threw in the conventional "blyssyd be God" (I, 261). He did not wax philosophically about God's providence or fortune's wheel, though John II does add that his brother "is a lyffe and fareth well, and in no perell off dethe," while John III himself is "in no joparté off my lyff." When John II addressed his mother it was with "Jesus have yow in hys kepyng" or "wyth the grace off God, who have yow in hys kepyng" (I, 291 and 308). Nor was Paston family usage noticeably difference from that of their correspondents; Henry Berry's letter to John I, with its "to the worsschippe of God and you all, wych euer haue you in his kepynge. Amen" (II, 682), was but one among many that talked in this vein.[8] Richard Calle, addressing his employers, was much the same: "Almyghty Jesu preserue you and send you the victorye of your elmyes, as I truste to Almighty Jesu ye shall" (I, 653). In his wording Calle differed but little from John Downing, writing to Edmund Paston I in 1447–48: "Almyty God have yow in his kepyn" (II, 704). This was what we can think of as boilerplate language—but it is also the way people wrote and, arguably, the way they spoke. If we should not make too much of it, given its frequency and its semireflexive nature, we should not dismiss it just because it was such common usage.[9]

How seriously is this all to be taken? In many respects, with adjustments for the brevity of phrasing and the fact that the writer was a lay person, we are on the edges of the world of liturgical formulae. Much of what can be said about prayer within the structured form of the liturgy can be applied to what we have here; repetitive, social as well as devotional, focused on thanksgiving or sacrifice, and as a form of discourse (between the living and the divinity).[10] We move here among people who heard the mass, who found time for private devotions, who attended sacramental occasions beyond the daily prayers, and whose speech was apt to be shaped to some extent by these experiences and by the culture or conventions of ecclesiastical discourse. Unfortunately for us, the Pastons were usually closemouthed about their commitments to the divine, and none ever cut loose in the fashion of Elizabeth de la Pole, writing to Sir Robert Plumpton in 1501. She hammered home all the themes we have touched upon and her loquacity is instructive; "your presperous helth, worship & welfayre, which I besech almighty Jesus long to continue, to his pleasure & your most comforth. Hartely beseeching the gud Lord that redemed me & all mankind vpon the holy Crosse, that he will of his benigne mercy vouchsafe to be your helper, & give you power to resist & withstand the vtter & malicious enmity & false craft of Master Empson, & such others your adversaries" (#159).[11] Would that Margaret or any of the other Pastons had ever felt a similar urge to open up.

In moving through other varieties of pious wording that were common and slightly more elaborate than the terse "god bless" tags, we encounter more fulsome invocations, those focused or directed appeals to heaven. Here Margaret shows a slight touch of her own. The invocation or the call for heavenly intercession is common, usually coming toward the end of the letter. More often than not Margaret called for aid in the name of the Trinity. It could be the basic "the blyssyd Trinteé have you in hys kepyng" (I, 172), or perhaps it was the "blissful Trinyté," or on occasion it might be the slightly more complex "The Trynyté haue yw jn his keping and sent yw gode speded in alle ywr materis" (I, 130: this being the young Margaret to John in 1448), or even "The Holy Trinité haue yow in hesse kepyn and send yow helth" (I, 127). But taking these slight variations into account, it was the Trinity, in some fashion or other, that we see as her usual choice. In most of her letters to her husband, Margaret closed with a prayer much along these lines: "The blissyd Trynyté have you in his kepyng and send yow helt and gode spede in al yowr materys" (I, 130). In contrast, the blessing she bestowed on her sons in letters written after their father's death came at the letter's opening rather than at the end.

Not even Margaret, a creature of habit and fixed in her ways, did or said exactly the same thing on every occasion. In addition to the invocation of the Trinity, she occasionally chose another of the alternatives so readily available: just plain "God" or "Almighty God" was certainly a reasonable choice, and this could run to "I be-seche alle-myghtty God have you in hys kepyng" (I, 174). Or it might take the form of "God have yow in hys kepyng and sen yow good sped in alle yowre materis," as in May 1464, when writing to her husband (I, 176). In a letter to her oldest son, she is simultaneously the mother who blesses and who scolds: "God kepe yow and yeue yow grace to do as wele as I woold ye dede" (I, 205). But beyond the Trinity and God (the Father, presumably) Margaret rarely strayed very far in choosing from the list of heavenly personnel. She offers but few direct invocations of Jesus; "Jesu have yow in hys kepyng," as to John III in 1472 (I, 218), which is unusual. When family fortunes were at low ebb after the loss of Caister she ended a letter to John II with "God bryng vs oute of it, who haue yow in his kepyng," this in a letter that had been "wretyn with onhertis ease" (I, 207). But basically, the two styles cover her usage: the Trinity and God Almighty.

Where she did depart from the basic text of invocation was when she issued a more focused call for divine aid. Her specific instructions to heaven and to those located there, hopefully keeping an eye on matters Paston, seem not inappropriate, coming as they did from one rarely at a loss in giving advice about earthly matters. In these invocations Margaret resorts to the kind of Manichean us/them view of life that characterizes so much of the Paston outlook.[12] She asked for such aid when writing to John II during the siege of Caister, surely a time when all the heavenly as well as earthly partisanship they could solicit was urgently needed: "God kepe you and send you the vittory of your elmyse, and geve you and vs all grace to leve in peas" (I, 202). When John I had been cooling his heels in the Fleet, she concluded in much the same style; "The blessyd Trinyté haue you in hys kypnyg and send you gode spyde in all youre maters, and send you grace to haue a gode conclusyon in hem in haste" (I, 184). But often it was the partisan style we associate with the Pastons: "And I pray God hertely send vs good tydyngs of yow, and send the victory of your enemys" (I, 191). Not quite the Sermon on the Mount, though in fairness the family was swimming in a sea of troubles (even if mostly of their own making). No wonder their calls for help were so parochial, so self-centered. In some of Margaret's more focused appeals for divine intervention—as in a letter to John of August 1465—she straddles the ridge between a request for reinforcements for our side and a malediction against the other guys: "The Holy Ghost kepe you bothyn and deliuere you of your elmyse," this being one of the few times she appeals to that elusive third person of the Trinity (I, 215).

Calls for divine aid were usually short and simple, if heartfelt. While a bit of cursing ones enemies and wishing them ill was a regular feature in these invocations, neither Margaret nor any other Paston ever came near the level of verbal hostility we encounter in "An Anonymous Account of the Case" in the Armburgh Papers. In this case all restraint has been jettisoned; if you were against them then nothing bad that befell you could be enough; you deserved whatever you got. The God of the Old Testament at his most smiting-inclined: "with inne a while after, for his vntrouthe and specialy for the offence that he dyde in the holy place, Godde chastised him and sent hym soche a disease in hys bak, that he went stoupyng, that his shuldres were as lowe as his myddell and neuer recovered that dissease." And if being disabled was insufficient as a weather vane of divine wrath, the writer follows up with "for his vntrouthe God smote hym with sykenesses with inne a day or two ate most and was dede beryed with inne fourtenyght after."[13] This kind of invective reduces the occasional outburst from Margaret Paston about "false shrews" into a virtual exercise in ladylike restraint.

Phrases designed to facilitate the synchronization of matters Paston and the turning wheels of heavenly intervention, as Margaret and others expressed them, are found in many letters. Such invocations have a formulaic quality and quantity, and they offer another way of eavesdropping on the articulation of lay piety, even if we get limited returns in a quest for insights into religious sophistication and sensibility. That one form or another of such wording was used so frequently, and by so many, reminds us that the invisible but protective and comforting world of Christian heroism and intervention was right out there, just awaiting the call. These invocations and call for intervention are speech acts—incantations to summon support and to bond human affairs with and into the larger agenda of divine schemes and programs. We can read them as a lay version of prayers, offered on the run; secular prayers uttered here and now and in the vernacular by men and women of the world who hold out great hope for the possibility of help from on high.[14] As secular prayers—by, for, and from the laity—these speech acts conform to the dynamics of discourse or prayer and even more concisely than the words of the liturgy. We have utterances and invocations, calls in praise of the magnificence and munificence of God (the Father). This, we might say, is a dialogue in which party B, the one praying (and writing the letter), indicates to A, the divinity, that B is fully cognizant of A's majestic status and power. Sometimes A's aid is solicited to provide aid on behalf of C (as well as of B)—whether it was sought for the recovery of the manor house at Gresham or the reduction of time in purgatory. B (in the person of Margaret, or another Paston) had few qualms about asking for aid for specific and parochial purposes rather than for the general welfare of Christendom. This is the kind of earth-to-heaven discourse that Pritchard has called "a tripartite conversation between the author, the recipient and God." In the Paston letters, of course, such aid was turned to a practical and partisan application: our own victory and our enemies' downfall.[15]

There are striking omissions in the way Margaret goes about these tasks, intended to bolster family fortunes as well as to gain whatever spiritual benefit was available. No matter which style of expression we track—from the simple "god bless" or "god kepe you" to the more the elaborate "The Holy Ghost be your gyde and send yow good spede and councell, and deliuere you ought of all trobill and disseas to his plesere" (I, 218: Margaret to John III)—she never invokes any of those many saints who figured so frequently in her letter dating. Nor did she direct herself and her causes to the Virgin (except in her last will). Neither St Margaret nor St Katherine were called upon, whatever we are told about their strong hold upon lay spirituality. Only male intercessors were on call, though the Holy Ghost might be considered as gender neutral. Other Pastons used the invocation clause rather less frequently than Margaret, though her sons, among others, seem to have been even more liberal with those "god bless" and "god be thanked" phrases sprinkled throughout their letters. Nor are we taken aback to discover that John I but rarely calls upon divine aid, either for himself or for the letter's recipient (let alone for many third parties). No reader of the Letters has ever found John I noteworthy for generosity of spirit; his approach to life seems to have been to give away as little as possible, even if it were only pious words and good wishes (though his will and some *inter vivos* generosity, discussed below, may argue against this harsh assessment).

But if John I was tight mouthed as well as tight fisted, we find in letters from the Paston men to the great men of the realm more than a whiff of spiritual as well as of the social and political cringing that was par for such exchanges. When John III addressed the duke of Norfolk in 1472, while Caister was still in the duke's grasp, young Paston was quite willing to use the language of subservience: "we shall prey to God for the preseruacyon of your most nobyll estate" (I, 359); we can imagine what he was really thinking. Nor was John III any less ingratiating a few years later, writing now to his patron Lord Hastings: "wyth Godys grace, whom I beseche longe to contenue the prosperous astate of your good lordshepp" (I, 370). And on the idea that obsequious wording had helped part the waters with Hastings, he continued in this vein with Lord Fitzwalter; "And your seyd besecher shall daylye prey to God for the preservacyon of your noble estate longe t'endure" (I, 390; dated by Davis somewhere between 1487 and 1495). By comparison, his verbal humility in addressing Edward IV seems fairly restrained: "preye to God for the conseruacion of youre moost noble persone and estate royall" (I, 294: from 1475, when the Pastons were pushing their case against Norfolk's continued possession of Caister).[16]

When other Pastons did insert a plea for heavenly aid or for a blessing, they might cast a somewhat wider net than Margaret had done. While no one else fell back so heavily on the Trinity (whether Holy or Blessed), other choices introduce us to a slightly wider roster of those whose intercession or guidance was being solicited. We certainly have the Holy Trinity, both early and late; Agnes Paston signing off in 1440 with "The Holy Trinité have yow in gouernaunce" (I, 13), and then her grandson John III, some 25 years later: "The Holy Trinyté haue yow in kepyng" (I, 323). As well as God (the Father?) acting in conjunction with but seemingly distinguished from the Holy Trinity (I, 420), we have appeals to the Holy Ghost (which Margaret also uttered from time to time): "I prey God send yow the Holy Gost amonge yow in the parlement howse," as John III said to his older brother (I, 361). "Alle-myghty God haue yow in guydyng" is only to be expected (I, 235), and there are innumerable references to Jesus, in contrast to Margaret's few pleas in that direction; a fairly simple pleasantry of 1461: "Owre Lord haue yow in hys kepyng" (I, 115: Clement to John I). Walter Paston, in the 1470s, also remembered the central figure of the faith: "Allmythy Iesus have yow in hys kepyng amen" (I, 402), and John III sang much the same tune: "I prey to Jesu preserue you and yours" (I, 374). Elizabeth Poynings, John I's sister, also lent her voice: "by the grace of Jesus, quo haue yow in his blessed keeping"

(I, 121), and John II said much the same to his mother: "Jeshu have yow in hys kepyng" (I, 279). Perhaps the various forms and personages of the divinity were interchangeable and the distinctions noted here reflect minor variations in expression, not anything deeper or more profound.

But if the other Pastons reached out beyond Margaret's narrow circle of helpers in their calls to heavenly intercessors, their choices were still quite limited, their dip into the ranks of holy men and women still fairly constrained. Where is that diversity we saw when we looked at the saints' days (or at church dedications, or at the patron saints of guilds, or even at baptismal names)? Those dozens of saints drawn from all ages and stages of Christian history—each and every one ready to respond to the call of every man, woman, and child who might be deemed deserving—are more remarkable here for their absence than their presence. Nor were other Pastons much more imaginative than Margaret, as we see with John III to his father (I, 322), "I pray God forther yow in all youyr materys to hys plesans and to youyr hertys desyir"—heartfelt but not particularly imaginative. On occasion the younger Paston could be more charitable, as when he said, "I pray God send you your hertys desyir and othyr pore folys thers" (I, 328: to his mother in 1467). He went a bit further in writing to her in 1478: "I prey God send vs good tydyngys, whom I beseche to preserue yow and yours and to send yow your most desyred joye" (I, 380). John's sister Elizabeth (Poynings) took a small step beyond the simple invocation, as her "Jesu for his grete mercy save yow," possibly a glimpse of the redemptive aspects of the faith (I, 121).

For all the tributes to the towering status of the Virgin in medieval religious life—a presence felt and encountered at every level from high theology of the schoolmen and the visions of the mystics to the popularized tales of *The Golden Legend* and tales like that of the Virgin and the Juggler, in addition to all those church dedications—Mary goes virtually unnoticed in the Paston letters.[17] In the wills we will find invocations of Mary as standard in the opening clauses: "lego animam meam omnipotenti Deo, Beate Marie, et omnibus sanctis" (I, 12: from William I's will of 1444).[18] But in their letters, despite all the formulaic invocations, blessings, and thanksgivings, no one pays her much heed. Was Mary's direct intercession something to be reserved for long-term needs—for something beyond the ephemeral agenda of the letters? Since her reservoir of intercessory power and mercy was infinite, there was no question of an economy of scarcity.[19] And given the proximity of her famous shrine at nearby Walsingham—a shrine boasting a phial of her milk and one we know they had personal contact with—we wonder at this consistent practice of nonmention. The Trinity may have been on everyone's lips, in the most literal sense, but this cannot be said for the Mother of God.[20]

It is always possible that I have been too willing to read these tags of verbiage as carrying more meaning than was intended. Certainly, to some degree these phrases and invocations are like kennings of Old English poetry, or perhaps no more expressive of individualized thought than messages on greeting cards today. We have the Holy Trinity instead of Homer's wine-dark sea or "get well." But this does not necessarily mean that such messages do not express sincerely held views and feelings; their standardized or prepackaged formulation does not have to discount what they say. They represent a choice of wording and, presumably, of thought or intention, just as one exercises choice regarding which Hallmark card to send. John III clearly meant the very best when he said to a brother with whom he was intimate, "I trust to God to ese your hert in some thynggys" (I, 334). He cast a wide net with his "I pray God send yow your herttys desyir in these maters and in all othyr," and in this case the recipient of his secular-voiced prayer (that is, his mother) could presumably fill in the "all othyr" as she chose (I, 343). Given the limited agenda of Paston wishes—the acquisition of property, success in lawsuits, the brokering of marriages and the like—it is not hard to vote for sincerity and credibility when Edmund said to his mother, toward the end: "I beseche God send yow the accomplyshment of your moste woorchypfull desyres" (I, 399: a letter of January 1481). Nor should we rush to assume a salacious interpretation in John III writing to "myn owne fayir Mastresse Annes" in a letter of 1474: "God geue yow good rest, for in feythe I trowe ye be in bed" (I, 362: nor should we search for any hidden symbolism in the date, "Wretyn in my wey homward on Mary Maudeleyn Day at mydnyght"). The most striking of all the well-wishings is in a letter of John III to John II; "but God kep yow thys Lent fro lollardy of fleshe" (I, 329). However, Lollards by now were figurative reds under East Anglian beds; sometimes a facetious comment between brothers is just a facetious comment.[21]

An instructive variant of the quasi-religious phraseology of the letters is provided by those blessings, bestowed by both Margaret and John I (and others). In them we can hear (or read) the lay appropriation of clerical speech, used here to reinforce and legitimate the social and familial hierarchy over which the letter writer presided. Taking a leaf from Old Testament blessings and birthrights, our Paston parents assumed a power to endorse or condemn both enterprises and individuals. This came as a matter of course, part of the privileges inherent in social hierarchy, age, and parenthood. These blessing are also a kind of speech act, helping us trace the articulated vectors of power and status that sanctified relationships and governed their direction—"an active process, a process of negotiation between the human world and the divine."[22]

We see, in letter after letter from John II and John III and others, that the Paston children explicitly sought to receive these blessings, and Margaret's practice of opening a letter with such good wishes served to soften the harder news she was often about to deliver. The children asked John I and Margaret for their words of favor, as from John III—now a father in his own right—to his mother: "Modyr, in as humbyll wyse as I can I beseche yow of your blyssyng. I trust fro hense foorthe that we shall haue our chyldyr in rest wyth-ought rebwkyng for ther pleying wanton" (I, 367). And no matter where our sympathies lie in the disputes between feckless but engaging John II and his hard-nosed father, or between the brothers in their concerted opposition to James Gloys, these grown children still were eager to be the recipients of parental words of approbation. A parent was always a parent, regardless of the age of the parties and the amity (or lack thereof) of their dealings.

Though women of rank could play the powerful blessing-card on their own, they were more likely to do so in the absence of their traditional male couverture. Both Margaret and Agnes dispensed such blessings, though when John I had been on the scene it had usually been his hand to play (as it presumably had been for William I in the preceding generation); John I's out-of-favor son and heir, John II, did his best to set things aright when writing to him in August 1461: "Most reuerent and worschepful fadyre, I rekomawnd me hertylye, and submytt me lowlely to yowre good faderhood, besechyng yow fore chertyé of yowre dayly blyssyng" (I, 231). But even while John I was alive Margaret could bestow a blessing, just as she was already the recipient of solicitations that she do so: "And Goddes blissyng mote ye haue and myn, so that ye do wele, etc" (I, 186). Alternatively, she might be receiving a plea for her good wishes; the newly married Edmund II wins the "most dutiful son" award for a letter of August 1481: "Ryght worchypfull and moste especialle good modyre, jn my moste vmble wyse with alle my duté and seruyse I recomawnd me to yow, besechynge yow of your blysyng, whyche is to be moste joy of erthely thynge" (I, 399). Young Walter, usually on the best of terms with his mother, was also moved to talk in the language of humble supplication: "I recomund me on-to yowre good moderchypp, I besechyng yow to geve me yowre dayly benedyiccyon, desyeryng hartyly to heere of yowre prospertyé, which God preserve to hys pleasure and to yowre hartys desire, etc" (I, 402). Of course, it may be that he helped ensure his special position with such a dutiful mode of address.

When John III was trying to make up with his mother, he kept it brief: "jn as humbyll wyse as I can I beseche yow of your blyssyng" (I, 346). In these utterances Margaret was following in the footsteps of her mother-in-law, Agnes, who had certainly squeezed all the advantage she could out of her role as matriarch and dowager.[23] Agnes expressed her approval in a language that made her a partner (and almost an equal one) in a two-party blessing, coming as it did from her and from God: "God make yow ryght a good man, and sende goddis blessing and myn" (I, 14, writing to her son Edmund in 1445, she then being a widow of about one year). Her son Clement, in addressing his brother John I, seemed to acknowledge the value of keeping on the right side of the old lady: "I pray yow recomawnde me to my modere, and that I prayed here of here blyssyng…I pray yow exscwse me to here that I wryte here no letter, fore thys way y-now a-doo" (I, 114). Nor was this line of discourse just from the men (boys) of the family. Agnes's daughter Elizabeth wrote to her in 1459 in the same vein: "besekeyng you dayley and nyghtly of your moderly blessing" (I, 121).[24]

What is striking about Margaret's freedom or power to bless is the way her benediction become a standard part of her salutation in writing to her sons after their father's death. Now—as the surviving parent, the matriarch, and the representative of the older generation—she bestowed her grace on John II and John III in a way she never had done to John I. To her husband, it was "Ryht wyrshypfull hosbonde. I recomannde me to you" (I, 183). But to her sons, it was "I agret you wele and send you goddess blissyng and myn" (I, 201) or "Ryght welbelouyd son. I grete you well and send you Cristes blissyng and myne" (I, 223). And she included such a blessing, usually as the opening lines of her letter, in all but 5 of the 29 letters she wrote to her two eldest sons. It was matriarchal privilege, exercised to the full.

We have touched on the frequent use of "god bless" in some form or other as a tag found in almost all the letters. If this was an in-the-midst-of-life talisman, there was another that was used to accompany the news of a death or the mention of the dead, even years after his or her decease. At the end of the road it was the semiautomatic iteration of "god assoil." Here again it is an instance of Margaret sounding much like everyone else in phrasing and in the frequency or regularity of her usage. Her phrasing was of the ordinary sort, and we can wonder at David Knowles's enthusiasm when he refers to her use of this phrase as one that conjures up "the beautiful old English language of death."[25] In a late letter to John II she observed the proper pieties while chiding him; "sythyn yowyr fadyr deyyd, whom god assoyle" (I, 227); dad in this case had been dead for 11 years—though his tomb was still unbuilt. A bit earlier she had been conveying (bad) news regarding current and local events: "fore certen Daubeney is dede, god assoyle hys sowle, where-of I am rythe sory, and yt had plessyd God that yt mythe be odere-wysse" (I, 205). This was along the same lines as "Ser Herry Inglose is passyd to God this nygth, hoys sowle god assoyll" (I, 141). News and the ritualistic phrase could go together, as in her talk to John I about an old death and a recent one: "yowre fadre and myn onkyl, whoys sowlys God assoyle" (I, 177).

Everyone wrote (and spoke?) in this vein.[26] John I told his wife that "your vnkyll John Berney is deed, whoos soule god haue mercy" (I, 56). John II, still procrastinating about his filial obligation touching the construction of his father's tomb at Bromholm, used a deferential form of reference in bringing up the unfinished business: "my fadre, god have hys sowle" (I, 279). When Edmund had sober news to report he too expressed himself in this fashion: "My syster ys delyuerd, and the child passyd to God, who send vus hys grace" (I, 397). We also find this usage in letters to the Pastons. We have the prior of Bromholm to John I in 1461: "what of yowr fader (William I), God blisse that sowle" (II, 624). And when a petitioner was filling John I in on some unhappy events, he used a formula that may hint at the doctrine of purgatory: "accordyng to the will of hym that is passed vnto Gode, whose soull I pray Jesu pardone, for truly, ser, thar was in hym no faute" (II, 646).[27] The most circumstantial account of news touching what we can think of as a "god assoil" situation or event comes when Agnes recounted the last moments in the life of "Ser John Hevenyngham," he who had fallen ill at nine "of the clok before none, and be too after none he was dedd" (I, 26). A gloom-and-doom affair, fully meriting the tag of "his soulys God assoyle," and closely echoed in a letter by Margaret on the same set of events. Her letter began by telling of the death of "myn vnkyl," whom "god hath purveyd for hym as hys will is" (I, 147) and then she moved on to the late John Hevenyngham, "His sekenesse toke hym on Tuewysday at ix of the clok before none, and be too after none he was dedd."

But even the ritual phrasing of "god assoil" was doled out within boundaries of sympathy and not so much beyond those boundaries. The newsletters that tell of other-than-Paston news and events sometimes give a list of those who fell in battle or who died shortly thereafter, now bare of any sort of blessing; no "god assoil" to soften their message.[28] Closer to home we have a letter from Thomas Playter to John I, reporting the death of Christopher Hanson, an agent of Fastolf and of John himself. "Cristofer Hanson is ded and beryed; and as for executor or testament, he mad non" (II, 673). Nor was Playter given to more pieties in his next letter: "Cristofer dyed on the Saterday nexst by-for Seynt Margret Anno E ijdo" (II, 674). A memo in Gloys's hand (II, 916) lists casualties at the Battle of Tewkesbury: nine dead in the field (including Edward "that was called Prynce"), with an additional 18 others "that were heueded." No editorializing, no pieties; news was just news. But a good word never hurt, and the least the Pastons and their correspondents could do was to note the death of Sir John Fastolf in proper style: "My Maister Fastolf, hoose sowle god assoyle," as Geoffrey Boleyn said to John Paston (II, 619).[29] Fastolf himself, boasting of his own good service to the crown, had referred to Henry VI's father: "…his noble fader, whom God assoile" (II, 570). And when Edward IV included John I among the recipients of a patent letter of 1461, the king referred to his own father, Richard of York: "oure fader, whom Crist assoyle" (II, 640).[30]

In our search for speech that opens the door on the mind-set and worldview of these good folks, we have hardly been overwhelmed by references to scripture or church history (beyond Margaret's choice of saints for dating), or by language that was obviously enriched by a familiarity with the prayer book (primer or psalter?), let alone the Bible. There are scraps of such material, as in Margaret's reference to Pilate and hand washing, but not many more to set beside this vivid flash in the dark: "Yf he do oght therin he doyth it closely, as he ys wont to doo, and wayshyth hys hondys therof as Pylate dyde" (I, 185). Only a few such references or allusions can be found, and for their rarity if not their profundity they are worth our notice. Friar John Brackley moved from English to Latin in a letter to William II, and he threw in a quote from the Book of Job (II, 705).[31] Whether it was a figure of speech or some deeper spiritual well, plus a need to emphasize depth of feeling, we have Richard Calle to John II in 1461: "And God knoweth it was never my wylle ner myn entent, as I not be saved at the dredful daye of Dome" (II, 737). But that these are the richest ore, given that we have almost 1,000 letters to mine, is an indication of the propensity on the part of almost everyone to utter the same clichés, the same pieties—even if heartfelt—over and over. The conclusion we have to accept is that when it came to matters of transcendental importance, neither learned allusions nor quotations from the wisdom of the fathers of the Church were part of the agenda or the idiom of the family letters.[32]

★ ★ ★

Now we move from the realm of things said to that of things done, and then to that of possessions, of things used and owned. Again, while Margaret is the centerpiece of this inquiry, others must enter in—partially in deference to the sources, partially in recognition that in such matters she was not a freestanding individual. That she laced her letters with references to the structure and personnel of heaven, and that she felt free to invoke divine support for Pastons and Paston projects, were integral parts of her belief system; no great surprises here. Her intertwining of the secular and the spiritual—of life as she knew it now and life as she anticipated it would be—was a basic factor in the way she and her contemporaries wove self and individuality into a cosmic framework and in how they legitimated their enterprise against those of others in the fierce scramble for divine support. Signs of a familiarity with biblical texts, or with passages from a book of popular devotion such as Nicholas Love's *The Mirrour of the Blessed Lyf of Iesu Christ* is not something we expect to come across. When Thomas Denys wrote to Margaret in 1461 he was hardly challenging her erudition when he said "I pray yow that it lyke you to send for my Maiser William Paston and shew hym all this, and that it were hastid; for on the aduersarie parte Judas slepith not." That Friar Brackley used more Latin than English in his letters—13 to John I, 1 to William II—and that he stretched his wings to include biblical quotations and references, does at least say something about what Brackley assumed an educated man of the day could be expected to follow. The Paston men had been to Cambridge.

But if words can only take us so far, what about behavior—things done—and material objects and possessions that also talk of ritual, devotion, and pride of ownership? Margaret Paston, like virtually all others of her world who were involved in public affairs and with a claim to property, had numerous dealings with the Church and church men (and perhaps church women). Such activity brought her into frequent contact with the Church as a propertied institution with a vast web and reservoir of personnel. These secular concerns and interactions, or related matters centering around property as such, will not occupy us at any length, though it is entirely possible that Margaret's feelings about such business and about the need to engage in it so frequently (and sometimes so contentiously) may have affected her feelings toward more spiritual aspects of the Church. Much of this contact revolved around the battles over the Fastolf will, and I will give them short shrift.[33] Those efforts proved very wearing. Margaret, late in life and in an unusually reflective mood, told John III that this matter of the Fastolf inheritance had virtually killed her husband: "I had leuer ye had neuer know the land. Remembre it was the distruccion of your fader" (I, 213).

If business dealings with the Church are out, and negotiations with William Paston II and the archbishop of Canterbury and William Wainflete over the Fastolf will and the proposed college (at Caister—no; at Magdalen College, Oxford—yes) are also out, where to begin? Pilgrimage seems a good point for a start. Either on an individual or a group basis it was a familiar feature of fifteenth-century life (as were pilgrim sites). One need not be as driven as Margery Kempe, nor as voracious in the search for new experiences as "The Wife of Bath" to have a yen to take to the road to visit some of the innumerable holy places of the Christian landscape, some near, some far. Though there was no injunction comparable to that laid upon Moslems to seek sites sanctified by the prophet, the roads, inns, and relic-laden churches of England were nevertheless thick with travelers who came and went with pious intent, even if the goal of many of their journeys can be dismissed as "man made shrines."[34] And against this larger landscape we can focus on East Anglia, an area especially rich in special sites and enriched by the benefits to be gained—by both pilgrim and holy site—by pilgrimages. Within a day's journey (or two or three days, if covered in a leisurely fashion) a Paston could leave a home base in Norwich or Paston or Caister or Gresham and take her or his pick from among the glories of Walsingham or Bromholm or Bury St. Edmunds, for the big-time sites and any number of lesser and localized churches and shrines for more provincial devotions. Nor should we neglect shrines even closer to home—those to be found in Norwich Cathedral or at St Leonard's priory.[35]

Given the proximity of so many pilgrim sites and given the Pastons' conventional and dutiful approach to religious activity, they have a rather thin record in this area. As always, we wrestle with the question of whether a great deal more activity took place but without trace in the letters. Margaret Paston's principal pilgrimage—in fact the only one about which we have specific information—was the one she undertook as a young bride. In 1443 John I, her husband of but a few years, had fallen seriously ill while at the Inner Temple in London, and both his wife and his mother were distraught when the news reached them (and we have no idea of the interval between illness and awareness back in Norfolk). Moved by the seriousness of his illness, and perhaps by the devotion of a newlywed, Margaret made her one recorded vow of dedication in September of that year: "and I have be-hestyd to gon on pylgreymmays to Walsyngham and to Sent Levenardys for yow" (I, 126).[36] Agnes, a worried mother and not one to be outdone by a new and green daughter-in-law, threw in her own contribution to the cause, though we only learn of her concern through the medium of Margaret's letter: "My moder hat be-hestyd a-no-dyr ymmage of wax of the weytte of you to Oyur Lady of Walsyngham, and sche sent iiij nobelys to the iiij orderys of frerys at Norweche to pray for yow" (I, 126). No reference, we note, to Agnes actually bestirring herself; cash and wax would suffice, though if she really matched John's body weight in wax it was a very sizeable donation. This expression of alarm by the women is familiar ground, and we assume that Margaret did indeed honor her vows; neither wife nor mother seems to have contemplated a trip to London to offer personal succor, let alone nursing care.

Though there is no reason to doubt that Margaret kept her vow, it is the only explicit record she ever left of such a journey. Nothing else—neither to Walsingham nor elsewhere—despite a long life of much East Anglian peregrination. From Norwich to Walsingham is but 25 miles or so, and the fame of the shrine sufficed to draw Erasmus in the sixteenth century, though he came with more inclination to make fun than to pray.[37] Moreover, as the letters guide us, none of the subsequent problems of John I ever moved Margaret to repeat her early experience and to take to the road to fulfill a spiritual quest. Nor did any scrape of John II or John III ever send her back to the shrine of Our Lady. No matter what help husband and then sons might have needed, and whatever they did get by way of support from Margaret—including those prayers, blessings, and heavenly invocations that we discussed above—it never entailed another vow of pilgrimage. A comment by Edmund II in a letter of 1478 might be read to indicate that his mother, now in declining health and burdened by age, either contemplated such a journey or actually undertook it. But her statement in 1481 that she "entende to ryde to Walsyngham" is too vague to let us pin it down (I, 399).[38] We do know that distances were short, the terrain familiar, and that if the journey of her later years was indeed undertaken some sort of pious purpose must have been at least one of its goals. For a nonpilgrim there was not much else to do in Walsingham.[39]

It is revelatory of Paston affairs and of a "conventional" woman's life to realize that Margaret did most of her traveling, in a life of considerable movement, within the narrow confines of the Paston-Mautby manorial universe. When she made one of her infrequent trips to London in 1465—and it may have been her only trip—it was undertaken to bring succor to John in what would prove to be his last summer. As she prepared for the unfamiliar expedition, she got advice from John III regarding what to visit in the metropolis; her son may have taken great pleasure, as a young sophisticate, in telling his mother of the you-must-not-miss sites; "I pray yow vysyt the rood of Northedor [of St Paul's], and Seynt Sauyour at Barmonsey amonge whyll ye abyd in London" (I, 323).[40] Though it is unlikely that Margaret would have been lost without such advice, as guides for pilgrims were a common and popular form of vernacular literature, if she did indeed lack personal experience, the guides generally were more concerned to steer people to Rome and St James in Spain, rather than to places just down the road.[41]

Other than Margaret's early pilgrimage to Walsingham and her visit to London, some 20 years later, the Pastons themselves add but little to this tale of pious tourism. Either they were not a family that rushed to take to the road, and certainly not on any sort of collective venture, or their activity fell into another of those cracks between their letters, though we might think a pilgrimage as something worth talking about—the kind of "out-of-the-loop" experiences we listen to today from those who have made more exotic if less cathartic journeys. It is possible that the men did enough traveling for secular affairs to satisfy their curiosity, and if they passed by and did homage at pilgrim sites along the way, they did not think to say so. The only relevant journeys, beyond those noted for Margaret, seem to have been two that were proposed, and presumably undertaken, by John III. He talked of going to Canterbury in 1470 and to St. James in Spain in 1473. In 1470 John II learned that his younger brother had recently been at Walsingham: "I vnderstande that Thomas Wyngffelde and ye were at Walsyngham to-gedre; God speede yow" (I, 208). Again, we know of the Canterbury visit as a proposal, rather than as a mission accomplished: "I purpose to go to Canterbery on foot thys next week, wyth Goddys grace, and so to com to London fro thense" (I, 342).[42] For news of a more adventurous trip to Spain, we rely on John II saying to his younger brother, "as for yowre goyng to Seyn James, I believe it but atwyen ij," and John II filled in some details in writing to their brother Edmund II: "to-morowe or ellys the nexte daye he takyth shyppe at Yarmothe and goothe to Seynt James warde, and he hathe wretyn to me that he wyll come homwarde by Caleys" (I, 276 and I, 278). There is but little more on this theme, and we cannot determine if Margery, John III's wife, was speaking literally or metaphorically when she said, "I have fulfyllyd myn pylgremage, thanke-it be God" (I, 420). In any case this ambiguous reference was only made in 1489, some five years after Margaret's death, so whatever Margery Brewes Paston had in mind, it was not in Margaret's ken. This seems about the sum total of reported activity, though it is reasonable to suggest that visits to Bromholm—with both the Holy Rood and the body of John I beckoning attractions—and probably to Walsingham might have been fairly common, if we but knew more.[43]

To set against this record, with its vague hints at additional journeys, the letters demonstrate a considerable interest in the journeys of others, especially as undertaken by people of note. Pilgrimages with celebrity value were clearly an item of interest, and information about them occupies more space in the letters than anything the Pastons said about their own activities (except for Margaret's early vow to Walsingham and those instructions regarding her visit to London). The kings and their families were given to making ceremonial journeys that touched down at pilgrim sites as a part of those processions that entailed feasting off other people's larders while overawing the locals. The Pastons were concerned to inform each other on these matters, though Margaret herself never had much to add. It was John II who reported that "as for tydyngys, the Kyng and the Qwyen and moche other pepell ar ryden and goon to Canterbury, neuyr so moche peple seyn in pylgrymage her-to-foor at ones, as men seye" (I, 264). And that the king might go to nearby Walsingham, or more precisely that he planned to be there next week, was of considerable interest (I, 117, in 1461: Clement to John I, and John III to John II in 1475, I, 365).[44] Henry VII's proposed journey of 1487—again, after Margaret's day—was to be by way of Stratford Abbey in east London and then Chelmsford and then Heveningham, Colchester, Ipswich, Bury, and, finally, "soo to Norwyche, and there woll he be on Palme Sonday Euyn, and so tarry there all Ester and than to Walsingham" (I, 409).[45]

Expeditions by some of local note were also considered newsworthy (which makes it even more likely that had the Pastons traveled more on their own, they would have mentioned such activity). The duke and duchess of Norfolk had gone to the shrine of Our Lady "on pylgrymage at Owre Lady on foote," as John II learned from a Norfolk man "that solde worstedye at Wynchester" (I, 263). The duke of Buckingham "shall come to pilgrymage to Walsyngham," as John II told John III in 1478 (I, 312). The duke and duchess of Norfolk were very much in Paston eyes and Paston concerns, and Margery, John III's wife, reported that "my seyd cosyn Gornay...seyeth my lady shal come on pylgremage in-to this towne, but he knowyth not wheder afore Cristmes or aftyr" (I, 417). Lady Calthorp, she of the prominent local gentry family, was also newsworthy: "My Lady Calthorp hath ben at Geppeswich [Ipswich?] on pilgry-mache, and came homeward be my lady of Norfolk" (I, 417).[46] Nor are we without references to more ambitious ventures. There had been talk of the king of France going into Spain, and John III said he would go with lord Rivers to "Portygall to be at a day vpon the Serasyns—I purpose and haue promysyd to be ther wyth him" (I, 350). And lower down the ladder we learn of some humble folk, also sheep in Christ's flock; a couple of pilgrims were mugged while on the road but received immediate restitution from their attackers when the highwaymen learned of their pilgrim identity (I, 20: Agnes to John I in 1450). William III, in telling John II of a young lady in whom he had an interest, reported that "hyr moder and sche wyl goo to the pardon at Schene" (I, 407). No other references to Shene: when our East Anglian folk did turn thoughts and feet to pilgrimage, Our Lady at Walsingham and her local rivals were usually sufficient for their zeal.[47]

Pilgrimage, we might say, was the cherry atop of the cake of lay religiosity. It was a highly visible form of activity, and though people of all walks of life might be pilgrims at some time or other, the journey stood well outside the round of routine activity. So while pilgrimage draws a good deal of our interest, as it seems to have done at the time, it is a limited guide to any sustained level of spiritual commitment. More tightly woven into the pattern of routine, and coupling the secular with the otherworldly, is the thread of the family's ecclesiastical livings and benefices, of their chapels and chaplains, and of what we can learn about attendance at church and of their interest in what went on there. It was in these areas of interaction and exchange that Christ and Caesar stood side by side, and in the eyes of the laity they seem to have made a good pairing. That the letters give few explicit references to the administration of the sacraments, or to the liturgy, or even to those saints' days that Margaret so assiduously noted in dating her letters, is disappointing but not surprising.[48]

A survey of these miscellaneous topics draws Margaret back toward the pack, and when she does speak of them her voice is not particularly distinctive. What can we learn about her role as the lay patron of churches and livings as well as an informed churchgoer? For this we have exchanges between her sons to set beside what she herself tells us. When she came to her marriage she brought the manors and estates of a considerable dowry, and this presumably meant the advowson of parish churches, along with the toil and tithes of the attached peasantry.[49] Of these scattered holdings, Mautby itself seems to have held pride of place; its acquisition (or life use, for John I) heralded the upward mobility that came to the Pastons by virtue of marriage to the Mautby heiress; control of Mautby also extended the Paston sway into the county south of Norwich and "happened" to put them within a mere stroll across the fields from Caister and from Margaret's kinsman, Sir John Fastolf, though we can say that this turned out to be a mixed blessing (I, 216).[50] John I seems to have been actively involved in affairs of Mautby, with a concern for the horses he kept there, for the condition of the stables, and especially for the state and progress of repairs being carried out on the manor house. In fact, keeping track of the profits and upkeep of Mautby was one of the regular questions he put to Margaret as well as to his servants and staff.[51]

It seems likely that John I assumed responsibility for the living and the upkeep of the church there, even though it would not be his for the long run. When the living at Mautby fell vacant in 1465, Margaret and John II both wrote to John I on behalf of Thomas Lyndis. Margaret was enthusiastic in her recommendation: "I truste verily that ye choulde leke hym right well, for he is rit a prystly man and vertusly dysposyd. I have knowe hym this xx yere and more; he was brother to the good parsone of Seynt Michellys that ye lovyd right well" (I, 192). John II offered much of the same: "I and he haue ben moch aquentyd to-gedere, and I vnderstond and knowe hys vertews leuyng and dysposicion right wele" (I, 235).[52] In addition to her endorsement, Margaret's letter touched a rather surprising and pragmatic side of the business: "And yf he myght havyt he woulde kepe an howsolde therevpon and bylde well the plase, and therof have it grete need for it is now rit evyll reparyd, and I wott well he woll be rulyd and gydyt as ye wyll have him" (I, 192). Her comments about affairs at Mautby do not end with an exclamation point here, but ours might. She goes on to reassure John that "I wott well he woll be rulyd and gydyt as ye wyll have hym." What had been going on at Mautby on Thomas Howes's watch—he who was about to resign—while John was preoccupied with other problems and Margaret was not yet spending the bulk of her time there?[53] Would that we had comparable information about the next time the living fell vacant, as it did in 1469, when Lyndes was dead and John I no longer on the scene. Whatever the problem, things seems to have straightened out, and in 1474 John II was writing to tell the parson there (as he reported to John III) "to dele curteyslye with Sawndre iff he woll please how ore me" (I, 274). Better days were at hand, and in 1481 it was Edmund II, writing his aged and ailing mother and referring to "the good parson of Mautby" (I, 399).

Margaret Paston, coming from a landed family, was no naive in the matter of choosing men to fill ecclesiastical livings; those chosen can be assumed to have been reliable Paston (and Mautby) partisans, and Margaret's say (or John's decision, probably made with her involvement) was an unquestioned part of the perquisites of the gentry, a peculiar aspect of lordship but very much part of the world of privilege and property. In 1461 she had communicated with John I about the living at Caister, concerning the priest's financial hardship amidst the confusion that followed Fastolf's death, and in 1469 John II asked that she recommend him to the "good mayster that ye gaffe to the chapell of Cayster" (I, 201).[54] Nor was the chapel and church at Caister her only dip into these waters, as she also expressed concern about the duke of Suffolk's claim to appoint to the living at Drayton, whereas her own candidate, Sir Thomas Hakon, currently parson of Felthorpe, was clearly preferable (at least in her eyes), he being "a right a gode man and wel dysposyd" (I, 190).[55] She seems to have understood the procedure whereby a priest who had been nominated for a living was installed or—if the arrangement did not work out—removed. She told her husband (I, 183) how a commission from the bishop had to be proclaimed three times in the church, by "a deen." Then, "yff he (the candidate) appyre not wyth-in vj monthys... then he for to be depryvyd and the patron to present wham he luste, and ells youre presentacyon ys not sufficyant." So the few references we have concerning her role in naming candidates to maintain the family's right to appoint looks to be another of those "tip-of-the-iceberg" issues, since we know nothing about the holders or fates of the other livings. In fact, other than Gloys the ecclesiastics of the Pastons' household and their churches are just additional blanks to add to the lengthy list of unknown aspects and people of Paston life. They performed the masses attended by the family, they heard confessions and gave absolution, they administered the sacraments, and they may well have been dispatched—as Gloys was—on secular business. Did they have their own opinions about the different levels of spirituality and commitment within the family? Someone, somewhere along the line, must have turned Margaret's interests toward those saints and their days.

Mautby manor and parish church will resurface as we follow Margaret into her later years, the 18 or so she spent without John I to stand beside her and guide her. Our references mostly zero in on her chapel in her house at Mautby, rather than to the parish church, and for the chapel we rely in good part on the correspondence between John II and John III, whom Margaret made her agents in her efforts to obtain and then to renew the necessary license.[56] There had been a family chapel (or chapels?) as far back as the time of William I: "Wetith of yowre brothere John how manie gystis wolle serve the parlour and the chapelle at Paston, and what lenghthe they moste be and what brede and thykkenesse thei moste be...it were wel don to thinkke on Stansted chirche" (I, 14: Agnes to Edmund I in 1445).[57] It sounds as though the family chapel was being built, or being rebuilt (which seems more likely) shortly after William's death. During John I's lifetime, when Margaret reported on the state of repairs underway at Mautby, she includes an account of work on the chapel as part of the whole project: "it is not lyke that there shal nomore be made there of this yer but the gabels of the chambers and the chapel windows," it now being November (I, 144). Certainly the example of Fastolf's lifestyle and domestic arrangements at Caister would have made a chapel at Mautby—virtually within sight of the old man's compound—a *sine qua non* for those claiming to be his heirs.[58] A chapel also meant a chaplain and devotional books and ecclesiastical paraphernalia, the appropriate furniture along with hangings, floor coverings, and other decorations, none of which ever get mentioned. It was apt to be relatively costly, though worthwhile for both social and spiritual reasons, and Margaret had no inclination to hold back.[59]

By the mid-1470s Margaret was feeling the effects of age and perhaps the social and psychological affects of widowhood. A partial withdrawal, or what we might think of as semiretirement, had its attractions: she was talking as early as October 1470 of moving to Mautby: "my lyffelode encreassite evill for I am fayn to takyn Mautby in myn owyn hand and to set vp husbandry ther" (I, 208). In 1472 John II said that "my modyr...purposeyth to go in-to the contré and ther to soiorn onys a-yen" though whether this meant Mautby and a semipermanent retreat is not spelled out (I, 353). We know that by 1474 Margaret had returned, more or less permanently, to her native ground, and a serious illness a few years later must have strengthened her desire to stay put; it would have made extensive travel—those peripatetic circuits from one Paston household to another—increasingly difficult and burdensome: "yt ys far to the chyrche and I am sekly" (I, 222, in January 1475). Thus when her two eldest sons talked of the need to renew the license for her chapel at Mautby, as they did several times in the 1470s, they were taking on a responsibility for something that had already been handled, perhaps by Gloys, for some years. As early as November 1472 John III reminded John II of Margaret's concern that the license for the chapel be renewed: "to get a new lycence of my lord of Norwyche that she may haue the *sacrament* in hyr chapell. I gat a lycnse for hym for a yere and it is nyghe wory nought. Ye may get it for the Byshoppys lyue and ye wylle" (I, 357).[60] Presumably her sons were dutiful and they obtained the license, though it may have come with a short shelf life, since by 1475 the brothers were again discussing the need to renegotiate the matter. In January 1475 John III was delegated—and now directly by his mother—to talk to the bishop of Norwich. Nor was Margaret unduly reticent about pushing the matter or pulling rank; "I wold ye shuld spekyn wyth my lord of Norwych and a-say to get a lysen of hym that I may have the sacrament her in the chapell, be-cause yt ys far to the chyrche and I am sekly, and the parson ys oftyn owt" (I, 222).

The distance between the manor house at Mautby and the parish church—which is atop a small hill—would not have been hard to negotiate, unless Margaret's health really was failing. In 1478 John Whetley wrote to John II telling him that "my meastres your moder hath ben gretly deseased, and so seke that she wened to haue dyed and hath made her wyll" (II, 782; this will was not the one we have from 1482). In this case Margaret recovered and continued, no doubt, to be concerned with both parish church and private chapel. Her earlier complaint about the parson—he is "oftyn owt"—is revealing for what it says about her perception (or self-pity) regarding her own condition as well as the quality of priestly care, given that he must have been her man. One of Lyndis's virtues that she emphasized in her letter on his behalf in 1465 had been that he could be counted upon to put the church back into some seemly order. But regardless of what was going on in the parish church, Margaret was determined to keep the chapel. In March 1475 she spelled it out once more: "Yf ye cannot getyt of the Busshop of Norwych getyt of the Busshop of Counterbery, for that ys most swyr for all plas" (I, 223). We assume that the quest was successful, if only because we hear no more of the matter.[61] And though Margaret was very much the lady of Mautby manor the indications are that she cared both for her own soul, as in the focus on her chapel, and simultaneously for the seemly role of the parish church in the village, as in her focus on the priest there and his obligations to his parishioners. No hints of any cleavage between the spiritual health of "upstairs" and that of "downstairs."[62]

But for all this concern about her chapel, Margaret is not very revealing. How was it furnished? We assume that Mautby-Paston pride guaranteed a level well above what was absolutely necessary, though this is a surmise.[63] Whatever furnishings and fixtures she wanted, they were dealt with by Margaret or her minions and lie outside the agenda of any extant letters. Even the identity of her chaplains, other than Gloys, ranks with all those other family and household mysteries. Until his death in 1473 James Gloys had served as her chaplain, and since he first served as her scribe in 1450 (I, 139) he may have done service for a full generation. He first made his mark in that letter of 1448 in which Margaret tells John I of the great slanging match in the street: Gloys threatened and attacked by Wymondham and his men, Margaret and Agnes castigated as "strong hores," at least as she told the exciting tale (I, 129). To his position in the family circles Gloys brought a good deal of partisan zeal, though he seems at one time to have held the living at Stokely, which was in the hands of the Berney family.[64] In terms of diligence, if not of accord, Gloys had seemingly earned his keep insofar as Margaret Paston was concerned, though by the time she and her sons had to deal with her petitions for the renewal of her chapel, Gloys—whose death was welcomed by John II and John III—had died (and no "god assoil" from Margaret's sons when they heard the news). Whatever influence he had had on Margaret in her years of widowhood and in her relations with her sons, he certainly had been a hard-liner on her behalf.[65] Though the numerous letters he scripted for John I and Margaret—7 for John between 1449 and 1454, 20 for Margaret between 1451 and 1472—tell us nothing of the man, one of his sermons has been preserved (II, 919). It is hard to judge him on the basis of one sermon, accepting it as his, but it supports the idea that his value to Margaret was for partisanship and versatility rather than for outstanding intellectual, rhetorical, or spiritual gifts.[66]

Though we have little regarding Margaret as active patron and personal overseer of ecclesiastical livings, there are indications that she considered her churchgoing and that of her immediate family to be a serious matter. Furthermore, as the mother who stayed home and worried about the children, she was responsible, in good measure, for their proper behavior as they grew up and moved out into the world. She seems to have taken considerable pleasure in the prospects of young Walter Paston, about to enter the ranks of the clergy with all the benefits of a wealthy family and an Oxford education behind him until his early death in the plague year of 1479 cut him short. At the same time, Margaret was not so blinded by the prospects of a son in the church that she was indifferent to the spiritual as well as the vocational aspect of this career, and she had told Gloys back in 1473, concerning young Walter, "I will loue hym bette to be a good seculare man than to be a lewit prest" (I, 220). Furthermore, to set against her support for Walter, who presumably evinced sufficient calling to meet his mother's standards, we note that no one else in the family ever was inclined toward a religious life, let alone toward that of the cloister. Secular law and secular affairs by pious and educated men (and women) seems the direction and limit of family interests and aspirations; recognition at court, no doubt, and cutting a swathe in the county, with parliament and the shrievalty as appropriate lines in their resumes. It probably would have shocked Margaret had John II come home and declared that, since the search for a wife was going nowhere and his success as a courtier and local squire was a mixed bag, he might as well turn his back upon the world. Such choices were for others, either more introspective or more spiritually inclined and with fewer worldly prospects than were any of the children of Margaret and John (except for Walter, second youngest of his generation).[67]

Not that Margaret's views about the importance of a proper measure of piety were confined to her support of Walter's chosen career path. Early in her married life, when John I's illness had inspired that vow for a pilgrimage to Walsingham, she also reminded him to bedeck himself with a small token as prophylactic against a relapse: "I pre yow that ye wyl werc the reyng wyth the emage of Seynt Margrete that I sent yow for a rememravnse tyl ye come hom"—which seems a combination of popular religious practice and conjugal intimacy (I, 125). But urging the men to pray was probably a standard element in what we can think of as feminist piety and rhetoric; "prey hym of hys grace and helpe, and entend welle to God and to yowr neybors" (I, 205). And on the material side, there must have been pilgrim badges as souvenirs of travel and reminders of the localized grace of the saints. That neither Margaret nor the others say much about charms and relics and other mnemonic signs of their faith is unlikely to point toward any touches of iconoclasm or Puritanism; silence is just silence in this case. Moreover, Margaret never makes any reference in any of her 100 letters to magic or miracles. From her letters we learn more about shirts and horses and hawks than about her collection of rosaries and crucifixes, let alone about her devotional reading.

When relevant for inclusion in a letter, there are specific references to churchgoing. That great Gloys-Wymondham quarrel that sent Margaret and Agnes to the prior of Norwich in quest of his support broke out while they were on their way home after a mass on Friday, a service presided over by the parson of Oxnead, "euyn ate leuacion of the sak-eryng" (I, 129). On one of those occasions on which Margaret was chiding a son, she referred to the advice she had given, and where she had given it: "And if ye wull haue my good wille eschewe such thynges as I spake to you of last owre in parish chirch." Such a casual mention might indicate that it was not out of the ordinary for her to lecture in such a setting (I, 186). When she asked for advice from Lady Morley about seemly activity in a house of mourning during the holiday season, was it a question of civil behavior or really an effort to ingratiate herself with the peeress (I, 153)? And as Margaret was cognizant of the procedure whereby a priest could be installed and removed, so she also knew the binding power of those private words that had, alas, tied her daughter Margery to Richard Calle. She feared for the worst when asking the bishop "whey there yt the worddys that sche had seyd to hym mad matrimony ore not" (I, 203).

Other letters reinforce the picture of men and women "doing business" in church, or on the way to or from church, or in the churchyard. All of this fits into the picture of church services and church space as such a common and accepted feature of life that a separation of the sacred—whether it was space, or dealings and affairs, or the sacred days of the calendar—did not loom large in the laity's view of how their world was organized. Elisabeth Clere, to her "worschepful cosyn" John Paston in 1460, on how "Stywardesson cam to me on Esterne Even to chirch and preide me to be his good mastras, and wold put hym-self in my rewle to do as I will bidde hym" (II, 600). She paraphrases Stywardesson's plea: "for if Judas, he said, wold an asked grace of God he schuld an had it, and for his sake that I had received that day that I wold take his submission." Though few other references are as poignant, it was while the family had gathered for the funeral mass for Walter in 1479 that they learned of Agnes's death in London, though this was just the coincidence of timing. Perhaps Agnes herself, in earlier days, had been easier to approach while on her way to mass; she told John I that Warne Harman had reopened his quarrel with her "on the Sonday…[when he] sayd oponly in the church-yerde that he wyst wyll that and the wall were puddoun" (I, 23). And was Agnes at home or in her chapel when "after euyn-songe Angnes Ball com to me to my closet and bad me good euyn…," this being another chapter in the prolonged dispute over a right-of-way and the building of a wall (I, 24)?

One reason for the silence around so many of these issues is that they touch commonplace activities that were so commonplace, so much part of everyday life, that they rarely make the agenda of the family letters. And because Margaret usually wrote from home, where being enmeshed in the routine of kitchen and solar and chapel was largely taken for granted, she has little incentive to talk about such concerns. But other Pastons, on the move or involved in more peculiar situations, do make references to that world of church and sacraments. We will pay attention below to the seven-sacrament font at Gresham as a reminder—to us and perhaps to Margaret—of the centrality of the sacraments. She did talk to John I of the value of standing as godparent: "I be-seche yow hartyly that ye wochesaf to be hys god fadyr, fore I hope he is schastysyd and wil be the warhere her-aftyr" (I, 176). But it was her older sons, writing to each other about the duchess of Norfolk's confinement, who open the window on the mysteries surrounding birth and the sanctification of a child's entry into the world. In 1472 it was John III to his brother: "my lady took not hyr chambyr tyll yesterday" (I, 356). Then, perhaps a few days later, he urged his brother to show up: "it is myn avyse that ye shall come home your-sylff as hastily as ye maye so that ye may be at the crystenyng of the child that my lady is wyth" (I, 357). Finally, in a letter of 18 December we get to the climax of the drama: "The Byshop cam to Framlyngham…and on Thursday by x of the clok be-for noon my yong lady was krystend and namyd Anne. The Byshop crystynd it and was godfadyr bothe" (I, 358).

Marriage, as the Pastons knew to their distress in the case of Margery and Richard Calle, needed no public ceremony; we know nothing of how Margaret and any of the others had solemnized their vows. We will look at funerals when we come to the Paston wills. The Stonor letters give us a reference or two to penance, as well as to keeping faith with the dead, but the Pastons are pretty reticent about such deep and serious matters.[68] The value and the power of oaths were accepted as binding both secular and spiritual affairs. Back in the days of William I, a petitioner (Alianor Chambre) said to him, "I pray how that they may be delyuerid vndure scripture and yowre sele," though she may have just meant the judge's seal on a document (II, 426). An account from John III takes us to the deathbed of "Mastyr Brakley," the friar who swore to the end that he had told the truth in support of John I's claim to be Fastolf's heir (I, 327). Brackley talked to John about "dyschargyng of my consyens ayenst God" and he seemed about to die. But he rallied ("he revyvyd a-yen…supposing to haue dyeyd for the-wyth"), making a final affirmation to his confessor: "in dyschargyng of my sowle, for I know well that I may not askape, but that I must dye in hast…" And as an indication that the laity knew the rules, Richard Calle wrote to Margery Paston to bolster her courage when the family worked to untie their clandestine marriage. The disapproving relatives knew that Calle and Margery had followed the proper procedures, unhappy as they were about it, and the groom assured his wife on this: "I suppose and ye telle hem sadly the trouthe they wole not dampen ther soles for vs…be pleyne to hem [the bishop of Norwich] and telle the trouthe" (II, 861). In a different setting it was the straight-laced and judgmental Margaret, now the disapproving mother when confronted with her daughter's marriage, who denounced the parson of Brandeston: "he shall be chaysteysid as conciens and lawe requerith" (I, 197).

★   ★   ★

A few more aspects of the religious life of the Pastons, though little of it rests very heavily on Margaret. We turn from behavior to material objects—from words and deeds to things owned—and ask what they might tell us about an investment in the trappings of spirituality. Ownership and display were important components of a family's social presence, a visible assertion of having "made it." Does a look at their collected books steer us toward religious feelings or expressions?

We have several inventories of personal goods, giving a glimpse of the possession (and use?) of items that might have been squirreled away in chests and strongboxes, some perhaps stored for safekeeping in monasteries or friaries, and some perhaps on display in the family's various living quarters and chapels. One inventory—from Margaret to John I—listed items lost or destroyed after the duke of Suffolk's men had looted the Paston compound at Hellesdon in October 1465 (I, 195), though we have no idea what proportion of the items looted or trashed are actually covered in Margaret's report. What we do see, in a negative fashion, is that very little of what she mentions pertains to anything with a religious or devotional purpose—little that cuts to the bones of what has been called "the material culture of piety."[69] Perhaps the ornaments of the church had been so thoroughly worked over that they were beyond recall, or perhaps Margaret did not want to elaborate on some of "the good stuff" that still remained for fear the soldiers might learn of it and come back for more. She does provide John with a detailed list of secular items lost when the duke's men had run amuck in the church, a nasty proceeding in which they "stode vppon the hey awtere and ransackyd the ymages and toke a-way such as thay might fynd, and put a-way the parson owte of the church tyull they had don." Some gear had been taken; "ij handgonnes, iiij chambers for gonnys," while the "chauntré [chamber?] of Richard Calle" had lost clothes, some personal items, and a "boke of Frensh, price iij s iij d" (I, 195). We know that various family treasures were stored, perhaps on a regular basis, with the Dominicans in Norwich, and it may be that valuable objects, along with important papers and coin would have been among the items kept from view in this fashion, but the items lost at Hellesdon were all everyday, secular ones. What the Pastons kept hidden from each other—as Agnes complained John I had done with papers and valuables after his father's death—would presumably also have been hidden from outsiders' eyes.[70]

That inventory from Hellesdon had been drawn up to cover details of what, they hoped, would be a one-time disaster. Hellesdon was not the main family headquarters and not a likely repository for the bulk of their prized possessions. Other lists are more useful for our purposes. We learn from a list or an inventory, "late that was in my cofir at Norwich" and dated from around 1464, in which John I enumerates some seemingly valuable items of a religious nature: cups for the sacrament, a cross weighing 5 pounds and 3½ ounces, a pot called "a cristamatorie to put in holy crème...a chaleys of guuld player weyng ij pound" and more of such (I, 68 and I, 69).[71] A list or inventory that John I and his brother William II had drawn up in 1459–60, "a remembrauns of the goodes that sometime were Ser John Fastolffes, mad be John Paston aftir such examinacions and writyngges as he can fynd," gives us a better look at items of interest in this discussion: "an jmage off Owre Lady wyth ij awngello sensing...a cross wyth a fott lx vnc...an ijmage off Sent Denys tiltte weyng l. vnc," and more of this sort, including "bokes Frenshe, Latyn, and Englyssh" (I, 87). John I and William II estimated a total weight for the haul of 67 pounds, 4 ounces; each of the seven items, plus one "crosse" is described in a bit more detail.[72] But nothing of this sort from Margaret herself, neither regarding the parish churches she kept an eye on for John nor from that chapel at Mautby that was of such concern. Nor, as we shall see, was she particularly forthcoming in her will. Her silence about the sort of possessions we are concerned with must have covered a goodly collection of items; Margaret's position as the Mautby heiress would mean family possessions—Berney and Mautby heirlooms—passed down from earlier generations, along with her share of Paston family treasures (I, 230).

There is a little, to be sure, but not much, and no hints of whether what we have really is a case of "that's all, folks" or whether many items of interest were just swept up by those general clauses that dealt with the residue of Margaret's sizeable estates. Since the will indicates the breakup of a dowager's household and the disposal of her goods, there are a lot of household and personal items—mostly steered to Margaret's daughter Anne Yelverton and her son William III as the major beneficiaries for this part of their mother's holdings. Some spiritual items do appear in the miscellany, mingled without special distinction among a considerable quantity of secular goods; we can pick out that primer and beads of silver for Anne ("my massebook with all myn awterclothes"), and we also have the bequest of "my peir bedys of calcidenys gaudied with siluer and gilt" for the lucky goddaughter. That the private or manor-house chapel might also serve as a storeroom as well as the center of domestic devotion seems peculiar, but such a possibility helps explain Margaret's instructions: "…and myn hole litel white bedde in my chapel chaumber at Mauteby, with the fetherbedde lich as it is nowe in the said chapel" (I, 230).

We do have one document in the collection of family papers that may be the break in the otherwise blank wall that surrounds Margaret. In Davis's edition of the Paston letters there is a document, an inventory, that while carrying no explicit attribution or heading is included by Davis in the "to Margaret Paston" group of documents. Davis's headnote says that "it seems likely that she was connected in some way with this document, evidently earlier than the death of Gloys in 1473" (II, 732). I offer a more proactive reading; I suggest that this inventory covers some of the personal possessions that various members of the Paston entourage had left with Margaret and, either after Gloys's death or in preparation for her planned removal to Mautby—and these may have been related events—it was now time to take stock of what there was and to determine the several owners. The inventory itemizes the goods of 20 different people—perhaps otherwise unknown or unnamed members of the Paston household, which might help unravel some of that mystery as well. We have 18 men plus Katherine Wilton and Jane Belton. Of these 18, 4 of the men are down for items of personal devotion or for church use (Gloys, Herré Bolt, Frere John Alderiche, and John Juddé; Gloys and Juddé are figures of prominence in Paston affairs, whereas the others are not otherwise named). Gloys and Bolt are also noted as book owners. If my reading of this is correct, we have some notion of the items with which Margaret was surrounded (whether hers or just left in her keeping; that is, on deposit in her household).

What does this mysterious inventory actually offer? The friar had some possessions we would expect to find: "ij quaris of prayers…a powtenere with a payre of bedys of jette," and Juddé (of his two items) had the same sort of beads. Bolt's longer list mentioned a "pater nosterys of corall" and a surplice and "a steynyd clother, a crvcifix" plus gloves, hose, a comb, and a lot of clothing, boxes and containers, and "a payre of beddes of segmore." Gloys was listed for "j crosse siluer." And for the books, the returns are a good bit richer. In all, the inventory enumerates 34 items for Gloys, 7 of which are books. This included some service or prayer books, as we would expect, as well as "j boke of xij chapetyrs of Lynccoln, and a boke of safistré" and "j boke of *Vitas Patrum*." Bolt, with a long list of personal items ("a payr of hernishede knyffes," etc.) had even more diverse books, including "a rod boke with

Hugucio and Papie, iij bokes of soffistré," and—to our frustration—
"maney other smalle bokes." These items do not exactly take us into
the world of affluence and display at show in such a document as the
Bedford Inventory, but they remind us of how among personal possessions there would be rosaries and crucifixes and primers and "a confes-
sional" as well as "a kerchey thered, and ther-in was vj s. viij d. of gold"
or "a payre of dowbyll glovys, furredde with lambe." Katryn Wilton
had nothing of interest to report, but Jane Belton, along with blankets
and sheets and hose and a smock and more of the like, was listed for "a
payre of beydys of jette with pater nosteris of corall."[73]

In the absence of Paston household books we have no recourse but
to accept that all sorts of goods that Margaret had inherited, purchased,
and accumulated just came and went the way of time and change, as did
those Margaret sent to John II in 1470: "syluer vessel that your grandma
maketh so mych of…I had [it] of myn husband and myn husband shuld
haue had it of his fader" (I, 208). Between the various members of the
family and their numerous homes and town houses, there surely were
a lot of valuables, some at least to be packed up and moved around and
redistributed in the normal course of life, let alone in what the wills
and postmortem partitionings must have set in motion—not to mention
intrafamilial and extrafamilial looting and raiding. The Pastons are not
going to help us on this score. There are still some touches in the church
of St Peter Hungate in Norwich that we can label as shown their taste
and crafted under their supervision, to be discussed below. Otherwise we
just have to assume that "typical" upper-class items on display at such an
exhibition as the Victoria and Albert Museum's "Gothic Art for England,
1400–1547" were in line with what Margaret held dear but about which
she never had occasion to speak.[74]

A brief discussion of a few of the items from the "Gothic Art" exhibition can give us some points for comparison—what people like the Pastons
were not going to own, and items of the sort that they probably did own,
or certainly could have had they chosen to. If we begin with what was
clearly beyond their reach, we can mention (from the catalogue's "The
Table and Feasting" chapter) Archbishop Chichele's salt or the Winchester
Election Cup. The former, of silver with gilt and rock crystal, stands some
44 centimeters and is "one of the most important survivals of medieval
plate in England and is of unique design," dating probably from the 1420s.
The Winchester cup, from the third quarter of the fifteenth century, is
45 centimeters and also of sliver gilt, with applied pastes, and it may be
missing some rich ornamentations or bejewelling it had when it was made.
Items clearly out of the Paston's league, but this is not the case with a bowl
of the 1480s, 17 centimeters in diameter and of silver and once decorated

with translucent enamel, or the flagon of c. 1500 in cast pewter, shaped with a bulbous form and a waisted upper section.[75]

This comparison can also be hinted at from items discussed in the catalogue's chapter on "Private Devotion." While the Bedford/Beauchamp Book of Hours was made in the 1430s for patrons of much greater wealth and an interest in cultural patronage and display, Memling's "Donne Triptych" was done for a merchant who was not likely to be in a completely different world, except as his taste and his continental contacts shaped his interest. But a simple mould from which pipe-clay Virgins could be turned might have been something a chaplain would have, and the window made between 1420 and 1435 for Sir Roland Lenthall at Hampton Court was not beyond what the Pastons would install in St Peter Hungate a few decades later, as we shall see below. The window depicted an Annunciation, and Susan Foster says "the joys of the Virgin were an ideal subject for the glazing of a private chapel," especially as Mary is reading from a book of hours.[76]

Do we fare any better, in the search for material objects that bespeak a spiritual turn of mind when we look at books and reading? Not much, at least not for Margaret herself, little beyond what I have offered as speculation about a primer or book of hours and those all-too brief references in her will. A little better for others in the family, or for the family as a group, though many of the positive marks are really due to John II—we having a partial inventory of his books (I, 316), in addition to his *The Grete Boke*. However, the contents of *The Grete Boke* are entirely secular and tell us nothing about the spiritual exercises of the book's owner, let alone those of his kin. After Gloys died in 1473 John II and John III communicated with each other and with Margaret about getting hold of the library of their old adversary. John II never got his act together, as we might say, and as other problems intervened it was unlikely he ever bought the collection or arranged to have it sent to him; "my mynde is now nott most vppon bokys" (I, 291). But the correspondence is about acquisition and shipping; no hint of what was in that collection, or why John II, rather uncharacteristically given his feelings toward Gloys, expressed so much interest. The library of a cleric that caught the eye of a country gentleman poses some intriguing questions.[77] If I am right about the nature of that inventory in Margaret's possession (II, 732), then we have an idea about Gloys' items that John II might have had his eye on. However, as his mother told him, "As for the bokys that ye desyryd to have of Syr Jamys, the best of alle and the fairest ys cleymyd, ner yt ys not in hys jnventory" (I, 221). What were they, and who had claimed or bought them? Margaret goes on to say that John II could have the rest: "the prys of the todyr bokys be-syd that ys xx s. vj d., the sych I send yow a byll of." This was not a lot of money; the best were gone and what was left was perhaps not so attractive. Margaret seems to have been the go-between; if she herself had cared about the contents of the items under discussion she managed to avoid saying so. We are also in the dark regarding the party to whom John II would have sent his check, had he made the purchase.

The other women of the family add but little to the story. Margaret herself did direct, after the death of her brother-in-law Edmund I in 1449, that his books be sent along to William II at Cambridge (I, 133). There are references to Anne's "sege of Thebes" (I, 352);[78] to French books among those items lost at Hellesdon (I, 195: one belonging to John I, one to Richard Calle); to John II's "Temple off Glasse," which John III was to send with the letter's courier on his return trip (I, 267); to miscellaneous French books that John II asked John III to send along, as he assumed that Ebesham, the scribe, was finished with the work (I, 245); several details in letters or accounts from Ebesham to John II about the making of *The Grete Boke* and other texts (II, 751, 755); and another reference or another copy of "the book of vij Sagys" that Gloys was to deliver to Walter "and he hathe it" (I, 353). But in all of this, nothing that is not secular, perhaps in reflection of Paston tastes for leisure reading.[79] Nor is there much in the wills to offer a wider view regarding acquisition or interest.

★ ★ ★

Any sort of conclusion to this survey of expression and behavior is going to be a tame one, largely repetitive of themes already explored. As Margaret Paston thought of dating her letters in terms of saints' days and moveable church feasts, she also expressed herself in a language that was embedded in an idiom of religious blessing and thanksgiving, of intercession and invocation. So was that of others of her world, or so the letters lead us to believe. In this regard, at least, Margaret Paston was very much one of the crowd, holding her own but distinguished in no particular fashion in style of speech or activity. If she regularly went through the verbal drill I have sketched out—blessings, invocations, words of thanks or of hope regarding heaven's interest in Paston projects—she was by no means the most effusive, the most given to having pieties roll off the page. On the other hand, her usage was regular, typical, and fairly constant. We can take one of her letters, chosen at random, and look at the weave of information and spiritual tags. In a letter to John II of October 1466 (I, 198), written shortly after the relatively early and unexpected death of John I, she sprinkles her prose thusly: "send you God ys blessing and myn...Youre fadere, wham God assole...and at the reuerens of

God, spede youre maters soo thys terms…God send you gode speke in
all youre maters." Nothing fulsome, nothing hinting at the feelings of
guilt and unworthiness that led Margery Kempe on her unique journey
(both physical and spiritual). We should also note in all the family correspondence the absence of much interest in the supernatural as we would
think of it today; no signs of concern for witches or magic, whether
good or bad, or for miracles, or for any aggressive search for relics. No
indication of winds of change that were to blow across her East Anglian
landscape. Though the sons knew the world of the Low Countries and
the Burgundian court, they leave no indication that either the elaborate
investment in cultural artifacts or the diversity of religious expression
one encountered upon crossing the North Sea was anything they chose
to carry home.

In recent discussion of the laity and the late medieval Church we have
seen differences of opinion about such concepts as the privatization of
worship and devotion and the alleged withdrawal of the gentry from the
common body of prayers and church attendance. I think much of this is
a red herring—an anachronistic attempt at assessment that does not mesh
with the world of lay religion I found when Margaret Paston is set as the
centerpiece. It is easy to fall back on the idea of a dichotomy—the world
of a public sphere and of a private sphere—and to accord each its due, its
proper share and realm of activity and loyalty. But I think this beclouds
the issue. Eamon Duffy has warned against confusing the privatization
of worship and devotion with personalizing it; that is, with thinking it
indicates any larger dissatisfaction with the going tenets of orthodoxy.[80]
We come closer to the contemporary approach by working from the idea
that there was no problem with wanting to (and being able to) lord it over
the parish and parish church and the priest therein, as was appropriate for
the gentry, and simultaneously pushing and shoving to get that license
from the bishop for the private chapel. Both sides of the coin were among
the proper perquisites of the landowning class. Letters from Margaret and
others tell us how they went to church and talked about all sort of business during and after the services, of what they thought of sermons and
preachers, and of negligent priests and untrustworthy monks and friars.
They put few on a pedestal, but they made no great efforts to knock anyone off that pedestal.

Margaret Mautby Paston led a long and busy life, one filled with drama,
crises, and its full measure of tragedy, disappointment, and (early) death.
She entered into a marriage that "worked" for a quarter of a century—one
marked by numerous children who survived to adulthood. She came to
the Pastons with "a private income," and she held and enjoyed a respect-
able niche in her world, though life often held some unwonted surprises.

It is easy if not particularly incisive to say that her faith sustained her, since her faith was such an integral part of her daily existence; it would like say- ing that her legs carried her or that her eyes enabled her to see. Hers was not a "born-again" or a "Jesus-is-my-personal-savior" sort of religion— any more than it was one of mystical vision, or one that impelled her to take the vows of chaste widowhood when that fate befell her.[81] If we put Margaret into one of those tired jokes wherein the recently departed goes to heaven and has to account to St Peter for her life on earth, it is hard to imagine Margaret Paston saying anything except that she followed the rules (which she seems to have known quite well), that she did her best to make sure her children knew and followed those same rules, and that she expressed her faith with her tongue as well as keeping it in her heart.

CHAPTER 4

FAMILY WILLS: MARGARET PASTON AND
THE REST

A look at the last wills and testaments of the Paston family—with
Margaret as our centerpiece—opens the window on many scenarios and agendas touching the world and worldview of the late medieval laity.[1] Reading the wills that have come down to us takes us into
the center of that circle wherein the individual and the family, the secular community, and those realms defined and governed by the Church
and spiritual life, were overlapped so they can be read as being (or as
having become) one entity, one sociocultural phenomenon. Thus, it is
not only unnecessary but also anachronistic to worry about whether the
Paston wills are more "about" family than they are "about" spiritual
expression and direction. Rather, we might think of the aggregation of
family wills as offering a kinship-linked case study, or a string of connected studies, that illuminate what John Bossy has characterized as a
church composed of a "body of believers," with both "body" and
"believers" as operative words.[2] And, lest this seem intrusive—an
agenda imposed by the historian upon the family—it was Margaret herself who spoke of the importance of writing a last will before bidding
the world farewell: "And for godsake advise hym to doo make hys will,
yeue it be not doo...els it were peté" (I, 220). It was a vital component
of "the good death."

To turn to the Paston wills is to deal with women and men in a
wide variety of last-days and last-wishes settings, many of them pointing us toward some well-known paradigm or model for the deathbed,
the funeral, and the last will. Because we have so many late medieval
wills, and because they are documents in which the formulaic and the
individualized mesh, we can say that there are various models that we
can point to regarding how the last days and the death were played out,

how last wishes were expressed. Though different Pastons fit or followed what I offer as a variety of different models, it is not surprising
that such a universal experience as death and burial and funeral conventions can be categorized in terms of analogues, precedents, and patterns
of performance. For many of these we can find a Paston, or even more
than one Paston, whose departure can be covered by a cloth much like
that cut at some earlier time and for some more distinguished figure—
perhaps someone the tale of whose last days would have been passed
down as part of the lore of their cultural or familiar tradition. Of the
many death-and-beyond scenarios of their world, those associated with
the death, funereal procession, and burial of Eleanor of Castile in 1290
were memorable and eye-catching. From her death in Lincolnshire
through the 12 stopovers, each commemorated by an Eleanor Cross,
to her burial at Westminster Abbey (with her viscera buried at Lincoln,
her heart at Black Friars in London), Edward I offered his realm a
model of public mourning and of a ritualized procession that would be
hard to match, and anyone who had spent any time in London knew
of this precedent. Or—if we wish and still within living memory for
the generation before Margaret—there was the elaborate routine after
Agincourt that involved bringing the parboiled remains of the duke
of York and the earl of Suffolk, the two high-level battlefield casualties, home for burial. Margaret's parents or her parents-in-law might
have seen this procession, and—had they seen it—they were even more
likely to remember the funeral of Henry V in 1422.[3] Could a mere
Paston emulate such a last journey? With the appropriate adjustments
downward for status and wealth, the answer seems to be yes, he could;
in the person of John I he did so, or certainly tried to do so, in 1466.
Nor do we only have upper-class models, and if we come down a peg
or two we can follow the reburial and attendant expenses involved in
putting the likes of Sir Thomas Arundell, someone not too far removed
from the Paston's social status, to rest.[4]

Beyond these there are other styles, other precedents and patterns.
There is the scenario of the deathbed that might be celebratory and
comforting or, by way of contrast, one that could be bleak and lonely.
On the bright side, it is hard to surpass the elaborate and performative
stages of the deathbed drama that was on display during the last days of
William the Marshal in 1219. His long dying gave family and associ-
ates and friends, including the young Henry III, much opportunity to
gather to pay last respects, to discuss the governance of the realm, and
to be involved in the division of a vast estate.[5] Such deathbed drama
was replicated, albeit on a considerably smaller scale, by Judge Paston,
William I (d. 1444), Margaret's father-in-law (whom she knew from the

domestic situation of her early years of marriage). Agnes Paston's account of William's will-writing and dying—considered below in some detail— gives us a rich tableau of sons and lawyers and others, running in and out of the bedchamber, scrambling to record the old man's last wishes, swearing to honor them, thinking of ways to trick the others.

Against these various pictures of reunion and ritualized farewell—the good death, as we are now apt to term it—we can also set some dark-side scenarios—lonely deaths, bereft of the comforts of the near and dear, usually taking place in unfamiliar rooms that lacked the comfort and reassurance provided by familiar possessions and faces.[6] For a Paston page from this book of grim farewells we have John II, dying in London (probably of plague) in 1479. No record of brothers or sisters to sit beside his bed, no wife or children; just the stark surroundings of a rented room and a will that talks about projects that he, as the heir of the family, did not live to carry out. Our analogy or paradigm here might be the deathbed of Henry II, the dying king buoyed up by the vain hope that Richard would arrive for a final reconciliation.[7] If John Paston II's lonely deathbed is not quite as moving at that of a great king, it was still a bleak way to go: "more than pathetic; it was shameful," as Colin Richmond has put his stamp on the scene.[8]

But there are still other models, other parallels to offer, and they are not all as lugubrious. One style of bidding the world goodnight was by using the will to make a final assertion of identity. We shall see this in Margaret's case, where she used her last instructions, at least in part, to reaffirm her pre-Paston identity and to return to the roots of her natal family. Nor was she alone in using her will and burial instructions for the creation or re-creation of an identity. To some extent her mother-in-law Agnes had done so, just a few years earlier. We can also turn to Alice Chaucer, duchess of Suffolk, for a final assertion of identity—one that in this case had but limited concern for where she had stood, as just a well-fixed commoner, at the start.[9] And if we wish to emphasize piety and contemplation or contrition as among cardinal virtues that one was supposed to embrace as death neared, we can turn to Isabel, duchess of Warwick (d. 1439), with both a will and a monument that pointed toward a costly version of a simple message.[10] There was no shortage of alternatives from which to choose, insofar as such models actually helped people shape the last act of the drama.

How did the Pastons, collectively or individually, exercise their final option, or how were these choices made for them if their own instructions were lacking or could not be fulfilled? Studies of burial patterns— whether from fifteenth-century England or from virtually any other historicized society—testify to the strength of family traditions and groupings, of church and churchyards as prized sites, and of the strong attraction of local over "national" institutions and burial places.[11] But when we turn to the Pastons we have a dilemma they do little to help us unravel. Though usually the various Pastons fit neatly into the mainstream of their class and culture when we analyze their activities and expressed interests, whether we find them engaging or not, their wills and burial patterns make little effort to plot or to follow any path of family tradition.[12] An aspect of wills to keep in mind is the way they set the stage for what has been characterized as a "theatre of devotion."[13] At an obvious level a will is a document of spiritual power, a document of transgression that crosses or ignores the boundary separating life from death. The wishes of the dead loom large over the living—be they executors or beneficiaries or witnesses—and those wishes become a form of posthumous social control. We can read the last will as the script of a drama, the testator is author and director and perhaps choir director and choreographer as well. The will's provisions specifying the number of poor men and/or women enlisted for the funeral procession to hold candles and to pray in exchange for a gown or a ha'penny, are stage directions. Furthermore, as wills provide instructions regarding the liturgy and the choice of prayers, often stretching into the indefinite future, they can be read as a lay interjection into and control over the words of the priest at the altar. The testamentary stipulations about the number of trentals and the occasions on which they are to be said, and the designation of who would say them, is a takeover of the prayer service by a testator, a layperson who is now paying the piper. That this intrusion aroused no problems about territoriality, with such instructions as "the iiij Ordres do singe for my soule…the hole seint Gregories Trentale…to do singe for me soule, and for the soules aforsaides, C masses in oo day," shows the unexceptionable nature of the interaction of lay and clerical, or living and dead.[14] The dying and the dead have some privileges usually denied to the living.

Several times I have turned to the question of how to set Margaret Paston in the context of "the religion of the Pastons." However, nothing throws cold water over the idea of collective family behavior like a discussion of Paston burial sites and last wills. There are numerous fifteenth-century families—royal dynasties, aristocratic lines, country gentry, wealthy townsmen—that saw collective burial and constructed traditions of testamentary benefaction and remembrance as making a visible and lasting way of creating or reinforcing solidarity and identity.[15] Such solidarity transcended the boundaries of time and even (to some degree) of mortality, substituting instead a permanence of place, one proclaimed by an ever-growing collection of tombs and memorials so arranged as to grace the chosen site.[16] The Pastons, however, are not to be numbered in these ranks. No lying together, awaiting the dreadful day of judgment. The kings and queens of England might turn their thoughts about death and burial in the direction of Westminster or Windsor or Canterbury. The Beauchamp-Nevilles had their great church at Warwick. The house of York made much of their collegiate foundation at Fotheringhay. Lesser families like the Scropes of Bolton could turn to Bolton, the Hungerfords to Salisbury Cathedral. Not, however, our East Anglian friends.[17] Paston bodies were scattered in death, perhaps appropriately enough, since it was their physical disbursement while alive that had created the need for all those letters in the first place. There never was any consensus, any agreement about one of those all-encompassing albeit posthumous family reunions within a given church or house. While the Pastons were not alone in this kind of behavior, we know so much about them as a group that their dispersal in death stands out.[18] The one qualification to this generalization is a regard for the White Friars, the Carmelites, especially for their house in Norwich. Ties between various Pastons and the White Friars were strong and persistent, and yet, in critical ways and touching some of the key players, they were limited. The will of Agnes Paston indicates that ties with the Carmelites were ties she had brought with her—a kind of spiritual dowery—from her pre-Paston days and her pre-Paston identity. Burial in the Carmelite house would have preserved and continued a link between the Berrys and the Pastons. But Agnes was never able to impose this invented tradition on many of the others, though there are strong indications that she tried to do so.

To anticipate my narrative, Table 4.1 shows the pattern (or nonpattern) of disbursal of the Pastons, their overarching paradigm regarding burial. The table lists nineteen individuals, Pastons by blood or by marriage, whose deaths spanned the better part of a century, beginning with Clement (d. 1419) and running to John III (d. 1504) and his second wife Agnes (d. 1510). Looking at the burial sites we can identity eight probable locations that were chosen for the well remunerated privilege of holding one or more members of the family. While the Carmelite order goes to the head of the line, with their house in Norwich claiming some pride of place in terms of numbers, none of the major players in the family saga excepting Agnes herself expressed much interest in resting within Carmelite confines. That Agnes died in London may have served to thwart her expressed intention to lie with the White Friars in Norwich; the plague, if that is what carried her off, had little respect for even the best laid plans and the strength of intergenerational traditions.[19]

Table 4.1 Deaths, Burial Sites, and Last Wills of the Pastons

Paston: By Blood or Marriage	Relation to Margaret	Dates (and Approximate Lifespan)	Burial Site	Source of Information and Date of Will[a]
Clement Paston	Grandfather-in-law	d. 1419 (probably long-lived)	Paston parish church (with wife Beatrice)	Will: Gairdner, III, 447–48 1419
William I	Father-in-law	1378–1444 (60+)	Norwich cathedral	Will: I, 12 1441
Agnes	Mother-in-law	c. 1400–1479 (80)	London Carmelites	Will: I, 31–32–33–34 1466
Edmund I	Brother-in-law	1425–49 (24)	London: Carmelites or the Temple Church	Nuncupative will: I, 80 1449
Clement	Brother-in-law	1442–d. by 1479 (37)	Norwich Carmelites	—
Elizabeth Poynings Browne	Sister-in-law	1429–88 (59)	London Black Friars	Will: I, 123 1487
William II	Brother-in-law	1436–96 (60)	London Black Friars	Will: I, 113 1496
John I	Husband	1421–66 (45)	Bromholm priory	Blomefield[b] and Gairdner, II, 266–71
John II	Eldest son of John I and Margaret	1442–79 (37)	London Carmelites	Will: I, 309 1479
Walter	Son	1451?–1479 (27)	St Peter Hungate, Norwich	Will: I, 405 1479
Margery Calle	Estranged daughter	1450–d. by 1482 (32?)	—	—
William III	Son	1450–alive, 1504 (54+)	—	—
Edmund II	Son	1445+–d. by 1504 (c. 60)	—	—
Anne Yelverton	Daughter	1450–1495 (45)	—	—
John III	Son	1444–5–1504 (60+)	—	—

Continued

Table 4.1 Continued

Paston: By Blood or Marriage	Relation to Margaret	Dates (and Approximate Lifespan)	Burial Site	Source of Information and Date of Will[a]
Margery Brewes, wife of John III	Daughter-in-law	d. 1495	Norwich Carmelites	—
Margaret, widow of Edmund II	Daughter-in-law[c]	d. 1504	Iteryngham	Will: II, 929 1504
Agnes, widow of John III	Daughter-in-law[c]	d. 1510	London Black Friars or in Kent	Will: II, 930 1510
MARGARET MAUTBY PASTON	—	c. 1420–84 (c. 64)	Mautby parish church	Will: I, 230 February, 1482

[a] Unless otherwise indicated the source is Davis's edition of the Letters.
[b] No will for John I, but Blomefield and then Gairdner publish the records of the receipts concerning John's funeral and testamentary benefactions.
[c] These "daughters-in-law" only married into the family after Margaret's death.

★ ★ ★

By the time Margaret was ready to put her last wishes to paper in 1482, she could look back and say that no pattern of coordinated bequests, let alone of burial, had prevailed. If her memories of Paston life began with her parents-in-law, William I and Agnes, they offered no lead in this regard. The deaths of William I and Agnes were separated by 35 years (though perhaps only by 22 in the making of their wills) and by the choice of burial sites. And though we will show many links or duplications between the bequests of John I and of Margaret, the interval of 18 years between their deaths, plus Margaret's own fortunes and feelings in those years, must have made it easier for her to go her own way at the end. How much of this dispersal of bodies and of testamentary benefaction was by policy, how much by way of indifference (which would seem uncharacteristic, given the circumstances), and how much of it was just by the chance and circumstance of where and when death occurred? Some of the Pastons just happened to die in London while there on business; others had moved there, and burial in the metropolis was either easier or in keeping with a stated preference. In some instances a dead Paston was brought from London back to Norfolk for burial, as were both William I and John I (and perhaps others, including Agnes). Two of the London deaths—those of Edmund I and then of John II—were the deaths of unmarried men, and responsibility for an East Anglian reburial was passed along to their kin but probably not to a satisfactory conclusion. And of those who actually chose burial in London, we can look to William II, brother of John I. He had married upwards (to Anne Beaufort), and his East Anglian roots seems to have withered as a fancier lifestyle in more exalted surroundings opened before him.

Nor does the pattern of disbursed burials end with these particular Pastons. Where we have wills or relevant information, some of it coming after Margaret's will of 1482, we see that the women of the family also went off in various directions, though some of the husband-wife comparisons are clouded because we would not have her will had she not outlived him. Some paths were charted by husbands, or by a now-deceased husband from a former marriage, or by their families. Elizabeth Paston, that ill-treated daughter of William I and Agnes and sister of John I, was twice married: first to Robert Poynings, second son of Robert, IV lord Poynings (young Robert dying at the second battle of St Albans in 1461) and then to Sir George Browne of Betchworth, Surrey (executed for rebellion in 1483, attainted in 1484). She had children by each marriage, and on her death in 1487 she asked for burial with Browne in the London Black Friars ("With my forsaid housband Sir George"), her burial to be accompanied by the handsome sum of £21 (xxj li) for bringing her body to the site ("feche me from the place where I die vnto thair said place") and then for "diriges and masses with all other obseruaunces…(including) vij trentallis" at her burial and other prayers over the succeeding weeks and months ("euerly weke following vnto my monthes mynde": I, 123). Other of Elizabeth's bequests went to the parish churches of Dorking, Surrey ("for prayer and reparacion of the forsaid churche"), to St Albans "Wodstret within London," to prisoners at the four London prisons ("to euery of those places, to be praid for, xx d"), and to various poor folk in London, including "bedred folks" and "most specially souche as haue knowen me and I thaym" (I, 123, printed from PCC Reg Milles, dated May 18, 1484). This was a marital rather than a natal identity, forged by and followed via her husband's family; two husbands makes it more complex, serving to remove her even further from her Paston origins. Her basic identity by the end—and in all likelihood from the moment of her first marriage—shows in the pattern of testamentary bequests that accompanied and expressed her new identity. She focused on the South and Southeast, with few traces of East Anglian roots, relatives, or reminiscences.[20]

If Elizabeth Paston-Poynings-Browne, daughter of William I and Agnes, was not to be drawn back into the nets of Paston tradition and testamentary bequests, such as they were, we would hardly expect to find many signs of such connections and traditions in the wills of two women who married into the family later in life and who only became

Pastons by virtue of a second or subsequent marriage. The 1504 will of Margaret, widow of Edmund II (son of John I and Margaret), pays due regard to her identity as his widow (II, 209: "wedowe, late the wife of Edmond Paston, squire, late disseasid") but she goes her own way with burial and related bequests.[21] Burial was to be at Iteryngham (Sherringham: referred to as "All Saintes of Sharington" in the manuscript) and bequests for repairs for the church, for its high altar, and for various guilds were distributed among the churches and communities with a strong Norfolk base: Sharrington, Manyngton, Saxthorpe, Barnyngham, Wolterton (with repairs to the highway there as well; 5s to "highe weyis"), and Wood Dallyng. A host of children were remembered, they presumably now all being adults, out in the world and begotten in marriages prior to that with Edmund Paston. A daughter-in-law Margaret Lomnour was to get a primer covered in green velvet, while daughter Anne was the recipient of her mother's best coral beads. This Margaret Paston had one of those complex martial records: a late husband (Thomas Briggew), children with three or four different surnames, a nephew who was remembered, and an overriding interest in disposing of the goods in her manor house at Manyngton. On her deathbed she cared neither for the Carmelites of Norwich nor the cathedral of the Holy Trinity there.[22]

Another will we can read as "a sort of Paston" will is that of Agnes, second wife and then widow of John III. She outlived him by about six years, and she too had a compound biographical record; in a will of May 1510 she asked for burial in the London house of the Black Friars beside her (former) husband John Hervey, were she to die in London; otherwise, in Kent, in Sondryche [Sandwiche?] parish church. The almshouse at "Sondryche" was to receive household items, while "my grete booke of prayers" was for daughter Isabel, and "myn other booke of prayers keuered with redde and having a siluer claspe" for "mistress Bygote, with my Lady Marquys." Her chaplain was parish priest at Sonderiche; he was to receive ten marks *per annum* for five years in return for prayers for John Harvey, Sir John Paston, and John Isley, "my husbands and other my frendes."[23] So in this case we see a life course that had some room for the Pastons but was hardly likely to accord them pride of place regarding burial, bequests, or references to family. Agnes may have been from East Anglia, though Kent seems a more likely alternative, either for her origins or for her earlier marriages and her child-rearing years. The pattern we trace for Elizabeth Paston Browne and then for the two women who were her great nieces-by-marriage is typical for women of affluence who married a number of times, who perhaps had children by more than one husband, who moved away from their original home grounds, and whose identities brought many separate strands into a pattern of their own design.

Nor was it just those wives who came into the family later in life, or Paston daughters who married out and never returned to the fold. John I's brother William II made a rather grand marriage with Anne Beaufort, third daughter of Edmund, duke of Somerset, and at his death in 1496 William said that (I, 113, from PCC Reg. Horne 12) "I will that my body be buried in the church of Blak Frerez in London at the north ende of the high altar there by my Lady Anne, late my wife," and it was there that "a large stone" for him and Anne was to be put in place. The £20 he left for charity was also London bound: "emonges pouer people and prisoners within the cite of London and withoute." And to further emphasize the way he ignores or dismisses the pull of the Pastons, an eight-year chantry, to be sung by "a preset of honest conuersacion" was to be established at Cambridge, where William had been a student.[24] The parish church of St Peter in "Wodenorton" (Wood Norton, Norfolk) received 5 marks for "a hole vestyment." In addition he instructed that debts owed him by his aged and poor tenants were to be excused: "none of my tenantes nor farmers suche as be of grete age and fallith in pouerté be in any wise vexed or troubled…for no maner of olde dettes due vnto me before the day of my deces." William did turn a bit toward familiar ground with a stipulation of some personal goods to cover bequests for "Castre Clere" in Norfolk and "in my place in Norwiche." Some recognition of old stamping grounds, but mostly it was William's lofty marriage and London years that really seem to have governed the direction of his choices.

★ ★ ★

A lot of Pastons had gone to earth before Margaret's eyes by the time she drew up her will in February of 1482 (two-plus years before her death in November 1484).[25] Since entering the family in the early 1440s she had seen the death of her father- and mother-in-law (William I and Agnes), of her husband, of two brothers-in-law (Edmund I and Clement), and of three of her own children: John II (1479), Walter (1479: a plague year[26]), and Margery Calle (accepting that the mention of Margery's children but not of their mother in Margaret's will is an indication that she was dead by 1482).[27] There had probably been instances of infant mortality—of Agnes's children and of her own—though no record remains to offer any details; no fifteenth-century monuments or brasses to display the lineup of those little bodies and souls—the boys and girls lined up separately in their decorous rows—for us to tally. Margaret does offer one of those tantalizing throwaway references, in writing to John I, of a dead brother

Harry (Henry—presumably born to Agnes and William I), no other reference fills in the blanks.[28]

In terms of fertility, survival, and longevity the Paston family record is a fairly strong one, and the long widowhoods of Agnes and Margaret may have helped to weaken any push for common burial sites for husbands and wives. Margaret's brother-in-law William II lived until 1496, her sister-in-law, Elizabeth Poynings Browne until 1488, and four of her own children who reached adulthood outlived her. Three were her sons: John III lived until 1504, Edmund II until at least 1504, and William III until sometime after 1504 (when he had to be relieved of any public role because of some sort of insanity). Her daughter, Anne Yelverton, whose marriage had been such a problematic issue in earlier years, lived until 1494–95; John III's wife, Margery née Brewes—she of the touching courtship and the valentine letter—lived until 1495 (after which John remarried; his second wife, Agnes, daughter of Nicholas Morley of Glynde, Sussex, she not dying until 1510, as above). And in the ranks of those who had predeceased Margaret, we can tally old Agnes's full span in terms of some eight decades. The plague year of 1479 claimed its victims—some already old but some hardly that full of years—and while John I had only been in his mid- or late 40s when he died in 1466, his father had lasted at least into his 60s, and maybe more by the time of his death in 1444. Table 4.1 sets this out and also indicates the relationship of each person to Margaret.

The table brings home what I have been saying about the absence of any single overriding tradition regarding burial. Whatever the Pastons proclaimed about their dubious social origins (and their good fortune in getting Edward IV to repeat such nonsense), they did little to take advantage of the opportunities offered by death and burial to cement the idea that they were of the ancient and honorable gentry of the county.[29] Presumably they would have understood what I have been saying about a common family site. If they knew not of the Capulets, as Juliet spelled out the macabre contents of the family vault, they certainly moved in a world of comparable statements about identity and tradition, as shown by their own insistence on their bogus lineage and their claim to ancient gentility. Did they know the biblical tale of Abraham, seeking a burial spot for Sarah, or of Jacob, asking to be carried back from Egypt for burial with his ancestors? In any case, the Paston men, and probably the women, would know of the program of royal burials at Westminster Abbey, or of such families as the de la Poles at Wingfield, or of the Howards at Thetford—to stick to East Anglia.[30] A chantry like that of Thomas Erpingham in the cathedral at Norwich would have been a familiar site on their spiritual landscape. We just have to accept that either their dispersal at death represents some sort of deliberate policy—or they just did not care, though that seems hard to accept, given the seriousness of such issues.

The pattern of disbursal began early, that is, between the first and the second generation. After Clement Paston's burial in 1419 no one else in the family went to rest in the parish church of St Margaret at Paston, where in a sense it all began. Why not? Why not a family chantry there? Perhaps the little church at Paston awakened too many memories of ignoble origins, and turning their backs on Paston was a sign that the family had made it into the world of more prestigious sites—or so they may have argued to themselves. But they did maintain their manor house at Paston. Nor, when the next turn came, did anyone in the family ever follow William I's lead of a chantry in the lady chapel of the cathedral, the most emphatic possible proclamation of "making it" on the staircase of social mobility.[31] The strongest single thread was that tie with the Carmelites, the White Friars, in both Norwich and London; Table 4.1 shows this. There were burials in Carmelite houses, endowments to the order, and some statements about personal ties. However, William I, John I, and Margaret—main players in the family drama—were never caught by this net.[32]

So far this has been more about family than about religion, though my basic premise is that these were pretty much two sides of the same coin. We can look at the wills in more detail, and to do this we properly open with Clement, he who began the family's climb upwards. Clement Paston, father of judge William I, had died in 1419, perhaps just a bit before Margaret's birth. He had had some success in the world but no great vaulting ambition; no indications of any inclination (or ability) to create some fancy identity by means of a last will or burial provisions. He asked for burial in the parish church at Paston, between the north door and the tomb of his wife Beatrice. He followed the usual practice of late medieval lay wills in that he divided his bequests into numerous small parcels, including those intended for his parish church.[33] There was a bequest to the high altar of the parish church, 3s 4d to its vicar, money for 6 pounds of wax for lights before the image of the church's patron saint, St Margaret, 12d for lights above the rood screen or loft, and 3s 4d for repairs to the church. Still a local boy in his loyalties, he left another 2s to the vicar of Bacton, 8d for repairs at Trunch, and 6d for the same for Mounslee (Mundesley) parish church, along with 6s 8d to the prior and convent at Bromholm, just down the road in the most literal sense (and holder of the advowson of the parish church at Paston). The residue of his estate was to be divided between Clement's sister Martha, married to John Bacton (whose very surname proclaims his local roots—as does "Paston" for the Pastons), and his son William (William I), with the usual clauses about the residue being used for the welfare of Clement's soul.[34]

The witnesses include a number of clerics: Nicholas, prior of Bromholm, Richard Jernemuth, "monacho" (a brother at Bromholm?), Richard, vicar of Paston, a chaplain, "et aliis."

As befits a man of some means but one who is by no means wealthy and whose major obligation is to family, this conventional will leaves its maker's mark on his community but stops well short of any sort of grand statement. For the first generation of a family on the rise, this sufficed, and it was not unimpressive in its way. Clement and Beatrice were destined to rest for many years in the parish church at Paston without the company of others of the family. On the other hand, links had been forged or consolidated with the prior of Bromholm, an important figure on the local landscape, as well as with a number of nearby parish churches and those who served them. Nor was Clement all that shrinking. Burial within the parish church, rather than in the churchyard, bespeaks some self-awareness regarding status (and displays his ability to afford something beyond the usual standard).

William I was the man who really put the family on the road upward.[35] He died in 1444, shortly after young Margaret Mautby had married into the family; the likelihood is that the newlyweds had spent their brief domestic life in the parental household, especially as John I was still at Cambridge and often away from home. William I left a will in which he stipulated burial in the chapel of the Blessed Virgin in Norwich Cathedral, by the south side or end of the altar (though he actually died while in the parish of St Brides, Fleet Street, London). A cathedral burial was a bold proclamation, indicating that the family had arrived; a chantry in the mother church of the diocese was a real leap forward in the family's assertion of identity and affluence: "ad finem australem altaris in capelle Beate Marie in fine orientali ecclesie cathedralis Sancte Trinitatis Norwici" (I, 12). Few could afford it, and few had the clout or the temerity to claim it, and William was playing at high stakes in the game that Paul Binsky has referred to as "the politics of space."[36] The chantry services he called for ("missam de Spiritu Sacto") were endowed for seven years, to be sung by the monks of the cathedral; the mass of the Holy Spirit for his soul, the souls of his wife (she to live for another 35 years), his father and mother, and "omnium consanguineorum et benefactorum nostrorum, et omnium."[37] Agnes tells us that revenues from the family's manor of Swainsthorpe had been designated for the support of this costly commitment.[38] Since the Lady chapel in Norwich Cathedral was demolished at some point in the late sixteenth or early seventeenth century we cannot gauge the size, let alone the splendor of the chantry, and physical evidence of William's handsome declaration of social arrival and self has gone the way of time and the wrecking crews.[39]

The other ecclesiastical bequests in William's will are of interest since they enable us to follow the family's move—in physical, socioeconomic, and psychological terms—from the hinterland of the Norfolk coast to its metropolitan center. While William chose the cathedral as his permanent resting place, he still recognized a commitment to the outer edge of the county whence he had come. Robert, prior of Bromholm was to receive 40s and each monk there 6s 8d.[40] In addition, he left money to the vicars of Paston and Bacton to square accounts still outstanding from his duties as an executor. Since Bacton and Bromholm priory are but a very short remove from Paston, these three loci of William's rural benefaction make a neat triangle—one covering the original home ground of the family and places his father had covered in that will of 1419. William's dealings as a judge and man of affairs had brought him into contact with great men of the church and with numerous regular and mendicant houses (including Cluny itself), but his will clearly was not the time or place for such connections. One unusual note is that William called for prayers that recited the five wounds of Jesus and the five joys of the Virgin Mary, a knowledgeable reference and set of instructions unique in the Paston wills.[41]

Though many years and many deaths were to intervene between William's burial in the Cathedral in 1444 and the death and burial of his widow, Agnes in 1479, a comparison of their wills is instructive. The various draft versions of Agnes's will are largely devoted to her fulminations about the way John I had taken advantage of his brothers in 1444 and had run off with the lion's share of his father's estate, including various treasures and critical documents she had thought safely squirreled away with the monks at the Cathedral: "swyche tresowre of on my husbons…the sayde John Paston owte of the seyde abbey vnknowyn to the Priour ore ony oder person…and wyth-owte my wetyn and assente…toke and barre awey all, and kepyng it styll…" (I, 397). In venting her anger Agnes was given to repeating William's saws about how to get ahead in life, as well as his worries—quite reasonable ones, as it turn out—that John I would take advantage of his brothers, who would have "no littill that they migt not leve theron wythougt they shuld hold the plowe be the tayle." But when Agnes had finally run through this litany and turned to a consideration of her own soul, she proved to be most informative.

Agnes's verbal re-creation of the scene of William's death is evocative; the family's version of the deathbed drama of William the Marshal. William Paston died on "Thursday night betwixt x and xij of the clokk." Various interested parties had been summoned both before and after his last breath, and on the Friday next they asked to see his will, which Agnes then produced; we wonder about clerics and secretaries and perhaps an attorney or two, but in Agnes's version, at least, she was very much the controlling figure. John Dam read the will, presumably aloud to all and sundry, and while he was so occupied John I "walkyd vp and down in the chamer: John Dam and I knelyd at the beddys fete" and discussed the future of the manor at Sporle and the shares of the estate that would go to the younger sons. It looks as though an interest in William's soul took a backseat to considerations of the division of his estate, at least as Agnes subsequently reconstructed the scene.[42] Certainly, in the pieces of her will that we have there is little indication that she reflected much on her husband's spiritual concerns. What John I had done to his brothers, or what he had not done, seemed to be of much greater importance.

We learn more about the end of William I, though little of it adds to our knowledge regarding his chantry, his concern for prayer services, or of the devotion of his worldly goods for spiritual purposes. What we have of William's own will is focused on real (and personal) property, and nothing in an undated inventory (I, 11) is any more enlightening; the document does not seem to have been part of a near-death stock taking. The inventory is rich in its list of tools, weapons, and secular household items, down to the last "j pykforke…j towayll…j fetyrlok." From the letters of William's descendents, written long after his death, we get some additional information, though here too it is property and procedures, not the old man's soul (or his religious goods) that are of concern. From the complaint launched by John III against his uncle, William II in 1483 (I, 387), we learn that the bishop of London (Thomas Kempe) had been a supervisor of William's will: "for keeping of the trewe jntent and will of the seid William Paston, justice." And of more interest, though again shedding no light on spiritual matters, is a letter of 1485 from Elizabeth, sister of John I, to her nephew, John III (I, 388). She says that she, age "xiij, xv yer, or xvj yer olde," was with her parents at St Bride's in London when "my fadyrs last syknes took hym." John I did not get to London from Norfolk until it was too late—shades of Henry II and that no-show, Richard the Lionheart—not coming "tyll aftyr that my fadyr was diseased."[43] She had witnessed her father's will, presumably as a spectator rather than a legal signatory, but nevertheless she has been present, some 41 years ago: "Any thys wyll I wyttnesse whyle I leve for a trewthe, as knowith God."

Agnes, William's champion of his last wishes, died in London in 1479, a very old lady. She was buried, in all likelihood at the behest of her son William II with whom she had been living, in the London Carmelite house. But the real strength of her ties with and affection for the Carmelites comes out when she talks of her Norwich connections. It is from her will—and *only* from her will—that we learn two things of importance regarding these ties. Talking of the Norwich Carmelite house, she says that "for I am there a suster" and so a cash bequest goes "to helpe to pay hir debts xx li." Her other statement, and of even greater interest, reveals the motive behind her bequest to mend their chapel of Our Lady "within the said place, wheras Sir Thomas Gerbredge my grandfather and Dame Elizabeth his wife and Sir Edmond Berry my father and Dame Alice his wife be buried, and Clement Paston my sonn" (I, 34). So in one stroke it all becomes clear: the Norwich Carmelite house had had ties with Agnes's mother's parents, and then with Agnes's mother after her marriage (and then with her mother and her father), and now with both Agnes and with the son who had predeceased her. This clarifies the reason for the four-generation chain, though it was never one to bind all the Pastons who, sooner or later, would be in need of a burial place.

The will of William I had named but few ecclesiastical beneficiaries; certainly, many fewer than the number of institutions and people with whom he had had contacts during his long and busy life. Agnes's will, or at least what we have of it, is even narrower. Beyond her Carmelite bequests and memories there was not even a reference to those advowsons and appointments that had been of considerable importance to her when she was playing her role as lady of the manor. William II, on his mother's behalf, had undertaken the fifteenth-century equivalent of running a job search, broadcasting details of the living and its resources, giving an assurance that the church at Oxnead was not a heavy burden for a capable incumbent, and going so far as to say that an enterprising incumbent might find time and opportunity to supplement that church's small (but guaranteed) income through other forms of activity.[44] None of this proprietarial focus is even hinted at in what we have of Agnes's will—no indications of how seriously she had been invested in those earlier quarrels over the right to appoint, or over the right to the right of way, or the building of a wall, or any of the other ecclesiastical *cassus belli* that had occupied so much of her time, energy, and epistolary agenda. Of course, we do not have the entire will; Davis's documents are labeled "draft will," "part of draft will," "part of draft will," and "extract from will." Nor is there any indication of *inter vivos* benefactions to take into account, though it seems likely that Agnes had been a significant patroness of and donor to the Carmelites in Norwich, as an affluent widow for over 20 years as well as an heiress in her own right.[45]

Agnes's grandson John III talked of bringing her remains, along with those of his brother John II, from London to the Norwich Carmelites, though there is no indication in the Letters that he carried through on this (I, 383).[46] We have no evidence that the family gave the London house anything beyond what was expected to cover burial costs, though this assertion rests on negative evidence. Whatever plans might have been contemplated (if not implemented) regarding Norwich as Agnes's ultimate burial site, there are absolutely no signs of any interest on the part of her survivors and heirs in putting her to rest beside William I in his chapel in the cathedral, whereas John II presumably would have gone to join his father at Bromholm ("I supposyd that he wold haue ben beryed at Bromholme") had he died nearer home or had John III followed through with his talk about reburial. William I had died long before and had said nothing in his own will about such a reunion, though his chantry endowment was to include prayers for Agnes's soul. Now Agnes, many years later, was no more forthcoming. And with her burial in London, her disregard of the dead William I is particularly interesting, since so much of her will—at least those draft sections we have—is concerned with his last wishes, at least as she recalled them so many years later.

There are other references to Agnes's will and related issues. In August 1479, which was shortly after Agnes's death, her grandson John II (also soon to die) asked his uncle William II about what seems to be a will of his grandmother, whether it was the version we have from 1466 (or at least parts thereof) or something more recent (I, 314); "off my granutdamys wylle, and whoo wrot itt, and whether she be buried or noo, and who weer present at hyre wylle making, and iffe she spoke owte off her landes." Again, on the likely idea that Agnes had provided sufficiently for her own soul, this is more likely to cover worldly affairs and possessions. And while John II was trying to get news about matters that were still waiting to be put to rest, he also reminded himself to ask Master Bele and his clerk "for my faderys wille," a document that has not been preserved but that can be inferred (as we shall see below). We have another reference to Agnes's death, when in August of 1479 her grandson Edmund II mentioned that the duchess of Norfolk was about to move with a group of 60 people, "whythere it is to convey my grandham hydere ore nowght he cowed not sey" (I, 397). Neither can we, though this may tell us of the otherwise unrecorded transfer of the body from the London Carmelites to the Norwich house.

Before turning to John I, and then to Margaret, we have a bit more that would have been noted in a family bible or book of hours, had they kept (and preserved) such a book. In 1449 Margaret's brother-in-law Edmund died, the first of the grown children of William I and Agnes to die. A draft of his nuncupative will survives, dated March 21, 1449 and witnessed by William May, "magister Noui Templi London," among others (I, 80). With no further elaboration, Edmund instructed that he be buried either in the Temple Church in London or in the Carmelite house there. So again the Carmelite theme can be heard, but not so strongly as to block any possible alternatives.[47] John I was to be his brother Edmund's executor and Edmund expressed full confidence that John would use his goods for the sake of his soul. No other institutions are mentioned, and that Edmund's soul was being entrusted to "Deo Omnipotenti, Beate Marie Virgini, et omnibus sanctis" is but conventional phraseology. Edmund does not say enough to allow us to judge whether he now thought of himself as a Londoner or whether his identity was that of an East Anglian who just happened to die in the metropolis. His trust in John I, his oldest brother, may indicate that the quarrel over their father's estate—perhaps blown to larger proportions as it was told by Agnes and William II, as the years passed—was not such a serious issue after all.

By the time Margaret drew up her will in 1482 two of her grown sons had died, John II and Walter both going in 1479. We know a bit about their last wishes, and a few details regarding burial add more chapters—albeit short ones—to the zig-zag pattern of family behavior. Since John II was in London and spoke of feeling ill just before his end came, his death may have been due to the same plague that perhaps had carried off his aged grandmother: "I was in suche feare off the syknesse" (I, 315), though this was long after his will had been written. Not surprisingly, under the circumstances, he was buried in London, in keeping with the provisions of that will of 1477 (two years before): "yf I dyghe ny the cyté of London...[to be buried in] Owre Lady in the Whithe Frerys there, at the northe-est cornere of the body of the chyrche" (I, 309: the gap is because of a defect in the manuscript). John II's death seems very much in the pattern of the "lonely-deathbed" scenario; the death of a young man of considerable charm who saw so few of his own projects come to fruition seems very poignant. He left quite expansive and costly instructions, though there is little indication of how much of this was ever carried out. He wanted something—probably a chantry chapel or a monument—to be built, "leke as ys ouer Syr Thomas Browne in the Frere Prechours, to the valour of xx li," and its purpose was to draw prayers, with another 20 marks being devoted to its upkeep. Providing for a chantry in a London burial house seems to indicate that, if he did die in the metropolis, he would be content to lie there. But he leaves us a mixed message regarding family plans and his role as eldest son; an inherited status or rank but hardly one he had played out either for its obligations or its opportunities. Were he to die in Norfolk, or so he stipulated, it was to be burial at Bromholm, "vn-to the founders toumbe, which arche is vn-to the north-syde and ryght agayn my fadyre toumbe with an awtere and a toumbe for me," with another £20 for a chantry there to go along with the new tomb. Also, and of some interest, John II either makes a plea for the creation of a family burial tradition at Bromholm or a more general plea on the idea that a good tomb and a chantry will turn people's thoughts to prayer: "so that owre cousyns…have the more deuocion to that place and the rathere reste there bodyes there the encresse of the…encrese and profite of the howse and reste on the religeus thereof lyke as owre auncetours have."[48]

John II talks of endowments to and support for the college that by now should have been established from the riches of the Fastolf estate, a four-chaplain affair under the supervision of the bishop of Winchester. The chapel of St John Baptist in Caister was to be incorporated within the Fastolf college; its annual revenues of "vij li. yerly" to cover a chantry priest's services; prayers for "the sowles of my fadere…" as well as those of Thomas Lyndes, one-time vicar at Mautby, and of John Daubney, killed while fighting on the Paston's behalf at the siege of Caister.[49] This will seems unusually pious and dutiful, but then again we have numerous indications that John II had his dilatory behavior over his father's tomb on his conscience. It sounds at though John's deathbed thoughts—or at least those in his will, which is as late as we can go—ran toward his inherited but as-yet unfulfilled obligations and his would-be role as heir of the previous generation, patriarch of the next. In many ways the story of John II and John III is very much a story of intentions—well meant of unrealized. John II intended to build the tomb that John I had wished for, and in turn John III intended to bring his brother's body (and that of Agnes) back from London to some resting place on the home grounds.[50] John III wrote to Margaret in November 1479 regarding his older brother; "if it had ben hys wylle to haue leyn at Bromholm, I had purposyd all the wey as I haue regyn to haue brought hom my grauntdam and hym to-gedyrs, butr that purpose is voyd as now" (I, 383). A month later, writing from London, John III told Margaret he needed money. Perhaps it was the cash-flow problem that thwarted his good intentions: "I haue myche to pay her in London, what for the funeral costys, dettys, and legattys" (I, 384). That John II died unmarried—and in that regard also failed his patriarchal duties—but reinforces our assessment of a life that often seemed to lack a sense of direction, perhaps in reaction to the aggrandizing, relentless tunnel vision of his John I.

Walter Paston, another of the family casualties of 1479, was buried in Norwich. Not, however, in the cathedral (with his grandfather), nor in the Carmelite house that had so many connections with his family through his paternal grandmother. Rather, Walter's burial site was the parish church of St Peter Hungate, on Elm Hill, before the image of St John Baptist to whose altar he left 3s 4d (I, 405). It is likely that the funeral arrangements, along with the church itself, were very much under Margaret's control; Walter's wish for burial there was surely one that was honored. Why St

Peter Hungate, we ask, it being low in the ranks of the city's churches? And the answer, of course, is that in 1458 John I and Margaret had acquired the advowson, and in (or by) 1460 they had subsidized extensive rebuilding resulting in the church that still stands, at least in its exterior frame, probably much as they knew it.[51] Since Walter seems to have emerged by 1479 as the apple of his aged mother's eye we can understand why he chose this church.[52] In some ways the question really is why *only* Walter, of all the Pastons—and especially of the sons who died after 1460—was buried there. At his death Walter was as yet an unbeneficed cleric, holding a brand-new degree from Oxford and a fair-sized estate on his own as his share of John I's holdings.[53] In his will he leaves instructions on the division of his sheep at Mautby, along with the profits of his manor (or his share thereof) at Cressingham. But for the most part, as a young man with aspirations for a clerical career, the bequests followed the dutiful and expected paths of testamentary distribution. Having just come down from Oxford, his remembrance of his burial church in Norwich was balanced by the list of beneficiaries who seem to have been fellow churchmen and fellow students of his Oxford days. One bequest was to a friar ("fratri Johanni Somerton, bachalaureo" for 5s) and others were to men identified as Masters and therefore likely to be academic friends. They were to receive various garments, with a further reference to possessions still at Oxford.[54] Walter also singles out his siblings; his brother Edmund, his sister Anne Yelverton, his sister-in-law Margery (wife of John III), and both John II (and John II's heirs, though there were no legitimate ones) and John III; no mention of his erring sister Margery Calle. John III was executor for the family bequests ("pro ista patria") while Master Edmund Alyard was so appointed for the Oxford side of affairs. The residue of Walter's estate, as was usually the case, was "pro anima mea," whether for prayers to be said at St Peter Hungate or at Oxford or elsewhere. None of Walter's bequests point to any greater spirituality or intellectual concern than we find in other family wills, university graduate and would-be cleric though he was by the end.

This brings us to the death and burial of Margaret's husband, John I, father of John II and Walter. The worldly end of John I offers a case study that opens all sorts of doors and that poses some intriguing questions. It also casts doubt, or at least some serious qualifications, on some of the assertions I offered above about Paston burials and testamentary bequests. John I died in London in May 1466. But he, unlike others of the family who had been caught short of their East Anglian origins, left provisions (and money?) for a most elaborate and complicated return to his native soil, as well as for exceptionally large-scale arrangements for the funeral and for a great scattering of testamentary bequests. His will has not been preserved, and what we have are a number of accounts, amplified by material in his sons' letters, and the whole package gives a fairly detailed picture of the external trappings of a procession and burial that went from the deathbed in London to interment at Bromholm with a lying in state in Norwich along the way.[55] The accounts tally the expenses of the procession, of the burial feast, and of the bequests for prayers, along with a lot of miscellaneous items. Though complying with the patriarch's wishes would have cost a great deal of money at a time when the family was cash strapped (as they usually were), things seem to have been carried out as he wished (except for the tomb).[56]

The whole affair was far beyond anything else in the family's record. Furthermore, John I picked up theme of family support for the priory at Bromholm and turned this into a whole cloth of impressive dimensions. William I, some 22 years before, had left Bromholm a modest bequest, as much a token regard for his roots and revelatory of local networking as of any great boon or special regard for the house. John I went to the other extreme, and that his sons were so slow to move on his monument may be explicable—and perhaps easier to sympathize with—when we think of what they already had had to shell out from the estate just for the grand affair that revolved around burying their father in an appropriate fashion; that is, in the fashion he seems to have arranged sometime before his death. John I left this world as the director (and leading actor?) in a gentry version of Eleanor of Castile's last journey; by contrast we know nothing of how his father's body had been transported from London to Norwich for burial in the cathedral. If we say that John's funeral was perhaps more appropriate for the likes of someone at the level of Sir John Fastolf, the irony is that it was the anticipated share of the Fastolf estate that was probably paying for it (though perhaps still in anticipation). I talked above of models for different styles of burial and testamentary distribution, and the indications are that John thought it all out in advance, and presumably in great detail, picking and choosing from a range of choices—as he must have done for the many beneficiaries who were to receive some tangible memorial of his departure.

The whole process of burying and commemorating John I was complex, costly, protracted, and—for us—enlightening concerning the image of self that he wanted to project. Because we have to rely on the accounts of expenses, rather than on a will, we lack the "living words" of John Paston: no invocation of saints, no first-person instructions about candles and the poor, and not even anything directly from his mouth about that famous and long unbuilt monument.[57] Thus a comparison of his funeral arrangements with those of the other Pastons has a touch of apples and oranges, as we know nothing about other processions or ceremonies to compare what we have for John I. In effect we are left with a trade-off for John I; rich details about the procession and funeral games, as against the lack of direct instructions from the testator about his soul, his saints, his executor, or the distribution of his personal goods. In terms of the sums spent and the display thereby subsidized, as measured in the hard language of pence, shillings, and pounds, the last journey of John Paston I from London to Norfolk may have run to more than all the other Paston burials put together.[58] And while we do not hear of John's death-bed pieties, we are informed of the obligation to pay for such worldly items as "a roundlet of red wine of xv. Gallonys, etc., xiis xid....for iiii bushels wete, xxxiid...for vii barrels of bere...for xli. Pygges...for xxxiii. Lambys...setting on the tents" and for much, much more of this sort (some of it just summed up as "vittelles bought by Richard Calle").

The bills that were turned do tell of John's last days and then of the processional aspects of his return to native soil; the long march with the body, the overnight rest stop in Norwich, and then final disposal of earthly remains at Bromholm. Moreover, apart from the ceremonial aspects of John's death, the accounts and receipts are rich in information about his extensive cast of ecclesiastically focused benefactions, they being steered to numerous institutions and to quite a few individuals who are mostly specified in an *ex officio* capacity, such as the vicar of Upton. In reality, as we would expect in view of the seamless garment of benefaction and gift giving that was spun in return for prayers, the categories of gifting and subsidized prayer spill over into each other a good bit. How much of the money designated for the prior of Bromholm and his monks and servants was in exchange for their prayers and how much was to repay the various parties for their roles, their out-of-pocket expenses, and the labor involved in hosting a large and messy series of meals and a house full of guests over the course of two or three days?

To follow events in the order in which they occurred—which is distinct from how their costs were registered by Gloys or Calle—we can begin with the expenses relating to John's last days in London and to efforts to get his body to Bromholm (by way of Norwich).[59] We can pick up the tale as he lay dying; a tale of mortal illness and death and entailing, among other commitments, the family's obligation to pay two men in London, for "awaytyng upon my master at London for vii dayes before that he was caryed, ii s. x d," though even before that the family recognized its debt: "to the keeper of the inne where myne husband dyed, for his reward vis viii d" (Gairdner, II, 270). The procession that brought the body to Norwich was composed (at least) of a woman "that came from London with the cors to Norwyche," a priest, 12 poor men who carried torches for a six-day journey (at 4d per day—and three days to return, at

6d per day), along with some "servitors" who were stationed somewhere along the route by William II, John's brother. A march of six days for the journey of 100 miles must have been a fairly stately one, making an impression in the villages through which it passed and in the churches where the burden was put down for the night (and where prayers said by the local priest and others would most likely have been encouraged and subsidized).[60]

When the cortege reached Norwich it headed for the church of St Peter Hungate and there John's body lay in state for one night or more. But even if the bier only rested in St Peter for a single night, what a night: 38 piests "at the dyryge at Norwyche, when the cors lay ther," they to receive 12s 8d, and to accompany or compliment their service the family also paid 39 children, "schyldern with surplyes within the schurche and without," and they to receive 3s 4d. In addition 26 clerks and four keepers of torches were emplyed, "for ryngers ageyn the cors." Few in the town would not have known that John Paston had died and that his body was passing through; did they ask why he was not joining his father in the cathedral? Then, after the elaborate and attention-catching ceremonies in Norwich, the body was ready for the final leg of the journey—from Norwich to Bromholm, and for a burial and for the monument that John must have worked out with the prior in considerable detail. As with other stages of the last journey, the body was but the centerpiece of a parade, and the friars from Norwich who now accompanied the body on this last stage came in for special mention (in contrast to guests who just assembled at Bromholm).

Once the whole company reached and/or assembled at Bromholm the accounts shift their focus to the problems that stemmed from the need to house and feed the gathering: to set up tents to shelter them, to pay for the huge quantities of fish, meat, drink, and the like. From a document among the receipts that is labeled "prior of Bromholm" we learn that he had been called upon to put up some of the guests, as well as some of the "blue-collar" laborers, over a weekend: three on Thursday, five on Friday, and so forth through the following Monday. The catering needs are impressive, as are the details of most medieval feasts ranging from a coronation banquet or the installation of an archbishop down to the daily fare set on the tables of the gentry. Those who came to pay their last respects were not likely to return with complaints about the fare they had been offered, having been able to choose from "xxvii gees...lxx capons...xli pygges...xlix calys...xxxiiii lambys" and a good deal more. This vast affair, combining sociability, John's assertion of an identity as a great man of the region, and the employment of clerics and lay mourners who said their prayers, is a typical example of how public life, family or private life, and spiritual concerns were sewn together with few split seams in the fabric. The mundane obligations that were part and parcel of this lavish display of sociability and piety also had to be taken care of: "For viii peces of peuter lost of the Priors, xx d." or "To the glaser for takyn owte of ii panys of the windows of the schyrche for to late owte the reke of the torches at the deryge, and sowderyng new of the same, xx d" (Gairdner, II, 267–68).

Beyond or perhaps after the ceremonial and festive parts of the funeral, we have a large number of accounts or obligations regarding money, sums to be spent on behalf of John's soul—all going to his impressively large network of subsidized well-wishers. The details about recipients and payments stand out in contrast to the actual Paston wills, where we generally find fewer bequests and are given little idea of how much was actually spent in keeping with testamentary instructions. John's bequests involved a mix of institutions and individuals, though I do not make much distinction in listing the beneficiaries in Table 4.2. There were bequests for numerous parish churches, for the four friaries of Norwich, for the college at Caister, and the like, while other payments singled out the individual recipients. The prioress of Carow was to received vi s. viii d., the vicar of Upton 2s, the parson of Mautby and Sir Thomas Lynes, "the prestes at the deryge at Bromholm," 44s, "the parisshe schyrche of Bromholm," 10s. Our categories do rough justice to the bequests and reciprocities of a pre-Reformation gala, and we can decide about "a cope called a frogge of worsted" for the prior of Bromholm as we wish, along with payments to the priory's staff of porters and the like. All in all, the house at Bromholm, between its vowed men and its lay laborers and servants, fared better than any other recipient or linked group of recipients. On the other hand, it was the chosen burial site—within a very few miles of the tombs of John's grandfather and grandmother at Paston—but was being treated on a wholly different scale and the visible indication (or so John had hoped) of the distinction between the first and the third generation of the Pastons.

As we tally the beneficiaries of John's largesse we see how he scattered his memorialization across Norfolk (as shown in Map 4.1), though we also note that it was confined just to Norfolk. Little nostalgia for the metropolis in which he spend so much time. Perhaps his involuntary visits to the Fleet Prison has given him enough of London's institutional life, though we did see money for the relief of prisoners as one category of bequest in the wills of his sister Elizabeth (I, 123, in 1487) and his brother William II (I, 113, in 1496), some years on. But what is striking about John's benefactions—particularly as the bequests of his widow are our real point of concern—is the high degree of duplication between

Table 4.2 Recipients of Bequests from John I and Margaret Paston

Beneficiary: Recipient Institution or Individual	Named by Margaret in Her Will (1482)	Named by John (from the Receipts of His Funeral—1466)
Mautby (Parish Church) and Villagers	X	X
Fritton p.c.	X	X
Bassingham	X	
Matlask	X	
Gresham	X	X
Sparham	X	
Redham	X	X
4 houses of Norwich friars	X	X
4 houses of Yarmouth friars	X	
Anchoress by ———	X	
Anchoress at Conesford	X	
Anchoress at Carmel	X	
Normans: sisters there	X	X
Chapel of Field	X	
St Giles Hospital	X	
Norwich Cathedral	X	
Lepers at the 5 gates	X	
Foregoers at the gates	X	
Leper at Yarmouth, north gate	X	
St Peter Hungate	X	X
St Michael Coslany	X	
St Stephen p.c.		X
Bromholm Priory		X
Bromholm Parish Church		X
Upton Parish Church		X

husband, dying in 1466, and wife, dying in 1484; this is shown in Table 4.2. Each was the only member of the family to be buried in their chosen sites, whether we look at John at Bromholm or Margaret at Mautby, and as far as our records go, no one else left bequests of any sort to these institutions after these two deaths (ignoring in this the good but unfulfilled intentions of John II about Bromholm as well as early bequests or gifts to that house). Of course, some wills have been lost (or had never been written?) and others exist only in fragments. Nevertheless, on the basis of what we do know there is a strong impression of John I following the trail of bequests that had in some part been laid out with Margaret, perhaps as

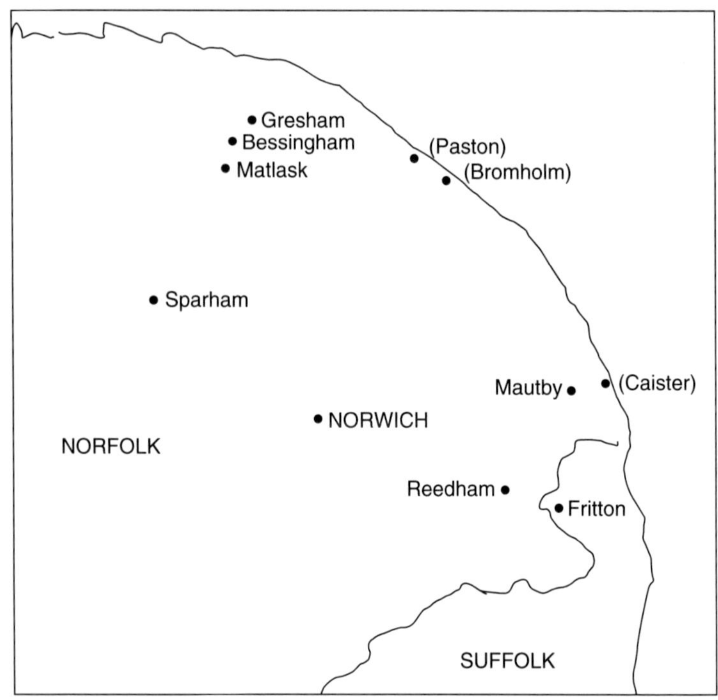

Map 4.1　Norfolk Churches and Manors Named in Margaret Paston's Will.

far back as when he took in hand the dowry that she had brought to their marriage. His bequests, as we reconstruct them from the receipts and instructions that accompany his funeral expenses, reflect a recognition of John's debt to Margaret, to her status as heiress of a more established family, and—or so we might like to say—to her years of unfailing devotion and duty on behalf of his causes and campaigns. If this is too romantic or sentimental, it does gain some support from his remembrance of money left for such a small and out-of-the way place as Fritton—one of Margaret's churches—on the Norfolk-Suffolk border and a place well "out of the loop" as Paston affairs and interests went.

One interesting issue we can touch before turning to Margaret herself concerns the institutional recipients whom we might expect to find in this list but who go unmentioned by either John I or Margaret (when her turns comes) or both. Unlike the neglected fairy in "Sleeping Beauty," they were not in a position that enabled them to cast a malediction on our testators; their exclusion from the list of beneficiaries offered no scope for getting even, just as they presumably had to suffer in silence. Nevertheless, some absences are noteworthy, and ignoring the possibility of *inter vivos* benefaction about which we know nothing—except for the rebuilding of St Peter Hungate—we are reminded of the thin thread of family tradition and of the wide scope for individualizing each will, each testators' circles of choice. We might expect an individual's circles to contain some recipients or beneficiaries found in other family wills, plus some choices that were unique. But the Pastons fall outside these perimeters of behavior, though it was recipients, not categories, that seemed individualized. That neither John I nor Margaret had much regard for the regular orders, with the exception of John's links with Bromholm, is pretty much in keeping with the standard pattern of fifteenth-century lay piety, as were those more generous bequests to a fair number of mendicant houses. But nowhere in John's huge web of benefaction and remembrance does Norwich Cathedral come in for mention, though Margaret would have something to give to what she refers to as the "mother church."

A different sort of omission, one that might have been rectified had we the text of John's will, pertains to our ignorance regarding any spiritual involvement or roles for his family—beyond the injunctions about building that infamous tomb. What we have is wholly impersonal: invite the following churchmen and women, feed them, hire the following people, etc., but little else. We know nothing about his distribution of those personal goods of ecclesiastical use, let alone his other possessions, though the inventories we looked at above support the idea of John as a typical member or representative of an acquisitive gentry class and culture. And in the absence of John's will and the conventions of expression, we have no words to the effect of "my wastrel son" is to sit in the front pew and say prayers in return for my soul and those of his forebears. At the end, even when John I turned out to be extremely and perhaps uncharacteristically open handed, he was not very revealing. Furthermore, with nothing directly from his own mouth or pen, we know nothing about the saints he would have invoked, though we assume the usual suspects, the Virgin, John the Baptist, and perhaps All Saints or the Trinity or St Catherine.

★　★　★

In a sense this is all table-setting for our look at Margaret, for her will of 1482. It has been a table bedecked with riches and much variety, though little by way of great and fabulous concoctions designed for the exotic palate we occasionally find among the fifteenth-century laity. It is more a case of a bit of this, a bit of that; a tomb, a new chantry, scattered bequests, burial in a family favorite, burial away from home, charity to prisoners and debtors, and the like. So when Margaret turned to write her will in 1482 her decision to "go home" in terms of burial at Mautby she was not snapping a chain of any strength regarding Paston traditions or practices. Though her decision, first to retire to and then ultimately to be interred at Mautby, tells us much about freedom of choice—at least for those who could pay for it—her burial preference was but her own variation on the theme of individualized and disconnected Paston burial patterns that she knew so well from her many years in the family. Her husband had not followed his father, nor that father his father; her mother-in-law Agnes had gone her own way, that of her natal family; her two sons whom we can track were in different churches (one in London, one in Norwich); her daughter (Margery Calle) perhaps in some unknown though doubtlessly some local parish church.[61] Who was to tell Margaret that her own choice was peculiar or unworthy or inappropriate for the matriarch of the Pastons, heiress as she was to the Mautbys? Helen Castor reads Margaret's burial and the wording that controls it as an indication of her "clear sense of the social superiority of her own family," a judgment with which it is hard to disagree.[62]

In previous work on Margaret's will I have suggested that we might read it in terms of a dialectic: thesis, antithesis, and then synthesis.[63] The first part, the thesis, covers ecclesiastical bequests she scattered around the county; the jewel in the crown being her burial at Mautby, in the chantry chapel that she described in loving detail. The thesis here is that she was not a Paston, but rather a Mautby. She expanded this theme (and subsidized it) at some length, for after the provisions for the church and the burial at Mautby she led her executors and beneficiaries on a tour, or a merry chase, around Norfolk (with a one-stop incursion in north Suffolk, at Fritton), and her route ran by way of some isolated and pint-sized villages (then and now). After that, in what I offer as the antithesis—still keeping the family on edge before turning to their bequests—she comes to Norwich (and even briefly to Yarmouth). But even in this she continues to tease the Pastons, moving slowly and deliberately through a long and generous string of bequests and good works in Norwich—touching both institutions and a variety of individuals. And only then, having teased her heirs, does she move to what I call the synthesis in which spiritual concerns and family bequests are joined. Now, at the end, does she turn to family. And in this she forgives and rewards and shows a generosity of spirit and purse we do not always find in her letters. Like John I, she may have given at the end with more warmth than she had spoken in life.

If we can say that the analogue for John I's elaborate and triumphant procession from London to Norwich to Bromholm was the funeral procession of Eleanor of Castile, for Margaret's burial the model was closer at hand; the burial and provisions for the tomb of Alice, duchess of Suffolk in her collegiate church at Ewelme.[64] Though the duchess did not rank high on the list of Paston friends, they knew her and knew of her, and Margaret in particular may have appreciated the way in which a woman who had begun life as Alice Chaucer had re-created herself and proclaimed a new identity—in Alice's case rising from that of the upper gentry to the status of a great noblewoman. The duchess had come a long way from a life that began as Thomas Chaucer's daughter, a girl from the Paston's own neighborhood.[65] But whereas Alice Chaucer wished to display how far she outstripped her early ties by creating her monument-to-self at Ewelme, Margaret Paston reversed the course and, at the end, reasserted her origins.

Given the various models and parallels before Margaret, along with the Paston family's lack of any strong tradition regarding burial, her decision to be buried at Mautby was not likely to have come as a great surprise (apart from the likelihood that she had been discussing it for years). She was also making a statement regarding her proprietarial hold on the village and on the power of her purse there, since the church at Mautby was hardly a very grand affair. Her bequests would have been very big news for its small and remote parish church.[66] Once we accept that her old-age withdrawal and then her burial in Mautby was a declaration of semi-independence from the Pastons and a reassertion of an earlier identity, Margaret's provisions fit a familiar pattern of lordship (or ladyship). Like duchess Alice at Ewelme, she left detailed instructions regarding the heraldry of the tomb: "iiij scochens sett at the iiij corners, whereof I wulle that the first scochen shalbe of my husbondes armes and myn departed, the ijde of Mawtebys armes and Berneys of Redham departed, the iijde of Mawtebys armes and the Lord Loveyn departed, the iiijte of Mawtebys armes and Sir Roger Beauchamp departed. And in myddys of the seid stoon I wull have a scochen sett of *Mawtebys armes allone*."[67] The prayers she specified did not exclude John I, but they hardly privileged him or placed special emphasis on the bonds that had been forged by some 25 years of marriage and the production of at least seven children (with three or four still alive): "synge and pray…for my sowle, the sowles of my father and mother, the sowle of the said John Paston, late my husbond, and for the sowlys of his aunceteres and myn during the terme of vij yeres next after my decesse…" For a woman who had marked the cycle of the year with all those saints' days, Margaret seems pretty secular and pretty laconic in this.[68] Mautby as headquarters, Mautby as permanent resting place, and finally Mautby as a projection of her image—now to be displayed through the tomb and special-built chantry. In that chantry would be her burial: "in the ele of the cherch…byfore the ymage of Our Lady there, jn which ele reste the bodies of diuers of myn aunceteres, whos sowles God assoile."

Margaret's burial and all that went with it were hardly on a scale to rival the great spectacle that had marked the departure of her husband some 18 years before. On the other hand, it was certainly notched pretty well up the gentry scale. As well as calling for a new south aisle in the church and an elaborate tomb with a legend to go with the escutcheons ("thise wordes wretyn: 'In God is my trust'; with a scripture wretyn in the verges therof rehersyng thise wordes: 'Here lieth Margret Paston, late the wif of John Paston, doughter and heire of John Mawteby, squire [and]...in the same scripture rehersed the day of the moneth and the yer that I shall decesse, 'on whos sowle God have mercy'"), there was to be money so 12 of her poor tenants at Matuby could attend the ceremony, clad in new white gowns and holding torches. And though the men would go home with an additional 4d apiece, the torches were, "for my yer day," and so it would be for 12 years. Priests in attendance were to receive 8d, plus 3d for "ich clerk in surplys" and 6s 8d to the priest who buried her, he to earn his half mark by reciting "ouer me at the tyme of my berying all the hole seruice that to the berying belongeth." Nor was this all; seven years worth of candles to burn each Sunday and holiday, four years worth of tapers, a seven-year chantry where "an honest seculer prest" would sing. And of interest to us, two books "yeven to abide" in the church, "aslonge as they may endure." One was a "complete legende in oon book," and the other an antiphoner for the church's use.[69]

The parish church at Mautby, though small, had not been without friends and benefactors from the ranks of Margaret's ancestors.[70] And now, having dealt with church, tenants, and village at what we might think of as her base camp, Margaret takes us on a leisurely tour of the countryside. Here the pattern of bequests as set by John I some 18 years before is pertinent, since Margaret also singled out village churches and the village poor in some Mautby-Paston manors that had gone unmentioned in other family wills (John I excepted).[71] Of the six parish churches and villages other than Mautby that she mentions in her spread of bequests, only Gresham had played much role, albeit an unhappy one, in the main saga of the Pastons—that being the headquarters out of which they had been driven in 1448. Given Margaret's emphasis on staking her own claim to identity, her testamentary focus on manors of her dowry comes as no surprise, despite the interval of almost four decades between her arrival and her departure.[72] In terms of the actual bequests, her practice was in keeping with accepted behavior; bequests just this side of miniscule, if that, mostly running to 6s 8d per church or even less. But when her thoughts turned to the parish church of St John Baptist at Reedham she was moved to pithy eloquence: "there as I was borne." This time, to match her warmer feelings, she raised the level of benefaction: "I bequeath v marc, and a chesiple of silk with an awbe with myn armes thereupon, to the emendement of the same cherche." But beyond these larger bequests to Mautby and Reedham, what we have are more examples of the hit-and-run style of giving; a small bequest, a few details, and on to the next recipient. The way in which Margaret enriched the parish churches and distributed largesse to the folk of her villages reminds us—as it did her contemporaries—that the dying sinner was simultaneously the lady of the manor. Every household at Mautby was to receive 12d, "as hastily as it may be conuenyently doo after my decesse." The church at Fritton in Suffolk was to get a "chesiple and an awbe," and each household, "being my tenaunt there" was to receive 6d. The same open hand to Basyngham (Bessingham), only now it was 8d to "euery houshold," and at Matelask (Matlask) it was 8d but now directed to "euery pore houshold that are my tenauntes." At Gresham it was church repairs and 6d for each poor household "that be my tenauntes," while at Sparham—the last of these little places—it was only "ich pore household late my tenauntes" with nothing explicitly devoted to the parish church of St Mary.[73]

These bequests compose what I have called the thesis segment of the will—the thesis being an assertion of Margaret's identity as a Mautby; the benefactions were part of this identity and, in a sense, they reified it. Though the degree of coincidence with John I argues for a striking level of marital accord on these matters, it was John looking to Margaret's places, rather than the other way. And now, having completed her testamentary version of the grande dame sweep through the countryside—her mental, physical, and testamentary version of a royal progress or procession—Margaret turned thoughts and purse toward Norwich (and fleetingly to Yarmouth as well). Here, in what I offer as the antithesis—the many clauses and provisions wherein she mingles her Mautby identity with Paston family sites and with her ties in the provincial metropolis—she moves from a rural or village identity to a more urban one. Her Norwich bequests carry a heavier tone; the affluent and socially conscious sinner and widow, now concerned to spread her largesse around the big town, not just in her own little villages. Though Margaret was not unimportant in Norwich, and the Mautby-Paston reach of some significance, she was hardly the dominant figure there that she had been in those scattered villages. In Norwich she spread her benefactions in an impressively wide arc; the cathedral, regular and mendicant houses (the four orders of friars in both Norwich and Yarmouth), secular or parish churches, the hospital, and a fairly extensive net of individuals (some in religious life, some just the deserving poor or the leprous).

While no one was likely to leave a bequest to more than a fraction of Norwich's many parish churches and ecclesiastical institutions, Margaret

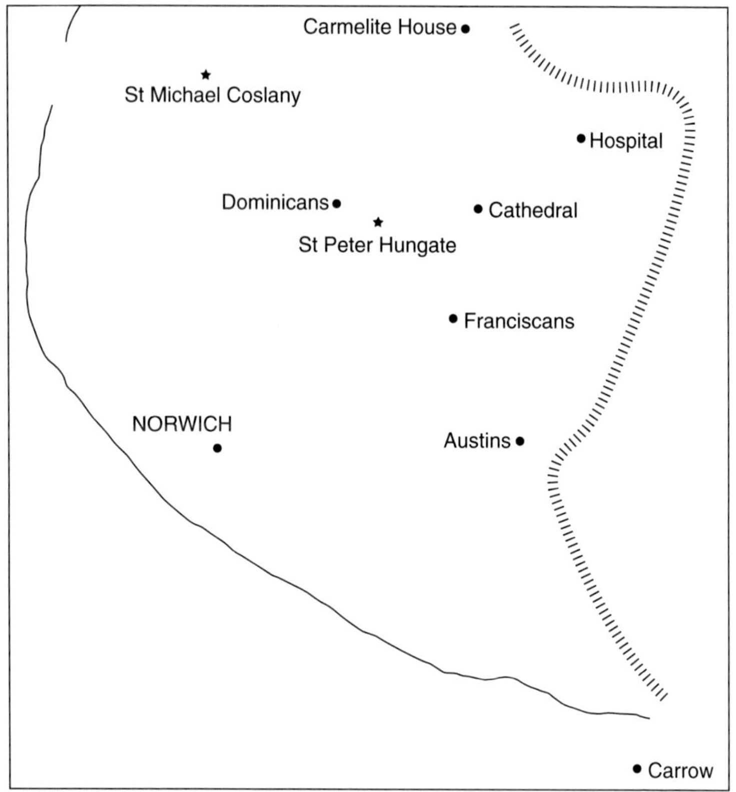

Map 4.2   Norwich Institutions Named in Margaret Paston's Will.

gave it a good try. Admittedly, in touching a large number of bases many of her touches were light and quick ones, their sum total very limited. And yet, given the number of potential recipients and in comparison with others in the family, Margaret—as a townswoman—wrote a generous and comprehensive will.[74]

Family links with the cathedral rested on the firm foundation of the bequests and chantry foundation of William I, though Margaret was able to control her enthusiasm: 20s "for a dirige and masse."[75] While hardly lavish, it is the only bequest from anyone in the family to the cathedral, apart from William I. Clearly, Margaret wanted to cover a fair segment of the urban landscape, and other institutions named included "ich of the iiij houshes of freres in Norwich," the same "iiij houses of freres" in Yarmouth, and the "Deen and his bretheren of the Chepell of Feld" and the hospital of St Giles, both the latter in Norwich.[76] In addition, there was an impressive focus on individual recipients, whether she was moved by innate sympathy or by the customary tactic of subsidizing as many prayers as possible for each shilling and pence that would be doled out. Norwich was unusually rich in its stock of anchorites and they evidently did make a mark on public consciousness (and conscience?): 3s 4d to "the ankeres at the Frere Prechours," the same to "the ankeres in Conesford," and again to the "anker" at the Carmelite house.[77] What Margaret terms "hole and half susters at Normans" got 8d each, and 2d was for "ich of the iiij pore meen and to either of the susters" of St. Giles hospital.[78] And still more of this sort: 3d to each "lepre man and woman at the v yates in Norwich," and 2d to each "foregoer" there, along with 3d to each leper at the north gate of Yarmouth.[79] In her bequests we might detect a slight tilt in favor of women, while the very limited appeal of regular monasticism is apparent (and the cathedral figures as the mother church, rather than as a Benedictine house).[80]

Where Margaret really hits her urban stride is when she turns to two particular parish churches. One is St Peter Hungate, and her generosity and enthusiasm here are easy to understand. However, there is no indication in the letters of why she felt such a strong pull to the parish church of St Michael Coslany. This was a handsome church in a comfortable neighborhood, a few minutes from the Paston town house but not otherwise known to be linked to the family. But whatever the motivation, Margaret directed that a "dirige and a masse for my sowle" be said there, with 4d going to "euery preste ther havyng his stipend being therat" and 2d to "ich clerk in surplys of the same parissh." The parish clerk came in for 6d, the "curat that shall seye high masse" 20d, and another 20d "to the sexteyn there, to rynge at the seid dirige and masse." She also left 6s 8d to repair the bells, this being a popular direction for bequests in the fifteenth century.[81] She was including a fair number of people at St Michael, perhaps a sign of the heavy clerical popular of a cathedral city in the late fifteenth century.

In light of this handsome treatment of the staff and personnel of St Michael Coslany, Margaret's bequests to the John-and-Margaret parish church of St Peter Hungate are likely to be of some note. Before she turned to the church itself she left 4d to each parish household there "that wull receive almes." For the church itself she left £20, but she made a break with the usual style of ecclesiastical benefaction. This large sum of money in effect was to be placed in trust, supervised by "the church reves of the same cherch for the tyme being, by the ouersight of the substanciall persones of the seid parissh," and the money was to keep the small parish going and to top up the annual income of the "seid parson or preste," until the "seid xx li. be expended." Clearly, whatever the Pastons had given to the church upon its rebuilding in 1460 was proving inadequate some decades later. St Peter Hungate was one of the smallest and poorest parishes in Norwich, with a marginal number of parishioners, and it had been on the financial ropes at various times in the past (as it would continue to be in the future).[82] There seems to be no record of how long Margaret's amplified endowment from 1482 lasted or whether it helped improve the "delivery" of spiritual succor for those of the neighborhood, but things were never especially comfortable at St Peters.[83]

The last part of Margaret's will is what I call the synthesis, for it is only now that she turns to the family, to the Pastons, and knits up personal bequests with personal bonds. To her as matriarch, the children of John I and Margaret, and then by extension the grandchildren, were the living incarnations of the union of Mautby and Paston. So now, after all those provisions for her soul and her declaration of independence, she distributes her worldly goods to the family of her body (and to a few others), and she does so with a fairly open hand as she embraces her kin and distributes her goods and directs the distribution or breakup of her estate. However, if our impulse is to say that the will now moves from the spiritual to the secular, it is probably more in keeping with Margaret's thinking to say it goes from the public to the personal, the private. Most of what was distributed can be set into the context of the disbursal of a wealthy and worldly household, of little interest to us for spiritual matters. Margaret's daughter, Anne Yelverton, was to get her "premer [and] my bedes of siluer enameled." Margery, wife of John III, received "my massebook, with all myn awterclothes," and Simon Gerard—one of her executors but an otherwise obscure figure in family annals—was to get various items from her "chapel chaumber." But since these were pieces of silver, a white bed, "the fetherbedde lich as it is now in the seid chapel," blankets and sheets, and "a pilwe of doun," the bequests are not much help in reconstructing that chapel that had so engaged her attention a few years before. In spelling out the landed income that would come to her son William, Margaret—having no doubt learned from the problematic legacies and provisions of her father-in-law and her husband—stipulated that the first priority was the completion of "the ele in Mauteby church" in which she was to be buried, plus the stipend "of the preste lymyted to singe for me to be yerly levied, aswell as the money be dispended vpon the keeping of my yerly obite." Only then, when those matters had been taken care of, would the land and its income come to young William. She had lived and she had learned. The example of the unbuilt tombs or monument of John I was something they all had had to live with.

There were still a few others to mention, like those who had stood at the bedside of William the Marshall in 1219. Toward the end Margaret turned her thoughts, and her words, to her spiritual kin, to godchildren (about whom we have never heard until this moment). Marie Tendell was specially privileged here, being singled out by name and given "my peir bedys of calcidenys gaudièd with siluer and gilt." Then, to "Ich of myn other godchilder"—though passed along to us with no hint as to identity, number, or sex—it would be as John III, his mother's executor, would decide. Approaching time for closure: last wishes, the end of a long life, the final distribution of worldly goods with the proper touch of conventional piety: "myn executours to parfourme this my testament and last wille, and in other dedes of mercye for my sowle, myn aunceteres sowles, and alle Christn sowles, to the most pleaser of God and profit of my sowle." God and profit made a good partnership.[84]

★   ★   ★

The whole collection of family wills that we have, including that of Margaret, is easy to read so as to reinforce the idea that fifteenth-century spirituality was apt to be conventional. Furthermore, it was apt to be expressed in conventional language, conventional terms, conventional bequests, conventional recipients. Paston wills are not likely to open the doors to large and innovative ecclesiastical projects, any more than they are likely to lead us to deep and idiosyncratic reflections about life, whether in this world or in the next. If any of the Pastons were inclined to undertake exciting journeys into the realms of contemplation and spiritual devotion, they managed to keep such journeys a well-hidden secret. Late-medieval lay religion, certainly in practice and probably in contemplation as well, is a mix of belief in transcendental spirituality and a negotiation or even a running balance sheet in deeds and words between Christ and Caesar, Canterbury and Westminster, Mammon and St Paul. Approaching these complex issues by way of lay wills puts heavy emphasis, of course, on what was articulated in a formulaic preface, as it does on what was being transmitted, and to whom, and in return for what. Worldly goods (and cash) were being translated into the currency of an extraworldly spirituality.

We can turn the page over and return to the question of what we did not learn; the eloquence of silence, or even of neglect, if we wish. For the Pastons as a group, the scattering or disbursal of burial sites can be thought of as an unvoiced policy of studied neglect, of seemingly choosing not to revisit ground once covered. William I did not go back—at least not in his will—to revisit the masses that his father had endowed, nor was he buried with his father. No more did John I or Agnes or Margaret or John II (or William II) re-enrich the chantry of William I in Norwich Cathedral, a move that we might think would have given a lot of visible (and audible) return for their money, as well as a boost to the filiopiety that they talked about but did little to support. Margaret Paston's will was striking, as was that of John I, for the number of institutions and individuals, both lay and clerical, that she did remember, but John and Margaret had gone off on their own. Moreover, Margaret had a few pence for the churches and poor tenants of Matelask or Bessingham; she makes no mention of Paston or Bromholm or Caister or Oxnead—neither the parish church nor her tenants in any of these familiar places. And in her will the Carmelites were not ignored but they were just included in the general distribution intended for the four mendicant houses of Norwich (and of Yarmouth). These omissions are especially noticeable because of the practice of small and widely distributed bequests that we see in almost every fifteenth-century will. Testamentary bequests at this level could be stretched to touch an exponential number of beneficiaries. And since Margaret drew up her will almost three years before her death, she had had more than ample time to correct oversights and or bursts of petulance that may have crept upon her at low moments in her long and lonely widowhood. Perhaps by the end she had had enough of the Paston's acquisitive and bellicose agenda. Her uneasy relations with her two oldest sons probably reinforced her interest in her ultimate reassertion of her pre-Paston identity, her own loftier origins. Given the burdens that the family's projects and plans and quarrels had put on her shoulders for so long, her last will proclaims no more Caister, no more litigation about the Fastolf estate, and even no more visits to the Holy Rood at Bromholm. There is a strong element of "free at last."[85]

Conventional lives do not make for exciting historical reconstruction. They are too close to the tale of that village that is fortunate enough to be without history, or to the familiar and routine events of today about which we will not read in tomorrow's paper. On the other hand, a detailed look at Margaret Paston's last will as an expression of her spirituality shows how thoroughly Christ and Caesar could be assimilated into the life course and the worldview and modes of expression of a pious, tolerably educated, and not insensitive or unduly secular wife, mother, and widow.

A close reading of Margaret's will steers us toward a more general reflection about women's wills—or rather, about widows' wills—that usually being the case when we have such documents. Because much of the family's real property was transmitted by the dictates of common law, Margaret had limited say in such matters. Furthermore, her children, by the time of her death, had their own households; her bequests to them topped up their resources and revenues but were not likely to be the basis of their first steps toward independence. Studies of widows' wills indicate that women of Margaret's day and status were usually inclined to distribute more small gifts, and more widely, than their husbands had done, particularly when parish churches and other small and local ecclesiastical institutions were the recipients.[86] Though John I was a hard act to top, given the great scattering of his last-wishes generosity, Margaret, as we have said, touched a large number of beneficiaries and in a deliberative fashion that fits quite comfortably under the rubric of "postmortem bossiness."[87] Her will shows every indication of being the result of much deliberation; we see this in all three of its sections, as I have explicated the text. We see it in the Mautby segment, in the Norwich segment, and then finally in the family segment. If the aging and isolate Margaret had gone through a period of depression and bitterness—and we know she had had at least one serious illness—she seems to have been over it by the end; no signs of scores to settle, of grudges to air. Not even very much by way of social control, except for that striking provision about her tomb being completed before William would receive his bequest.[88] She went to her end, an old lady—a rich one, on her home turf, and surrounded figuratively if not literally by two generations of descendents. Though we know nothing of the actual circumstances (or theater) of the deathbed, the paper trail that she has left us tells the tale of a good death. In that, as in quite a number of other ways, Margaret Mautby Paston stood out from most of the family.

CHAPTER 5

WHAT DID MARGARET SEE?

The Pastons are dead and gone. Though they eventually would rise well beyond the gentry-fueled aspirations of John I, the sands of time that were to grind down Mowbray and Bohun and Plantagenet would get to them as well. Their later eminence as earls of Yarmouth was but fleeting, even with their share of the Fastolf inheritance; when Charles Paston, II Earl of Yarmouth, died in 1732, having already out-lived his son and heir Charles (who had died without surviving progeny in 1718) the line was at an end.[1] Little was left beyond memories, some heavily mortgaged property now destined for the local market at knock-down prices, and a lot of old family letters and papers that, by good fortune, would eventually come into the hands of James Fenn and then Francis Blomefield and finally into those of the British people in the form of the British Museum/British Library (excepting the items that have gone elsewhere).[2] The manor house at Paston has disappeared, the great barn at Paston dates only from the 1580s, and the family's sites in Norwich were eventually abandoned for more appropriate houses out-side of town as the family moved up in the world, and what is left at Oxnead postdates the Pastons who have been of interest here.[3] Were it not for the fortuitous preservation of their letters the Pastons of the fifteenth century would be just another of those gentry families we would note in passing—perhaps as a footnote to the tale of the Fastolf estate and the creation of Magdalen College, Oxford, and of minor interest were we concerned to trace the roots of a family that rose to a minor peerage in the seventeenth century.[4]

What remains for us in this effort to follow whatever trail of religious utterance and practice Margaret Paston has left behind? We have worked to unravel the world of her saints and saints' days, the world of her reli-gious expression and practice (and her personal possessions), and finally the world of her spirituality as she spelled it out in her will, an enterprise that showed how she directed the transmission of worldly goods for spiritual purposes and happened, while doing so, to unpeel layers of one woman's life course and identity. In all of this, iteration and activity family and self (and perhaps gender) were tightly woven into the fabric of Margaret's faith. They gave us a social fabric that was not easily divisible, if it was not quite a seamless garment of faith and identity. Margaret Paston's will certainly can be read as a case study of this coupling, just as the will shows how a sense of place and of social status can—and perhaps must—be factored into the equation.

In our quest for the realities of Margaret Paston's spiritual life we are always conscious of the fact (or problem) that we can almost never run down a question about the Pastons to a conclusive ending, to closure. Nothing ever seems to be resolved beyond dispute or doubt, nothing is ever-so clear-cut that no exceptions and no further qualifications can be offered. This is the case whether we turn to what John I asserted about what Sir John Fastolf "really" intended regarding his will, or what Margaret "really" believed about the saints in her epistolary references to their days, or what the family "really" had in mind as they studiously ignored the social (and spiritual) benefits of a common burial site. With no way to estimate the proportion of their letters that has been preserved, and always at pains to stress the pragmatic and hard-nosed raison d'etre that guided the creation and content of the letters in the first place, we can never lose sight of those boundaries within which all our judgments and speculations must be contained.

In summing up the lessons presented by an analysis of Margaret's testamentary bequests I thought it of some value to pay heed to what she did not cover or mention: no bequests, no gestures, no touching sentiments in the direction of Paston or Caister or Bromholm, nothing of special note to distinguish the Carmelites, those favorites of her mother-in-law Agnes and of Agnes's family, from the other mendicant orders. There are no references in any of the family wills to the guild of St George that so dominated and helped defined Norwich's collective identity and civic voice in those middle years of the century.[5] Nor, with a few exceptions, were lay beneficiaries outside the family brought into her loop. Whatever we might wish to make of these omissions, beyond the insoluble issue of lost letters, they just have to be accepted as Margaret Paston's way of drawing her own boundaries. I suspect there was a considerable element of withdrawal, even of rejection, in some of these silences and omissions. It seems a bit much to say that her silence has to speak for itself, but a roll call of what she did remember does make one wonder about an unvoiced policy of deliberate neglect, and for reasons we can only guess at. Neither her years of widowhood nor her withdrawal to Mautby seemed likely to rekindle warm feelings about places and people of those last troubled years of John I and then of her difficulties with her two eldest sons. She had rocky relations within the family, and she does not seem to have found another intimate after 1473 to play the role that James Gloys had played for so long. In addition, she probably outlived many of her friends and collateral kin. However, to set against this idea of loneliness and bitterness or self-pity, it does not seem a great stretch to read her will—especially its last sections—as a statement of reconciliation and of affection. In her last throw she cast a very wide net.

We have come about as far as Margaret's own words will lead us. Accordingly, in this final essay I turn to a search for what we can recapture of the physical and material world in which she lived and moved. What is still there? Beyond the places to which her words as set down in her will have led us and the way in which her behavior has steered our inquiries, what more can we learn by trying to re-create or recapture this material and physical context of her world as it surrounded her but was not dependent for its existence upon her articulation—unlike the world created by her dating clauses and those "god bless" and "god assoil" throw-ins that we played with above? The search for "what did Margaret see" is a search or a quest that will follow her lead, with her testamentary bequests blazing the trail. It is a sort of Mautby-Paston pilgrimage, running first through the countryside and then into town—in keeping with the order she laid out in her will. Even given all that has befallen those places and buildings, what still stands after so many centuries and so many separate acts of destruction and restoration suffices for an evocative journey, guided as we are by Margaret's tersely worded bequests to churches and places, by her occasional snippets of memory or nostalgia, and by her explicit and deliberate instructions. We follow in her verbal footsteps; the extent to which her words can guide us on a circuit that might have been an actual physical journey undertaken at one time or another by our heroine is impossible to know.[6]

★ ★ ★

In an effort to capture and visit some of what remains of the world that Margaret Paston actually knew, saw, visited, and even made a little bit richer by way of endowment or testamentary benefaction, we must not attribute more agency, more interest, more cultural sensitivity to her than the records permit or than her general approach to such matters seems to merit. In my introductory chapter I took a brief look at some of the varieties of cultural and spiritual experience and activity that figured so prominently in the tale of upper-class women of fifteenth-century East

Anglia. A treasure chest, but not one stamped with the name of Margaret Paston; she was notable for her absence from (or at least her silence about) virtually every list and every kind of activity we could offer, whether it was guided by a feminine or feminist interest or one dictated more by considerations of class and status. This means that if a final journey, designed to follow in her footsteps as the course we set, it is not going to be a journey with many way stations and rest stops where we pause for an inquiry into literary patronage, certainly not as far as Margaret Paston mapped out our journey. Nor is our journey with Margaret going to halt so we will have time to spend with those intriguing women who were deeply engaged in circles of pious reading, or of book lending and borrowing, or of book purchasing. Nor will we have occasion to pass the time of day with those women and men who could fill us in regarding the pageants staged by the guilds or about the drama cycles of East Anglia—cultural, social, and religious activities and events that Margaret Paston must have known and probably witnessed but to which she never makes any allusion. Were the festivals and pageants and drama cycles high points of the year for Paston children, or for Paston parents? But, as we know by now, intellectual and cultural interests and re-creations almost never made their way into the epistolary vocabulary, whatever role they might have played.

Though less focused on spiritual matters than on the realities and practical considerations of daily life, a household account like that of Dame Alice de Bryene for 1412–13 would certainly flesh out some aspects of our inquiry—were any such documents extant for the Pastons.[7] But there are no comparable documents, nothing that sheds any useful light on the domestic situations of any of the branches of the family, let alone on that household over which Margaret presided during her life with John I and afterwards as its head. Dame Alice's household book gives a running account of who and how many came to meals, of their social and clerical status, and often of the basis for their claim to her hospitality. Though Dame Alice's household would have outstripped that of Margaret in size and social prominence, there are enough parallels to make us reflect, rather sadly, on what we do not have. We learn that Dame Alice—or rather the staff at her command—offered meals to 40 or 50 or 60 people on a regular basis, and to more than that on the odd occasion. Though clerics only compose a small proportion of the year's tally of guests, there were friars from major houses who showed up for a meal (and probably a bed); Austins from Clare or Gilbertines from Rochester, among others. Furthermore, if their numbers were small, such men seemed to have turned up on feast days of special meaning for their order—the felicitous choice of the feast day or anniversary perhaps offering them the opportunity to seize the day and to dominate family prayers and dinner table conversation.

The guest list from Dame Alice's household shows the mixed composition of those at her table; family retainers and servants, old friends, relatives of various linkages, passing travelers, and men of the cloth on a variety of errands. As a widow of considerable wealth, her household was a natural meeting ground and resting place for people from many walks of life, many corners of the realm. Can we see Alice as a model or a grander counterpart for Margaret, a widow of some wealth and of serious piety? Dame Alice's village household was probably at a more conspicuous crossroads in geographical terms, since in Norwich the Pastons were but one of many. But the Pastons certainly did not lack guests and mouths to feed. While we know little of the atmosphere of Dame Alice's domestic scene with its mixed and ever-changing company, the impression we have of Paston life is that it was fairly secular in a social sense. Gloys was Margaret's chaplain and confidant of many years' service, but his influence seems pointed more to family affairs and partisan interference in mother-son relationships rather than to instilling an air of piety. And back in the days when John I and Friar Brackley had been close, it was the Fastolf estate, not the catechism being taught to Paston children or the private devotions of their mother, that was the common bond between the men. Margaret herself does not refer to grace at meals or to a prayer afterward, and the sermons she mentions now and then were those heard in church, not in a domestic setting.

So in comparison to the Alice de Bryene whom we can see in high resolution, at least for one year, Margaret Paston's domestic scene is never more than a dim and cloudy picture. And if there is little to be learned about Margaret's piety by contrasting her with others whose high points of patronage or prayer or ecclesiastical benefaction or hospitality can be charted at home, what picture emerges when we follow her away from home? Our imaginative or imaginary journey, our virtual pilgrimage, now picks up the trail she blazed with her testamentary bequests. That we go from rural to urban seems in keeping with life in the fifteenth century, and until we come to Norwich near the end of our wandering, it is very much a journey through the countryside with a series of stops at small churches set in very small villages (with Gresham as perhaps the one exception, being a somewhat more substantial place). And yet in this journey—Margaret's own journey as spelled out in her will—Margaret Paston is very much the insider at each and every way station. If she has to stand out in the cold when we talk of patrons like Isabel Bourgchier or Katherine Howard, in their support of Osbern Bokenham, or of Margaret Purdons and women reading and then discoursing about devotional literature and hagiography, Margaret Paston is now clearly in her element for each parish church and village that she mentions in the will. Now she is the lady of the manor, the lady who had the right to be there, the lady who could (and did) claim a privileged status at each stop along the way. This focus on a rural identity and on an insider's identity is reaffirmed by the string of small but directed bequests we find in her will.

We can offer another contrast that helps sharpen our focus. Margaret Paston as insider, as the lady of the village and its church invariably stands in stark opposition to the identity and role projected by her near-contemporary, Margery Kempe, as the latter woman tells us of her travels over the course of her uneasy years. The contrast brings out the extent to which Margaret Mautby Paston was a village girl who, through her marriage, happened to spend much time in Norwich but who perhaps never quite saw it as her real base. It was marriage that had taken her to Norwich, and it was the end of married life that eventually allowed her to leave Norwich. Such a tale of relative physical stability, and the identity that went with it, can be compared with the difficult peregrinations of Margery Kempe of Lynn, an eternal outsider. If we construct an "index locorum" for Margery Kempe, we touch down all over Christendom: Norwich, Leicester, York, London, Canterbury, Bridlington, Ely, Bristol, among others, and this is without regard for journeys to Jerusalem, Rome, Compostella, and elsewhere, not to mention the many intervening towns. And in each of these places, including her native ground in Lynn itself, Margery Kempe was usually a foreign presence, an uninvited alien, arriving to trouble the waters. That she brought as much or more grief to herself than to others may gain her some sympathy as we read her tale, but it also reinforces the idea that an open road might bring home a traveler who was often less than welcome. Margaret Paston, by way of contrast, mostly stayed home and showed little desire to see much of the wider world. Her mother-in-law wound up living in London, her sister-in-law left East Anglia for the metropolis and the South, her husband and sons were on the road a great deal. Margaret stayed put.[8]

Before picking up Margaret's trail of testamentary memory and looking at what we can still see in the East Anglian landscape that might have been familiar to her, there are two further considerations, two things to remember before we set out on the road. One is the sad tale of the physical and material fate of many (or most) of the places we visit; much that we might ask to see is gone. We can track burial sites and read wills, but no Paston tomb or grave remains for us to visit; so much for homage and souvenirs. Whether the burial site had been a parish church or the cathedral or a regular house (either in London or Norwich), nothing stands today to fill in the blanks. For Pastons buried in regular or mendicant houses this is as we would expect; the "age of plunder" was very thorough. But various other fates have also conspired to bring us to a complete halt, factors in addition to or beyond the rapacity of Henrician go-getters and seventeenth-century iconoclasts. Neither the chantry chapel of William I in Norwich Cathedral nor the parish church burials of Margaret and her beloved Walter are to be found. The family's physical remains and memorials are no more with us than is the peerage they once held. Bricks and stones may last, but not the Pastons once buried within or beneath them.

The other form of loss is more understandable, if even more sweeping than that of buildings and bodies. Here I refer to the disappearance of any and all personal or household items from the Pastons, be they of religious use or any other that—in the best of all possible worlds— might have made their way into such collections as those of the Victoria and Albert Museum or the one in Norwich Castle Museum.[9] Though finding "MP" (or even better yet, "MMP") engraved on items intended for use in a private chapel is a bit much to hope for, the family did talk of such possessions in various of their letters, wills, and inventories. Obviously, between family heirlooms that had come down from William I or the Mautbys or the Berrys and their looting of the Fastolf estate, with its vast inventory of household and personal possessions, and the normal course of purchasing and acquiring, the stock of family treasures would have mounted up over the years. But few items are described in striking detail—as we saw in those snippets from John I and William I—and without family wills from the very late fifteenth and the sixteenth century, the chain of transmission snaps after a link or two.

In our interest in the family's stock of personal possessions of value or interest, it is possible that we place a greater premium on their books than did men and women of the day, and Colin Richmond has argued that Margaret Paston was not a great reader—nor, by extension, a serious collector of books. But by the provisions of her will the church at Mautby was to be enriched by "a complete legende in oon book and an antiphoner in an other book," both to abide there "as long as they may endure." Beyond this we have "my premer" for her daughter Anne Yelverton and "my massebook, with all myn awterclothes" for daughter-in-law Margery (Brewes) Paston. Not an impressive library, but there were some books and some concern for their fate. The books Margaret designated for Mautby parish church would move outside any line of family transmission and would no doubt succumb to the wear and tear of many hands, whereas the "premer" and "massebook" were to be kept within the family and might have gone down the generations. Furthermore, if Margaret herself was not deeply attached to the world of books, they were fairly familiar items in her immediate family: the "grete book" of John II, the books that went to William II upon the death of Edmund I, and that mysterious library of Gloys that was being disbursed to unknown recipients before John II could get hold of some of its prize items and for which Margaret had been the intended go-between.[10]

But none of these books can be traced down through the years, and the letters that tell of them are the only indication of their existence and ownership (except for the "Grete Boke" of John II). Other items of religious usage were also elaborated in Margaret's will; they too disappeared without a trace. Daughter Anne received "bedes of siluer enameled" along with her primer, though again they may have had no more special value than "ij peir of my finsest sheets ich of iij webbes" and other such household items. Margaret's goddaughter Marie Tendal was to receive "my peir bedys of calcidenys guadied with siluer and gilt," and her executor Simon Gerard came in for a little bed "in my chapel chaumer at Mauteby" and a featherbed "lick as it nowe in the seid chapel." But this argues that the chapel was also a sort of lumber room for miscellaneous goods, rather than pointing us toward a collection of pilgrim badges or a jeweled pyx that Margaret's cousin Sir John Fastolf might well have left her—had he only been good enough to say so.

Though we cannot put them into Margaret's hands or the safekeeping of her chest, there are items of interest that we can track from the inventories that John I and William II made when they surveyed some of Fastolf's vast world of possessions (I, 64). Relevant here, among the "goodes that somtyme were Ser John Fastolffes" would be the "ryng of Sent Lowes with a ston therin" and an arras with scenes of the Coronation and the Assumption of Our Lady. Though this latter item seems a goodly catch, we should note that it also had scenes of "the sege of Phalist...another of the Morys daunse, an other of Jason and Launcelet, an other of a batayle." Another inventory mentions a "table of gold with an jmage of Sen James set with precious stonys weyng xiij vnc....(a) box of siluer and gilt for the sacrament, with a crosse in the height and chased with lilijs" (I, 68). But no links that we can trace between the Fastolf estate and Margaret in terms of personal bequests, no will of John I, and nothing in the other family wills that offers much help. All we can do is generalize and say that these are the sorts of items that members of a wealthy household could be expected to have and then to transmit. A bit out of the ordinary would be the "pece of the Holy Crosse" of Elizabeth Poynings Browne, sister to John I. It was eventually passed along, with a great quantity of pedestrian household goods, to Elizabeth's daughter Mary (about whom we know nothing). Even when we learn a bit more, as with Elizabeth's instructions about "an image of saint Antony apon it" and her "auter clothe with the jmage of our Lode" we have to set these occasional reference against the long lists of linens and kitchenware spelled out in the will. Religious items, like all that bedding and furniture, were a normal part of a household, and their transmission was unlikely to be specified in a way that makes them stand apart from the vast quantity of secular items now passing along the line. Our focused interests give these items, as with books, a privileged place that they did not have to those involved in the transmission. The bequest of a pyx and of a pillow may have been equally valued and esteemed, despite the pecking order we are quick to assign to these items.

Buildings, we might say, should be made of sterner stuff; the sad fate of so many of those that once held Pastons can serve as an object lesson about the passing of all things. If we begin with an other-than-Margaret journey, we will not be on the road for long. Since the family really got started with the rise of Clement and Beatrice, we can begin by turning to their joint burial site—the parish church of St Margaret at Paston. Not only is there no sign of their grave (or graves), but the coffin that may contain the remains of John I, brought to Paston from Bromholm at the dissolution in deference to his standing in the neighborhood, is a putative burial at best. Pevsner described three "plain tomb-chests, no doubt of Pastons, the one at the east end said to have been brought from Bromholm Priory and may well be what is left of John Paston." The current guidebook for the church is just about as circumspect: "if (tradition) is correct this tomb is no doubt that of John Paston," and as for the other tombs in the church, they have been moved around so that "there is apparently no authority for stating to which particular members of the family they belong." The great glory of the church, and one that would have been familiar to Margaret, is the large wall painting of St Christopher. Even though Christopher was among the most commonly depicted saints, and even though he was to be found throughout East Anglia, the wall painting at Paston is impressive.[11] In addition, though hardly to be seen in anything like its original glory or moral impact, there are visible remnants on the walls of what probably was a scourging of Christ and a Three Quick-Three Dead. So if we follow the "what did Margaret see" theme, in the parish church at Paston, dedicated to her own patron saint, she would have seen the burial site of her grandparents-in-law and some powerful fourteenth-century art. If such memento mori were too familiar to inspire horror, they were at least sober reminders that the family into which she had married was of some stature in this world, though the message in the church was also that all such triumphs were but fleeting ones. However, Margaret never refers to the church at Paston—it being one of those notable omission in her will—and her references to other members of the family do not go further back in time than her father-in-law, William I.[12]

If we felt cheated by the condition of the parish church at Paston, do we fare any better when we look to the cathedral of the Holy Trinity, Norwich Cathedral? Here, in a purpose-built chantry in the lady chapel, Margaret's father-in-law William I had been buried in 1444. Once again, the fates are against us. It seems that the cathedral, desperate for revenue in the late sixteenth or early seventeenth century, demolished parts of itself that were no longer needed for the simplified liturgy of Protestantism.[13] The sacrifice of the lady chapel was not so much for the purification of prayers but rather for the cash realized from selling the stones of which it was built. In any case, and in some fashion that somehow went unchronicled, the lady chapel is no more, a fate it shared with what had been the attached parish church of St Mary of the Marsh and the cathedral clocher. Chantries in the cathedral, other than those of its bishops and of a few great men of the region like Sir Thomas Erpingham, seem to have had short lives, at least when compared with the hopes and intentions of their founders.

For those numerous Pastons who had been buried in regular houses, whether we look at the London White Friars or Black Friars or the Cluniac priory at Bromholm or the White Friars of Norwich, total disappearance is what we expect, all swept away by the tides of dissolution. Of the London houses—where Agnes and perhaps Edmund I and John II had been buried—nothing remains but some historical markers to tell of what once had been. John I went to burial at Bromholm amidst much splendor and expenditure, as we have seen, but there too nothing remains of the glories of a venerated if middling-level pilgrimage site. Set somewhere in the fields of what is now a working farm are some visible ruins, but they stand on private land and neither tourist curiosity nor archaeological work has gotten much of a return. Since John III did not seem to carry through his talk about moving John II from London to Bromholm—so father and son could be reunited—and since it seems difficult to determine whether he or his uncle William II moved Agnes from her first interment in London to the Carmelite house in Norwich, we can say

Figure 5.1 The Church of St John the Baptist, Reedham—"There as I was born".

Figure 5.2 St Mary, Bessingham.

Figure 5.3   St Christopher Wall Painting, St Edmund, Fritton, Suffolk.

Figure 5.4   Seven Sacrament Font, All Saints, Gresham.

Figure 5.5 Danse of Death, Rood Screen, St Mary, Sparham.

Figure 5.6 Elm Hill, Norwich—where the Pastons lived in town.

Figure 5.7   Arch of the Gateway, Carmelite Friary, Norwich.

Figure 5.8   St Peter Hungate, Norwich: exterior view.

Figure 5.9 St Peter Hungate: interior view.

Figure 5.10 St Peter Hungate: interior view.

that none of it made much difference at the end in terms of our search for physical remains and reminders.

★   ★   ★

Having gone down a series of dead ends in terms of revisiting the burial sites of Margaret's family-by-marriage, let us return to her own trail as she blazed it in her will—that pilgrimage of self and identity about which she was so deliberative. As Margaret began it, the trail picks up at Mautby, or more specifically, with the parish church of St Peter and St Paul at Mautby. Before we look at the church itself, as Margaret detailed how it was to look when her bequests had been carried out and as it stands today, a few more general reflections on the style of her will and the pilgrimage on which it is now leading us. In many wills of the day the testator's most favored institutions and beneficiaries, and especially the burial church, are named toward the head of the document and then, as we move toward the end and the disposal of the residue of the estate, they reappear for some further share of what still remained. But this is not Margaret Paston's style. Her will is a straightforward progression; no doubling back. Once a church or a village here and tenants there or some deserving individual or institution had been dealt with, that particular beneficiary of her largesse never reappears. No second thoughts, no inclination to return to give out any leftovers—which is why I use the term "deliberative" in describing her style. It was all thought out in advance; those deemed worthy of a bequest were named, rewarded, and then dismissed.

Margaret's testamentary journey began at Mautby, in its church. It was here, with church and manor house and its chapel, that Margaret had made her headquarters for the last decade of her long life. Despite this, as we have noted, there is no indication today of the family matriarch, let alone of her distinguished forbears. The parish church, atop a small rise that might explain some of the aging Margaret's insistence on her own domestic chapel, has but few features of great interest; the anti-Paston vandalism of some unknown time and for unrecorded reasons has removed all traces of that south aisle that was to be built to accommodate her chantry with its elaborate monument. Nothing remains except a visible scar in the wall to tell us of the aisle, "newe reved, leded, glased, and the walled thereof heyned conuenyently and werkmanly." Vanished are any and all markers of that Mautby lineage that Margaret had traced back to Lord Loveyn and Sir Roger Beauchamp and the Berneys of Redham. A few bits of heraldic glass still remain—Mautby arms, azure, a cross—small hints of splendor and the pride of family that had once towered over this little and rather isolated place—Mautby being a bit off the main road to Yarmouth, though but a short walk over the fields to Caister and the headquarters of the Fastolf world. Though we might like to say that Mautby was meant to be Margaret's personal Westminster Abbey, we also have to recall that no one else of the Pastons was buried there.[14] This reinforces the idea that her removal to Mautby was a step in the construction of an invisible wall between Margaret's natal family and her marital one.

After Margaret made her bequests to Mautby she moved through her litany of bequests toward "Fretton in Suffolk" (and she inserted the county designation, Fritton being just across the border) and then back to Basyngham (Bessingham), Matlask, Gresham, Sparham, and Reedham, before coming to and winding up in Norwich (with some parallel bequests to Yarmouth recipients). In casting a net that includes Matlask, Bessingham, and Gresham in Norfolk and Fritton in Suffolk she alighted on four of the 160 or so round tower churches that dot the East Anglian landscape, though this bit of architectural lore is of interest to us but presumably not to her. The round towers themselves were all much older structures, though there is disagreement over their approximate age as well as their purpose.[15] Except for Gresham these churches are in tiny villages, so far off the beaten track that they may have suffered less damage and fewer changes than churches located in more central locations (though they too generally underwent "restoration," mostly in the nineteenth century).[16] Restoration, but pretty certainly not much rebuilding or significant enlargement since Margaret's day, which means it is possible that these little parish churches may not be so different from their fifteenth-century incarnation, as Margaret knew them (with Redham as the exception, treated below). If we are poorer for the loss of the wall paintings and colored images and rood screens and stained glass in the windows, we may, as visitors, get some compensation in the form of electric lighting and rudimentary heating systems. These churches were cold and dark when Margaret's tenants sat and stood in them, no doubt offering the women and men of her villages an interior setting that was more conducive to turning thoughts to the mystery of the mass than to bodily comfort.

Since Margaret Paston is leading us, following her entails taking a look, after Mautby, at the church of St Edmund at Fritton, tucked just below the Norfolk border near Lowestoft. As it is largely a fourteenth-century church with a round tower that probably antedates the rest of the structure, it is just possible that we see pretty much what Margaret saw, though we trust that its powerful scheme of wall paintings was easier to follow then than it is today. The chancel is attached in a asymmetrical fashion to a tunnel-vaulted nave and it leads to a low, dark Norman chancel. The asymmetry is a reminder of the piecemeal building that was not uncommon, in this case a sign of how the church was extended, probably in the fourteenth century. There is a screen of that vintage and a very impressive group of wall paintings, now badly faded. In the curve of the chancel we have the tale of St Edmund, local king and martyr. Still discernible are the king himself and the wolf that led his followers to his mutilated body, plus some faded images of what may be his pagan persecutors. Along the walls there is the familiar St Christopher and what is perhaps Thomas of Canterbury (whom we know from Margaret's letter dating had some regional cachet). Depictions of Edmund seem natural for churches in the region and they are well distributed in the area.[17] Fritton was a part of Margaret's Mautby inheritance but it is nowhere mentioned in the family letters (as far as the indices of Davis and Gairdner are a guide). It should be thought of as another small bit of that private or personal pre-Paston world over which she was, at the end, reasserting herself (though only to the tune of 6s for "ich household being my tenaunt there" and the church itself to receive "a chesiple and an awbe" for its emendation).

Basyngham (Bessingham), both as a church and as a village of Margaret's tenants, was next as she arranged the queue; another of that group of round tower churches that had come her way. Unfortunately, the parish church of St Mary suffered the unhappy fate of being "severely restored" in the 1860s, though the carstone (rather than flint) tower is probably true to its medieval exterior. Given the church's small size and what must have been a perennial shortage of funds, the triangle headed doorway and the fifteenth-century pulpit and font still in place may be much as they were in 1482 when Margaret singled the church out for "emendement" in her usual bequest of a "chesiple and an aube." The village of Bessingham seems so isolated that it evokes a feeling of an earlier world, though it is quite possible that the rural poverty that blankets so much of contemporary Norfolk has come to replace a medieval prosperity that rested on the rich fields of corn and the flocks of sheep one would have seen from atop that rounded tower. The present church has been characterized as "very plain" and its tiled roof is probably later than Margaret's day. The windows are mostly perpendicular, though as we see them they reflect that Victorian restoration rather than their medieval identity. The sanguine attribution of the round tower to the tenth century tells us more about local pride than serious architectural history.[18]

From Bessingham the journey to Matlask is but a few miles at most, though we have no idea if Margaret herself ever paced it out. The church of St Peter, Matlask, also boasts a round tower and one that incorporates what may be Roman tiles among its flints, offering some return to the visitor to make up for the disappearance of the medieval chancel. The story is that during services in 1726 the chancel walls just gave way and collapsed, though no parishioners were injured, as the walls fell outwards rather than inwards—either a sign of divine providence or of a very small congregation that day. The church does have eight medieval corbels that are of reasonable quality, at least by the standards of a small and remote parish church; a tower arch and some fifteenth-century pews also add to its charm.[19] The summation of the place as "a very attractive little church with a feeling of warmth and calmness" seems a reasonable one, well deserving of that "chesiple and an aube...to the emending of the church" that it was to receive under the provisions of Margaret's will.

Gresham was a larger place and, as one of the Paston home manors until they were driven out in 1449 by Lord Moleyns, a place that loomed much larger in the family's history than did the remote villages through which we have been passing so quickly. Moreover, Gresham was not one of the Mautby dowry manors, but rather one the Pastons had bought from Thomas Chaucer earlier in the fifteenth century. When she moved on in the course of her bequests from Matlask to Gresham, Margaret may have had mixed feeling, given the humiliation and defeat she and her partisans had suffered there. However, as far as her will opens the window on her feelings (apart from her piety), it was business as usual, that is, another terse bequest of "a chesiple and an awbe...(for) emending of the church." No comments about the good old days, or the not-so-good old days. As Gresham is a more substantial place, so its church is a more substantial house of worship. The church of All Saints is another of those round tower churches (and it too was "renovated" in the nineteenth century). Features of interest, other than the tower, include a two-story porch that offers "an imposing entrance," an east window with flowering tracery, and a fourteenth-century chancel. But the church's best claim to something out of the ordinary—"the pride of this church," as the guidebook says—is the octagonal seven sacrament font, one of 25 still to be found in the country.[20] The font, probably preserved from destruction because its depictions of the sacraments had been plastered over at a critical time, may have been in place by 1480—when Margaret might have seen it, had she made a last visit to Gresham—though closer to 1500 is more likely. Again, it is nice to speculate that at least one of "ich of myn...godchilder," as she refers to them in her will—might have been baptized in this font and in Margaret's presence. The odds, or cold reality, argue against this.[21]

From Gresham Margaret's spiritual meandering next takes us to Sparham. Here we find the attractive little church of St Mary, "entirely restored" to its present condition in the 1880s, though with various bits of ornamentation that might have been seen by Margaret, had she come

this way. Because of extensive but oddly or poorly planned rebuilding in
the fifteenth century, the chancel is (once again) out of line with the nave,
as was the case at Fritton. At Sparham the building operation progressed
from east to west and the width of the arches varies, which probably gives
an insight to the quality and architectural planning of small-church construction, as well as to the shaky budget on which such enterprises rested.
The tower, probably from the mid-fifteenth century, was separate from
the church at first and only integrated with the main building when the
nave was rebuilt and lengthened, probably in Paston times. Bits of glass
have been preserved in some of the windows and there is a medieval pulpit, again perhaps one that has suffered a good deal through restoration.[22]
The most interesting feature of the interior—far and away ahead of any
of the other features—is a rood screen depicting the various saints and
the dance of death. Duffy talks of "fashionably well dressed cadavers who
leered at the congregation," a touch by the artist that would no doubt help
convey their grim message.[23] The depictions of Becket and the local hero
St Walstan were powerful reminders of the imminence of earthly death,
as well as of heavenly reward; the monumental brass of a late-fifteenth-
century rector, William Mustarder, added further verisimilitude to the
theme. Though the churches of East Anglia are still rich in rood screens,
Sparham stands alone in this regard among those on Margaret's list of
recipients, at least as her churches now present themselves.

In what seems a kind of "saving the second best for last and rating only
below Mautby," Margaret concluded her rural peregrination at Redham
(Reedham). Here, and only here, did she step outside her own laconic
boundaries: "there as I was born," as she says in her will, and the church's
reward for this came in the form of more generous bequests, running to 5
marks and a chesiple of silk with an awbe, "with myn armes thereupon."
The church of St John the Baptist may well have housed tombs and monuments of the Berneys, since Margaret's maternal ancestors had had their
roots here. Alas, a serious fire in March 1981 destroyed most of the medieval interior; the present church, handsomely rebuilt and modernized and
well illuminated, is literally an era away from "what did Margaret see."
Much of the exterior withstood the fire and the attractive outer walls,
composed of blocks of freestone interlaid with bricks and (Roman?) flat
tiles, probably look much as they did when Margaret was presumably
christened there in the early 1420s.[24] A tower that was built around 1447
was probably subsidized by a bequest from (her uncle) Thomas Berney,
and the brass to Elizabeth Berney, a cousin, dates from the late fifteenth
century. Tiles from the church's fourteenth-century floor are now in the
Norwich Castle Museum; the mermaid corbel still to be seen over the
chapel door would no doubt have smiled upon Pastons and Berneys in

Margaret's day, as she does upon the occasional visitor today. The village of Redham, still served by a local railway line, has moved about a mile down the road from the medieval waterside site that made this handsome church a good deal more accessible for those who sought its services in the days of the Berneys and Mautbys than it is today.[25]

This completes the rural component of our pilgrimage. The late medieval riches of rural Norfolk made Margaret's inheritance a valuable one, and its intrinsic value, plus her esteemed genealogy, made her a good catch for William and Agnes Paston's oldest son and heir. We have seen that the inheritance was very much a rural one, a phenomenon that tells us something about the geographical distribution of wealth and serves as a warning against seeing too much of fifteenth-century Norfolk life as being centered in Norwich. This latter view—like that of overestimating the importance of books when we talk about material possessions—may push us toward an anachronistic reading of late medieval county society. It may also be the key, or at least part of the key, to why Bromholm and Mautby, and not the cathedral in town, beckoned to John I and then to Margaret when it came to choosing a burial site. The bequests in Margaret's will show us someone divided in her allegiance and even in her identity; partially a maiden/wife/widow of the countryside, partially a proud and influential townie. Following Margaret's pathway through the little places to which she left her string of small but deliberative benefactions takes us, today, to isolated churches in isolated villages. Though the landscape was probably livelier and more populous in her day than in ours, touching all these Paston-Mautby bases evokes the idea of deep roots and of unchanging or slowly changing life patterns. That conventional beliefs and conventional lives drew their strength from this background is easy to understand. What might puzzle us, though it is hardly our problem to deal with in these essays, is why and how so much heretical, radical, and rebellious thought and action could more or less coexist in this same corner of the realm.

When we get to town the situation changes. Here, as we noted when looking at Margaret's will, she abandons the role of lady of the manor and seems to accept that she now is but one out of many; that is, but one of many matrons and widows of comparable wealth and status. This was hardly an insignificant identity, but it was a step down from her rural persona. Margaret touched a lot of bases in Norwich, widely distributing her bequests and showing a fairly thorough knowledge of what was going on in town. She opened the urban section of her will with a bequest to each of the four friaries of Norwich and of Yarmouth. In Yarmouth nothing remains; archaeology has filled in a few details about the Franciscan house. In Norwich, by good fortune, the Dominican house has been partially incorporated into the parish church and church hall of St Andrew, and some of the arches of the imposing Dominican cloister stand in the courtyard of a nearby office or factory block.[26] Supposedly the arms of John and Margaret, from the 1450s, are carved into the great south door of St Andrews. Of that Carmelite house that loomed so large in the tale of family burials and of Agnes's influence (or would-be influence) upon those around her, a handsome stone arch from what may have been the gate or the cloister can still be seen, standing guard duty just above the banks of the Wensum. The Great Hospital not only stands but has had the good fortune to have its own tale in detail and at length.[27] If Margaret would no longer recognize the institution to which her bequest had gone, she might be proud to be found among the long list of patrons. The house of nuns at nearby Carrow has gone the way of the world, and if there are successors to "iche leper man and woman at the v Yates," they are the homeless and the street people who still ask for alms and freely offer a "god bless you" in return, just as did those "ankers in Consford" to whom Margaret left 3s 4d.

The "mother church," as Margaret says in her will: the cathedral church of the Holy and Undivided Trinity. Family ties with the cathedral went, in a personal or direct sense, at least as far back as the arrangement made regarding the construction of the chantry of William I in the Lady Chapel. John I left nothing to the cathedral, as the scattered documents about his wishes guide us, and no one else in the family other than Margaret has left a record that tells of a different tale. But her bequest of 20s for "a dirige and masse" suffices to put this great building into the category of "places seen" (and of places endowed). Margaret had lived very near the cathedral, over the years, while it was undergoing one of those great bursts of building and rebuilding that are part of the long history of such structures. The fifteenth century was an eventful and busy one in its history: a major fire in 1463, the majestic Erpingham gate and Sir Thomas' chantry finished some years before the fire, the wonderful program of bosses in the great cloister (into which we assume Margaret had access, whatever St Benedict had said), and the choir stalls that were being built under the lead of various bishops.[28] There is some uncertainly regarding the roll of different bishops concerning these stalls, but whether it was the lead offered by Wakeryng (1416–25) or Lyhart (1446–72) or Goldwell (1472–99), they were in place for Margaret to admire (if she entered the choir) before her final farewell. Though we know nothing about the chantry that William had staked out for himself, we are told that the revenues of the family's manor at Sweynthorpe were dedicated to its support: "the anuyté fore hys perpetuell masse," and there were no complaints about procrastination or short dealing toward its upkeep, unlike the interminable controversy regarding building the tomb of John I.

In approaching the cathedral, coming a short way downhill from the Paston town house, Margaret would have seen a façade perhaps not too different from the one of today, though this too is a matter of some debate.[29] Atop the structure was that great new spire, now nearing completion and being built (or rebuilt) to replace the steeple that had recently come to ground. The choir vaulting was built on Bishop Goldwell's watch. The wall paintings still visible in what is now the cathedral's treasury were already old as far as decorations go, and the Despenser Retable was probably on display somewhere in the church's interior. It is hard to imagine that most of these various features, including the newly made bosses for cloister and nave, would have been unfamiliar to Margaret, or that the almost constant stream of building projects would not have made an impression on her. After all, she knew what was going on. She was a woman who had access to the prior of Norwich without notice or appointment when she and Agnes sought his help in their celebrated street quarrel in 1449, and if Margery Kempe could come into town and have an audience with the bishop we can assume the Pastons had his ear when they sought it. We can think of Margaret's bequests to the cathedral as a sign of her understanding of how one made a mark in the town beyond the small boundaries of one's own parish. The "mother church" was a marketplace of spiritual exchange; where better to display one's wares?

Of the many parish churches of Norwich, two were singled out in Margaret's will: St Peter Hungate and St Michael Coslany. The latter comes as a surprise, it being near the Paston's neighborhood or parish but, to the best of our knowledge, with no other or prior recorded connection with the family. Margaret was quite openhanded toward St Michael Coslany, again perhaps on the idea that if one wished to make any splash in Norwich it had to be a bigger splash than what was sufficient when dealing with Sparham or Bessingham. Her bequest of 4d to each priest, 2d for "ich clerk in surplys," 6d to the parish clerk, "the curat that shll seye high masse [to] have xxd," 6s 8d for "reparaction of the bellys of the same church," and finally xxd to the sexton to ring bells was a fair sum in all, well beyond what she had left to her own manors and those little parish churches of the countryside. What Pevsner refers to as "the enthusiastic display of flushwork" on the exterior walls of St Michael is handsome enough to rate a picture in his *Buildings of Norfolk* (Plate 16A), though the walls we now see were built at the very end of the fifteenth century or very early in the sixteenth, therefore seeming to add nothing in a literal sense to the quest for "what did Margaret see." Entering the church today, thoughts readily turn to the large number of children produced by John and Margaret—that full nursery with its demands on time, the family budget, and the hiring (and firing) of nurses and tutors and servants—since the empty and presumably deconsecrated nave of St Michael Coslany is now the children's science museum of Norwich, filled with young sages playing games with gravity and optics.[30]

The real plum of Margaret's urban benefaction, as we might expect, was the small and much-abused parish church of St Peter Hungate, the clear winner of the Norwich segment of the "what did Margaret see" treasure hunt. This was the church whose living John I and Margaret had acquired in 1458 and had then moved, around 1460, to rebuild in an extensive and elaborate fashion. In 1460 John was on the brink of getting his hands on the Fastolf estates, and he must have anticipated some of the Fastolf money to cover the large and ambitious plans that he and Margaret were subsidizing for the church of their parish, just up the street from their town house on Elm Hill. As a small church, located in one of the smallest and poorest parishes of the central city, it was easy for the Passtons to play the role of heavy patrons, and it would be here, in 1479, that Margaret buried her favorite son Walter.

What is so striking about the rebuilding—doubtless the result of much consultation between wife and husband and others drawn into the project—is that nothing about this project has left any record in the Paston letters. Whatever discussions went on between the Pastons and craftsmen and glaziers and masons and clerics about costs, style, ornamentation, iconography, etc., they were either conducted face-to-face or in correspondence and business-cum-legal documents that have not survived. Nor are there building accounts or church records to help us out. The long-term fate of St Peter Hungate has not been a happy one, and those years when it was warmed by the sunshine of Paston munificence were its brightest moments, whether we look before or afterwards. When Margaret's bequest wore out, as such things are wont to do, the church gradually but steadily declined into genteel poverty and neglect. By the early twentieth century it was held that "it was again so ruinous that it was declared unsafe and threatened with demolition." After World War II it served for some years as a church museum or repository for the miscellaneous bits of ecclesiastical furniture, sculpture, glass, and ornaments—most items taken from the surplus churches that Norwich could no longer afford and/or from those so damaged by bombs that restoration was unrealistic. Eventually the museum function was terminated and St Peter stood locked against all comes, until a recent decision to reopen it to visitors on select days and—most recently—to give it a new lease on life as a stained glass museum.[31]

Walking into the almost empty building today is as close as we can come to what Margaret would have gazed upon, perhaps for the last time in those sad moments of that funeral in 1479; she may never have returned to Norwich. The frame of the church and some of its external decorations are almost certainly those put into place under the critical and cost-conscious eyes of John I and Margaret, and the roof bosses hold their own against those of more elaborate and famous churches of the county. Though the stained glass in the windows has been rearranged or collected from elsewhere in town, most of what there is—and there is a very considerable amount—dates to the fifteenth century, and a fair amount of it is Paston glass, if we will. The roof bosses and carving would seem to be those made to order for Margaret and her husband, and the just-visible carving into a beam by the north door has usually been read as saying "1461," giving us a cornerstone dating for the work, though it takes a bit of imagination or the advice of a guidebook to be certain about the numbers.[32]

There are no indications of where the burials were sited, no indication of where in the church Margaret had Walter interred, though somewhere near the high altar would seem likely. What stands today, much as it did in the late fifteenth century, speaks to the idea of a proprietarial claim issued by a gentry family, now staking out its special space in central Norwich. Given how small the center of the town was, we can say that the Pastons were but five minutes from the great marketplace church of St Peter Mancroft, and they certainly would have been (envious?) spectators as the monumental east window was installed in the greatest of Norfolk's parish churches.[33] But at a level the Pastons would have considered to be affordable and befitting their own status, they offered their assertion of self in stone and glass and wood, even if no one other than Walter would rest there until the Second Coming. This church stands as the family's contribution to the glories of Europe's "most religious city," as Norman Tanner has termed it, and at least we can say that Margaret was going to leave her mark in town, even if her body was to go elsewhere, back to one of those little villages where she felt more at home and, perhaps, more in control.

The expertise and devotion of David King have given us an idea of the glass that probably was in place as a result of the Paston's rebuilding project of the 1460s, as well as a survey of what was installed in the early years of the sixteenth century (much of it in place when described by earlier historians and antiquarians but no longer to be found). Most of the fifteenth-century glass that remains, though as fragments and border decorations, dates from 1460–65. As such it is a reminder or remainder of what John I and Margaret supervised in their rebuilding of the church. In addition, some of the work, both in the church's architecture and some of the window design, is "almost identical" to work at Stody, whose donor Ralph Lampet was an active figure in Paston affairs, and many similarities between the St Peter Hungate work and the more elaborate work at St Peter Mancroft can still be identified. Beyond what we can see today, printed records and a fragment here and there tell of early-sixteenth-century glass with the heraldic devices of John II and John III, of a shield of Paston quartering Berry. There is a fragment of glass in a window with the word "marger" and this—or so King speculates—may have been from a window or a scroll bearing the name of Margery Brewes, the first wife of John III. This evidence of sixteenth-century additions, set in place a generation or so after Margaret's death, does indicate a sustained Paston interest in St Peter Hungate. King dates much of the sixteenth-century work to around 1522, which, insofar as it was a Paston project, would put it in the hands of those who were of the generation after Margaret's own children. But this sustained concern, as well as subsequent burials that might have taken place there, is but another of those many issues that leave no trace in the family letters.[34]

We have come to the end of the trail. Following Margaret's footsteps, as she has blocked them out in her will, has led us on a journey to rather modest and out-of-the-way churches and places, to one of the great cathedrals of the kingdom, to two urban parish churches, past some broken arches and odd remnants, given us a passing reference to a long-lived hospital, and kindled memories of such lost glories as town gates, anchoresses, lepers, and a chapel or two. Not as rich a journey as we might have hoped for, given the specificity of our knowledge of the relevant places. Nor did we actually come upon any Paston burials or tombs. Nevertheless, it is a not unimpressive pilgrimage—the historicized path of someone we otherwise know from the written word—for what she says and what others say about her. We began the inquiry into Margaret Paston's religious life and universe with a look at her calendar. Then we turned to what we could distill from her words. We have come to the end by way of a search for bricks and mortar that could be integrated into the fabric built on words. In this respect, we have had mixed luck, though we knew from the start that this would be the case. There are no remains specific to the Pastons, let alone to Margaret herself, but much remains that is evocative and perhaps not so different from what it had once been.

★ ★ ★

Having already played fast and easy with Margaret Paston's life, beliefs, and physical or material world, I end with some speculations about that which she kept most private of all—her emotional life and its unspoken links with her religiosity. An institutional church is not hard to reconstruct, but when we come to the realm of belief we enter a realm that is ever-so malleable and shifting. We can look at actions and we can take words at something like or close to face value, but how people internalized what they were saying and doing are mysteries that are in large part beyond us. If those saints whom Margaret named in her dating clauses took on a reality, let alone a historicity through her noting of their feast days, they would also have done so through the visual and oral presentation of their lives, miracles and martyrdoms—all as seen in churches or as known from devotional reading or as heard in countless sermons.

Beyond assertions of this sort we cannot say how Margaret felt, in any personal sense, about the faith that clearly was bound into her daily life in so many respects. To probe a bit at this speculation about emotion and conviction, we can revisit the death and last wishes of John I, only now it is to try to imagine something about Margaret's emotional and spiritual condition, rather than to see how the bills were paid and the subsidized prayers apportioned. When John died, 22 May 1466, away from home and amidst all sorts of unfinished business, he left a widow in her early 40s. She had a brood of seven children to worry about, ranging in age from the early 20s for John II to about seven for William III and all of them as yet unmarried. The extensive if unsatisfactory documentation about John's costly funeral process and burial, with its full measure of baked meats and fish and barrels of wine and all that went with this, proclaims the lavish nature of the proceedings. It was showy and expensive, something we also see in the rebuilding schemes John and Margaret had recently authorized for St Peter Hungate. These were both ways in which John made a declaration of his identity and his position as the Fastolf heir, now free to spend accordingly. It was not out of keeping with the culture of his world that he saved his most lavish display of self and identity for the last act of his drama—his funeral procession, his burial and the accompanying feast, and the prayers that would help him bridge that chasm between purgatory and heaven.

But a funeral is not just a socioreligious affair orchestrated to fuel the local economy, good as it may be for business and for personal reunions. It is also about saying farewell, about burying the dead and severing his or her ties with the living. The ritualization of grief and loss is designed to soften or obscure the finality of death and to offer an emotional bridge between the sorrow and pain of departure and the need of the living to get through to better days. So let us turn to the living, to the survivors of John I, instead of just being bemused by how much it cost to put the Paston patriarch to earth; John's wife, his children, his siblings

(Elizabeth, William II, and Clement II), and his mother, as we can reach back to them in the spring of 1466. The documents we have talk of the responsibility of meeting costs, of obligations incurred and of purchases made and now to be paid for.

What about the widow's feelings? We have nothing that even hints at tender or conjugal words, since John died in a rented room in London and Margaret learned of it, a few days later, while managing the household in Norfolk. Was she given special husband-to-wife instructions regarding prayers, or the distribution of possessions, or the care of the younger children? And if so, how was the message conveyed: word of mouth from the messenger who brought the bad news, or from others who followed, or by way of a John-to-Margaret letter that did not wind up in the collection? Had there been some agreement, worked out between John and Margaret about what to do in case of his death, unexpected as it was when it actually came to pass? We just do not know; nothing about his executors or supervisors, nothing about his personal goods. The focus on John's infamous and long-unbuilt monument and the mother-son tension that centered in part around her sons' procrastination regarding their father's injunction deflects us from other aspects of a situation that gives us an absent husband, sudden death in early middle age, and a grieving widow-cum-overburdened mother. And in her grief and mourning, Margaret was accompanied or surrounded by a difficult mother-in-law and an intrusive brother-in-law, by children just at or not yet at legal age, and by a household staff and servants of unknown numbers and costs, not to mention legions of friends, supporters, creditors, partners in business enterprises, people of all ranks and callings who saw a possible opening for profit and advantage, along perhaps with cousins and others who might show up and expect to be given their own share of attention and a portion of the baked meats.[35]

To what extent did Margaret's religious convictions, her conventional · spirituality, offer her a measure of consolation, hope, or stoicism with which to face the problems now dumped, without any warning, into her lap? Of this—perhaps the key moment of her emotional life, at least up to that time—we know nothing. Margaret's letters take a chronological leap; her last one to John was dated 27 October 1465; her next, to John Berney (and written while John I was still alive, according to Davis's dating) is dated sometime before 1 May 1466; the following letter and the first we have after her husband's death, was written from mother to son, to John II on 29 October 1466. Nothing coming hard on the heels of John's death, nothing from Margaret's greenest and sharpest days of mourning and grief, nothing bespeaking the early woes and burdens of what was to be a long widowhood.

A little more in this vein. When John I died in 1466 the family was deeply mired in the agenda he had created; the Fastolf estate, the recovery of various other estates and manors being contested, the search for friends and partisans in high places, the choice of men for the shrievalty and for parliament, the opposition of some great figures, and so forth. The Pastons coped, if not always very successfully or cheerfully. By the time Margaret made her will some of these old issues had perhaps lost their urgency, while others had slipped from Margaret's shoulders onto those of the men of the next generation. But once again, in 1479, emotional crises compounded the socioeconomic woes. Margaret was not called up to deal with the death of old Agnes nor, with more pain and less expectation, the deaths of John II in London and of Walter in Norwich. Again, her resolve was certainly being tested, her faith once more called upon as a bedrock on which she cold rest. Was Walter her favorite by the end because his brothers were so problematic, or because he was destined for the church? Or, conversely, was he destined for the church because he was his mother's favorite?[36] Or are these unrelated issues: sending younger sons into the Church was mainstream behavior for the gentry. It suffices to say that if religion had been constructed to offer personal answers and consolation when fate dealt one a bad hand, Margaret had occasion, certainly in the painful and critical years of 1466 and 1479, to look to those answers; consolation at least, if not a glimpse into the great mysteries. In the assurance of the words of the liturgy, in the repetition of prayers, in the reception of the sacraments, and in the tolling of the anniversaries she had to find what strength her faith gave her. That she might be facing a long widowhood was something she might have imagined from the start, though how much this probability softened the actual blow when it fell is another matter.

Though it is not easy to wax sentimental about the Pastons, if any one of them evokes some sort of sympathy it is apt to be Margaret. Soft hearts may be captured by the clandestine marriage of daughter Margery and Richard Calle, but Margery fades from the scene too quickly and too quietly to compete with her mother, neither does she leave a paper trail to allow us see her up close. Margaret knew that she kept the home fires burning, and for this unfailing devotion she has won plaudits ever since Fenn first published the letters in the 1770s. Wedgewood referred to her as "the indomitable Margaret," and Gairdner—moved to fulsome tribute perhaps beyond what the record really can support—said that her will shows "how strongly she felt the claims of the poor, the sick, and the needy as well as those of hospitals, friars, and parish churches."[37] Kingsford too has his turn: "the careful, wise, and prudent mother, feminine and practical but withal human, helpful to her husband, strict but affectionate with her children."[38] I have tried to show that the personal and the private were woven together in a garment that covered both her public activities and her matriarchal role within the family. Whether she would have been flattered by my metaphor, or my compliment, or my view of her spirituality, or whether she would have found my assessment presumptuous and even blasphemous is the last mystery I present and for which I have no answer.

The written record that has been preserved has not served us nearly as well as we might have wished regarding matters of faith within the family, wonderful as it is to have the letters at all. We might say the record indicates that Margaret Paston kept her own counsel, despite her many letters. I conclude this search by looking back at the premise with which I began—that Margaret Mautby Paston was pious and conventional, that the evidence argues that she took her faith very seriously, and that she never felt any need or desire to express herself in terms of personal revelation, let alone by raising awkward questions about life and devotion as it was taught and/or received. She was the typical and conventional lady on the Clapham omnibus and she rode it to the end of the line (though she might well have said she was entitled to ride first class). When she reached that end of the line, she probably crossed herself, clutched her book of hours, and prepared to get off when it was her turn to do so.

NOTES

1 Reading the Religious Life of Margaret Paston

1. Norman Davis, ed., *The Paston Letters and Papers* (2 vols., Oxford: Oxford University Press, 1971–1976). This is the basic edition I use and the letters are cited throughout these essays by volume and number, not by pages. The older edition by James Gairdner is used on occasion: James Gairdner, ed., *The Paston Letters, 1422–1509 A.D.* (3 vols., Westminster: Constable, 1895). There is now a third volume to round out Davis's work: Richard Beadle and Colin Richmond, eds., *The Paston Letters, III*, EETS, s.s. 22 (Oxford: Oxford University Press, 2005) (referred to as III, below, when cited). For a brief summary of Margaret's life, see my pamphlet, *Margaret Paston, Matriarch of the Paston Family* (Dereham, Norfolk: Larks Press, 2009).

2. Though the data rarely lend themselves to an individualized case study, there are some useful papers: Michael Hicks, "The Piety of Margaret, Lady Hungerford (d. 1478)," *Journal of Ecclesiastical History* 38 (1987), pp. 19–38; W. Mark Ormrod, "The Personal Religion of Edward III," *Speculum* 64 (1989), pp. 849–77; Rachel Gibbons, "The Piety of Isabeau of Bavaria, Queen of France, 1385–1422," in *Courts, Counties and the Capital in the Later Middle Ages,* ed., Diana E. S. Dunn (Stroud: Sutton, 1996), pp. 205–24; and for a longer and more discursive treatment, Jonathan Hughes, *The Religious Life of Richard III: Piety and Prayer in the North of England* (Stroud: Sutton, 1997). On the limits of "know-ability" in such matters, Deborah Youngs, *Humphrey Newton (1466–1539): An Early Tudor Gentleman* (Woodbridge: Boydell, 2008): Despite the preservation of Newton's commonplace book, we have the caveat: "It may not offer a window into his soul but it does shine a spotlight on several aspects of his spirituality and the influence the Church had upon his everyday actions. We can see what he knew of Christianity, what he was particularly devoted to; we can consider his contemplative and active piety and assess the relationship between is person devotion and communal practice."

3. Agnes reported to William about the meeting between the couple, probably in the spring of 1440 (I, 13): "as for the furste aqweyntaunce be-twhen

John Paston and the seyde gentilwomman, she made hym gentil chere in gyntyl wyse and seyde he was verraly yowre son."

4. Helen Castor, writing about John I in the *ODNB*: "His partnership with his wife, Margaret, seems to have been a successful one." For Margaret's dower, see the Inquisition Post Mortem on John I (II, 900). Gairdner seems to side more with the Pastons regarding the social balance of the marriage: Gairdner, I, xxviii, "no disparagement to the fortunes or rank of either family."

5. The interesting story of the preservation, publication, dispersal, and reunification of (most of) the letters is told by David Stoker, " 'Innumerable Letters of Good Consequence in History:' The Discovery and First Publication of the Paston Letters," *The Library,* sixth series, 17 (1995), pp. 107–55; Davis also covers this ground, I, xxiv–xxxv. Charles L. Kingsford, *English Historical Literature in the Fifteenth Century* (Oxford: Oxford University Press, 1913), p. 199, suggesting that it was John I, trained in law and apt to have an eye for any opportunity that might come along, who saw the wisdom of collecting and preserving the papers. I naturally lean toward the idea that it was Margaret's idea and her initiative.

6. Gairdner, I, xxix; Colin Richmond, *The Paston Family in the Fifteenth Century: Endings* (Manchester: Manchester University Press, 2001), p. 88; Roger Virgoe, *Private Life in the Fifteenth Century* (London: Macmillan, 1989), pp. 140, 158. Kingsford, *Historical Literature*, p. 206 for a positive assessment of Margaret as wife and mother. For another assessment, Joan W. Kirby, "Women in the Plumpton Correspondence: Fiction and Reality," in *Church and Chronicle in the Middle Ages: Essays Presented to John Taylor,* ed. Ian Wood and Graham A. Loud (London: Hambledon Press, 1991), pp. 219–32; p. 220, "Margaret Paston, for example, emerges as loving wife, hard-headed manager, harsh parent and stout-hearted defend of the family's 'livelode'."

7. Typicality, of course, is the presumed bedrock of social history. For some skepticism about Margaret's typicality and the pitfalls of generalizing from her life, Helen Jewell, *Women in Medieval England* (Manchester: Manchester University Press, 1996), pp. 229–32, and Rowena E. Archer, "Piety in Question: Noblewomen and Religion in the Later Middle Ages," in *Women and Religion in Medieval England,* ed. Diana Wood (Oxford: Oxbow, 2003), pp. 118–40. However, Colin Richmond argues for her typicality as one of her strengths or positive aspects, *Endings*, pp. 88–127.

8. Norman Davis, "The Language of the Pastons," *Proceedings of the British Academy* 40 (1955), pp. 120–44. Davis had a particular interest in the letters and writing of the women (which primarily means Margaret and then Agnes) and he held that the language of their letters, despite their consistent use of scribes, was much like their spoken language; Davis, "The Text of Margaret Paston's Letters," *Medium Aevum* 18 (1949), pp. 13–28; Davis, "A Scribal Problem in the Paston Letters," *English and Germanic Studies* 4 (1951–52), pp. 31–64; Davis, "Margaret Paston's Use of 'Do'," *Neuphilologische Mitteilungen* 73 (1972), pp. 55–62.

9. Defending Margaret as an author worthy of attention, in Davis's edition of the Paston letters, 167 pages are devoted to her letters (with the usual editorial additions) and she offers us some 60,000 words. In pages, this compares with 96 pages devoted to John I, 126 for John II, and 112 for John III (and the men all have many more other-than-letters among their documents). In recent surveys of women as authors and of medieval authors in general, Margaret has finally begun to receive some notice: Janet Todd, *British Women Writers: A Critical Reference Guide* (New York: Continuum, 1989), pp. 529–30; Lorna Sage, *Cambridge Guide to Women's Writing in England* (Cambridge: Cambridge University Press, 1999), pp. 491–92; Paul and June Schlueter, eds., *An Encyclopedia of British Women Writers* (New Brunswick, NJ: Rutgers University Press, 1988), pp. 505–6. Margaret Paston was omitted from Virginia Blain, Patricia Clements, and Isobel Grundy, *The Feminist Companion to Literature in England* (New Haven, CT: Yale University Press, 1990), though Margery Kempe and Julian of Norwich were both covered. The *ODNB* devotes space to Margaret but only as she is folded into the general entry on the family (written by Colin Richmond); John I and John II merit individual entries.

10. Richmond, *Endings,* p. 92. The days of the week and the hours at which she wrote, when indicated in a letter, are topics worth more investigation; topics on my agenda for a small project.

11. Ian Jack, "The Ecclesiastical Patronage Exercised by a Baronial Family in the Late Middle Ages," *Journal of Religious History* 3 (1965), pp. 275–90; Nigel Saul, *Death, Art, and Memory in Medieval England: The Cobham Family and their Monuments, 1300–1500* (Oxford: Oxford University Press, 2001); Michael Hicks, "Piety and Lineage in the Wars of the Roses: The Hungerford Experience," in *Kings and Nobles in the Later Middle Ages,* ed. Ralph A. Griffiths and James Sherborne (London: Sutton, 1986), pp. 80–108, and Hicks, "Four Studies in Conventional Piety," *Southern History* 13 (1991), pp. 1–21.

12. H. S. Bennett, *The Pastons and their England: Studies in an Age of Transition* (first edition, Cambridge: Cambridge University Press, 1922): chapter 14 for "Religion," chapter 15 for "The Secular Clergy," and chapter 16 for "The Regular Clergy."

13. H. S. Bennett, *The Pastons and their England*; David Knowles, "The Religion of the Pastons," *Downside Review* 42 (1924), pp. 143–63; Gillian Pritchard, "Religion and the Pastons," in *Daily Life in the Late Middle Ages,* ed. Richard Britnell (Stroud: Sutton, 1998), pp. 65–82. Colin Richmond comments on the various Pastons, in passing, *Endings.*

14. Colin Richmond, "Religion and the Fifteenth-Century English Gentleman," in *The Church, Politics and Patronage in the Fifteenth Century*, ed. Barrie Dobson (Gloucester: Sutton, 1984), pp. 198–208; Richmond, "The English Gentry and Religion, c. 1500," in *Religious Belief and Ecclesiastical Careers,* ed. Christopher Harper-Bill (Woodbridge: Boydell, 1981), pp. 121–50. For a contrary view, Christine Carpenter, "The Religion

of the Gentry in Fifteenth-Century England," in *England in the Fifteenth Century: Proceedings of the 1986 Harlaxon Symposium,* ed. Daniel Williams (Woodbridge: Boydell, 1987), pp. 53–74, and, more recently, Christine Carpenter, "Religion," in *Gentry Culture in Late Medieval England,* ed. Raluca Radulescu and Alison Truelove (Manchester: Manchester University Press, 2005), pp. 134–50; Eamon Duffy, "Religious Belief," in *A Social History of England, 1200–1500,* ed. Rosemary Horrox and W. Mark Ormrod (Cambridge: Cambridge University Press, 2006), pp. 293–339; Colin Richmond, "Religion," in *Fifteenth-Century Attitudes,* ed. Rosemary Horrox (Cambridge: Cambridge University Press, 1994), pp. 183–201; Hilary M. Carey, "Devout Literate Laypeople and the Pursuit of the Mixed Life in Later Medieval England," *Journal of Religious History* 14 (1987), pp. 361–81; Peter Fleming, "Charity, Faith, and the Gentry of Kent, 1422–1529," in *Property and Politics: Essays in Later Medieval English History,* ed. Tony Pollard (Gloucester: Sutton, 1984), pp. 36–58; Nigel Saul, *Knights and Squires: The Gloucestershire Gentry in the Fourteenth Century* (Oxford: Oxford University Press, 1981). Eamon Duffy, *The Stripping of the Altars* (New Haven, CT: Yale University Press, 1992), still at the head of the queue for the treatment of popular and lay religion and belief in the fifteenth and early sixteenth centuries.

15. Frederick Maurice Powicke, "The Reformation as an act of state," as his summary statement for chapter 1 of his *The Reformation in England* (Oxford: Oxford University Press, 1941).

16. A quick survey of women in East Anglian religious life: Joel T. Rosenthal, "Local Girls Do It Better: Women and Religion in Late Medieval East Anglia," in *Tradition and Transformation in Late Medieval England,* ed. Douglas Biggs, Sharon D. Michalove, and A. Compton Reeves (Leiden: Brill, 2002), pp. 1–20; Norman Tanner, *The Church in Late Medieval Norwich, 1390–1532* (Toronto: Pontifical Institute of Medieval Studies, 1984). For the neighboring county, Judith Middleton-Stewart, *Inward Purity and Outward Splendour: Death and Remembrance in the Deanery of Dunwich, Suffolk, 1370–1547* (Woodbridge: Boydell, 2001).

17. Edmund College and James Walsh, eds., *A Book of Showings to the Anchoress Julian of Norwich* (Toronto: Pontifical Institute of Medieval Studies, 1978); Nicholas Watson and Jacquiline Jenkins, eds., *The Writings of Julian of Norwich* (University Park, IL: Pennsylvania State University Press, 2006), to scratch the surface of recent work; for guidance to recent work, Liz McAvoy, ed., *A Companion to Julian of Norwich* (Cambridge: D. S. Brewer, 2008). For the historian, for help amidst the deluge of Kempiana, Anthony Goodman, *Margery Kempe and her World* (London: Longman, 2002); John H. Arnold and Katherine Lewis, eds., *A Companion to "The Book of Margery Kempe"* (Woodbridge: D. S. Brewer, 2004); Rayn Possell, "Margery Kempe: An Exemplar of Late Medieval Piety," *Catholic Historical Review* 89 (2003), pp. 1–29, with thanks to Maryanne Kowaleski for this reference. Much still of interest in the

introduction to the Penguin edition: Barry A. B. A. Windeatt, trans., *The Boke of Margery Kempe* (Harmondsworth: Penguin Books, London, 1985).

18. For an alternative lifestyle and choice, Kim M. Phillips, "Desiring Virgins: Martyrs and Femininity in Late Medieval England," in *Youth in the Middle Ages*, ed. P. J. P. Goldberg and Felicity Riddy (Woodbridge: Boydell, 2004), pp. 45–59; Sarah Salih, *Visions of Virginity in Late Medieval England* (Cambridge: D. S. Brewer, 2001). Helen Castor, *Blood and Roses* (London: Faber & Faber, 2004), p. 95, on Margaret's unhappy condition during her fifth pregnancy.

19. Samuel Moore, "Patrons of Letters in Norfolk and Suffolk, c. 1450," *Publications of the Modern Language Association* 27 (1912), pp. 188–207, and 28 (1913), pp. 79–105; K. K. Jambek, "Patterns of Women's Literary Patronage: England, 1200–ca. 1475," in *The Cultural Patronage of Late Medieval Women*, ed. June Hall McCash (Athens: University of Georgia Press, 1996), pp. 228–65; Mary Serjeantson, ed., *Osbern Bokenham: Legendys of Hooly Wummen*, EETS, o.s. 208 (1938); Simon Horobin, "Politics, Patronage, and Piety in the Work of Osbern Bokenham," *Speculum* 82 (2008), pp. 932–49. For Capgrave, Karen A. Winsted, *John Capgrave's Fifteenth Century* (Philadelphia, PA: University of Pennsylvania Press, 2007).

20. Mary Erler, *Women, Reading, and Piety in Late Medieval England* (Cambridge: Cambridge University Press, 2003); Jennifer Bryan, *Looking Inward: Devotional Reading and Private Self in Late Medieval England* (Philadelphia, PA: University of Pennsylvania Press, 2008).

21. Richmond, *Endings*, p. 116, Margaret Paston was "not a reader."

22. For an example of other issues that can be pursued and of other questions we can address, when the extant material permit, Elizabeth Noble, *The World of the Stonors: A Gentry Society* (Woodbridge: Boydell, 2009). Both social networks and domestic arrangements are explicated at some length in this study.

23. For the other collections of family letters: Christine Carpenter, ed., *Kingsford's Stonor Letters and Papers, 1290–1483* (Cambridge: Cambridge University Press, 1996) (cited hereafter as "Stonor"); Joan Kirby, ed., *The Plumpton Letters and Papers*, Camden Society, fifth series, 8 (1990) ("Plumpton"); Alison Hanham, ed., *The Cely Letters, 1472–1488*, EETS, o.s. 273 (1975) ("Cely"); and all references below are to the letters as numbered by the respective editors, not to pages. Also, Christine Carpenter, ed., *The Armburgh Papers: The Brokholes Inheritance in Warwickshire, Herefordshire, and Essex, c. 1417–c. 1453* (Woodbridge: Boydell, 1998). For some general reflections that extend to the various collections of fifteenth-century family letters, Joel T. Rosenthal, "The Paston Letters," in *The Oxford Encyclopedia of Medieval Literature*, ed. David S. Kasten (Oxford and New York: Oxford University Press, 2006), 5 vols, IV, pp. 184–87.

2 Margaret Paston's Calendar and Her Saints

1. H. Maynard Smith, *Pre-Reformation England* (London: Macmillan, 1938), p. 165; "men did not think of saints as spiritual beings in a far-off and inaccessible heaven, but as beings close at hand, still at work on earth, interested and active in the everyday concerns of life," coming in a chapter entitled "Superstitions and Abuses"; "Saints are like the mountain peaks of human nature," Mary D. Anderson, *Imagery in British Churches* (London: John Murray, 1955), p. 151. On prayers to the saints, John Harper, *The Forms and Orders of the Western Liturgy from the Tenth to the Eighteenth Centuries* (Oxford: Oxford University Press, 1991), pp. 47–54; for the prayer to a saint on his or her day, J. Wickham Legg, *The Sarum Missal, Edited from Three Early Manuscripts* (Oxford: Oxford University Press, 1916; reprinted, 1966).

2. For different views on whether the ritual half of the year outstripped the second half in terms of impact on lay consciousness; Charles Phythian-Adams, "Ceremony and the Citizen: The Communal Year at Coventry, 1450–1650," in *The English Medieval Town: A Reader in English Urban History, 1200–1540, 1200–1540,* ed. Richard Holt and Gervase Rosser (London: Longman, 1990), pp. 238–64 (essay first published in 1972); Eamon Duffy, *The Stripping of the Altars,* pp. 46–52. Robert N. Swanson has no doubts: "the unimaginative succession of Sundays after Trinity, apparently having no function other than to be Sundays after Trinity," p. 94 of his *Religion and Devotion* (Cambridge: Cambridge University Press, 1995); Gail McMurray Gibson, *Theater of Devotion* (Chicago, IL: University of Chicago Press, 1989), pp. 166–68, noting that most of Marian feasts fell in the second half of the year.

3. Paul Brand, "Lawyers' Time in England in the Later Middle Ages," in *Time in the Medieval World,* ed. Chris Humphrey and W. Mark Ormrod (Woodbridge: Boydell for the York Medieval Press, 2001), pp. 73–104. As was Margaret's wont, the dating could actually run to a few days either side of the saint's day—the morrow or the eve and the like.

4. Robert N. Swanson, *Church and Society in Late Medieval England* (Oxford: Blackwell, 1989), pp. 285–90 on saints and private devotion; Duffy, *The Stripping of the Altars,* pp. 179–80 on the special attributes of saints and how these were invoked.

5. For the relevant obligations of the patriarch, William A. Pantin, "Instructions for a Devout and Literate Layman," in *Medieval Learning and Literature: Essays Presented to Richard William Hunt,* ed. John J. G. Alexander and Margaret T. Gibson (Oxford: Clarendon Press, 1976), pp. 398–422; Felicity Ridley, "Mother Knows Best: Reading Social Change in a Courtesy Text," *Speculum* 71 (1996), pp. 66–86; Patricia Cullum and Jeremy P. J. Goldberg, "How Margaret Blackburn Taught her Daughters: Reading Devotional Instruction in a Book of Hours," in *Texts and Contexts in Late Medieval Britain: Essays for Felicity Riddy,* ed. Jocelyn Wogan-Brown et al. (Turnhout: Brill, 2000), pp. 217–36; Sue Powell,

"The Transmission and Circulation of the *Lay Folks Catechism*," in Alistair J. Minnis, ed., *Late Medieval Religious Texts and their Transmission: Essays in Honour of A. I. Doyle* (Woodbridge: Brewer, 1994), pp. 67–84; Robert N. Swanson, *Religion and Devotion in Europe, c. 1215–c. 1515* (Cambridge: Cambridge University Press, 1995), pp. 10–41 (the chapter being entitled "Faith and Its Demands"); Eamon Duffy, "Religious Belief," in *A Social History of England, 1200–1500,* ed. Rosemary Horrox and W. Mark Ormrod (Cambridge: Cambridge University Press, 2006), pp. 319–23.

6. Richard Pfaff, *New Liturgical Feasts in Late Medieval England* (Oxford: Oxford University Press, 1970); E. S. Dewick, "On a Manuscript Formerly Belonging to the Abbey of Bury St Edmunds," *Archaeologia* 54/2 (1895), pp. 399–416, for efforts on behalf of new cults.

7. Colin Richmond, "Religion," in *Fifteenth-Century Attitudes,* p. 190. Gibson says that "hagiography is about recurrence," p. 95 of her "Saint Anne and the Religion of Childbed: Some East Anglian Texts and Talismans," in *Interpreting Cultural Symbols: St Anne in Late Medieval Society,* ed. Kathleen Ashley and Pamela Sheingorn (Athens: University of Georgia Press, 1990), pp. 95–110.

8. John A. F. Thomson, *The Later Lollards* (Oxford: Oxford University Press, 1965); there was no Lollard presence in Norwich between the end of Alnwick's persecutions in 1431 and the dawn of the sixteenth century.

9. Donald Weinstein and Rudolph M. Bell, *Saints and Society: The Two Worlds of Western Christendom, 1000–1700* (Chicago, IL: University of Chicago Press, 1982). Eamon Duffy, *The Stripping of the Altars,* pp. 155–205.

10. Richard Pfaff, "Why Do Medieval Psalters Have Calendars?" in his *Liturgical Calendars, Saints, and Services in Medieval England* (Aldershot: Ashgate, 1998), paper vi. On books of hours, Roger Wieck, *Painted Prayers: The Book of Hours in Medieval and Renaissance Art* (New York: George Braziller, 1998), for their components and arrangement; for calendars, pp. 26–33. Also, Lawrence Poos, "Social History and the Book of Hours," in *the Book of Hours in Medieval Art and Life,* ed. Roger S. Wieck (New York: George Braziller, 1988), pp. 32–40 (p. 35: "the best seller of the Middle Ages," looking at women owners); L. M. J. Delaisse, "The Importance of Books of Hours for the History of the Medieval Book," in *Gatherings in Honor of Dorothy E. Miner,* ed. Ursula E. McCracken, Lilian M. C. Randall, and Richard H. Randall, Jr. (Baltimore: Walters Art Gallery, 1974), pp. 203–25; Paul Saenger, "Books of Hours and the Reading Habits of the Later Middle Ages," in *The Culture of Print: Power and the Uses of Print in Early Modern Europe,* ed. Roger Chartier (Princeton, NJ: Princeton University Press, 1989), pp. 141–73: p. 146, the book of hours helped foster silent reading in "the shift from the mouth to the heart"; Margaret Aston, "Devotional Literacy," in her *Lollards and Reformers: Images and Literacy in Late Medieval Religion* (London: Hambledon, 1984), #iv, on private reading, "independent of the liturgical cycle." Kathryn A. Smith, *Art, Identity, and Devotion in Fourteenth-Century England: Three*

Women and their Books of Hours (London and Toronto: University of Toronto Press, 2003); Bridget A. Henisch, *The Medieval Calendar Year* (University Park, IL: Pennsylvania State University Press, 1999) for the calculation of dates and the depiction of female saints; Charity Scott Stokes, *Women's Books of Hours in Medieval England* (Cambridge: D. S. Brewer, 2006); Eamon Duffy, "The Book of Hours and Lay Piety in the Later Middle Ages," in *Elite and Popular Religion,* ed. Kate Cooper and Jeremy Gregory, *Studies in Church History* 42 (2006), pp. 140–61, and Duffy, *Marking the Hours: English People and their Prayers* (New Haven, CT: Yale University Press, 2006). Marjorie C. Woods, "Shared Books, Primers, Psalters and Adult Acquisition of Literacy," in *New Trends in Feminine Spirituality: The Holy Women of Liège and their Impact,* ed. Juliette Dor et al. (Turnhout: Brepols, 1999), pp. 177–93: p. 185, "If a woman owned or bequeathed only one book, it was most often a primer" (that is, a book of hours).

11. For the family chapel in the time of William I (I, 11). H. S. Bennett points out that the chapel was part of the Paston claim to gentility, *The Pastons and Their England,* p. 206: "We are frequently reminded of the presence of a chaplain…although we hear little of his religious duties." *Calendar of Papal Letters, vi,* p. 434, for the indult to hear mass before daybreak.

12. Diane Watt, *The Paston Women: Selected Letters* (Cambridge: D. S. Brewer, 2004), p. 2, quoting Colin Richmond to the effect that Margaret "wrote at any time and at all hours." I interpret this gnomic wisdom to mean hours of the day, not days of the month or year, though these latter alternatives also seem to be the case.

13. Norman Davis, I, xxxvii–xxxviii, "It is legitimate to conclude that the women of the [Paston] family whose letters survive were not, or not completely literate," though since Davis wrote this (1971) the pendulum has swung toward a more sanguine view of women's literacy, at least for reading if not necessarily for writing. There is general agreement, however, with Davis's view that all of Margaret's letters were dictated to a scribe; Diane Watt, "'No Writing for Writing's Sake'," in *Dear Sister: Medieval Women and the Epistolary Genrem,* ed. Karen Cherewatuk and Ulrike Wiethaus (Philadelphia, PA: University of Pennsylvania Press, 1993), pp. 122–38; Watt, *The Paston Women,* p. 134: Margaret Paston was "the most prolific writer…yet, paradoxically, she was certainly illiterate." I find this hard to accept, though conclusive evidence in either direction is thin.

14. Margaret's letters with an existential date are: I, 128 (April 1448); I, 159 (2 July 1461); I, 170 (March 1462, at 11 o'clock); I, 173 (1463); I, 186 (30 June 1465); I, 187 (6 July 1465); I, 191 (August 1465). They are pretty straightforward: (I, 128) "Wretyn at Norwyche on the Wedenys-day nexst after that ye partyd hens"; (I, 159) "Wretyn in hast, the same day that ye departyd hens"; (I, 173) "Wrotyn this day"; (I, 186) "Wretyn the Sonday next after your departing"; (I, 187) "Wretyn in hast on Satyrday."

15. One of John I's letters to Margaret in 1465 is so dated: (I, 74) "wret the Satirday." John II used this styles on three occasions: (I, 233) "reten at Leyn the morrow aftermy departing from you" and also in I, 241 and I, 285. John III dated seven letters in this fashion, three of them to his mother (I, 367, 371, and 386). There are also such datings in the Stonor Letters (#83, 190, 240, and 249), those of the Plumptons (#81, 130, and a few more), and the Celys (#32: "Wryt at Calles the Thursda after your departing").

16. Norman Davis, "The Text of Margaret Paston's Letters," *Medium Aevum* 18 (1949), pp. 12–28, and Davis, "A Scribal Problem in the Paston Letters," *English and Germanic Studies* 4 (1951–52), pp. 31–64. Mary Erler (in conversation) pointed out that had the date come at the head of the letter it might well have been part of the scribe's preparatory arrangements, but coming near the end it was more likely to have been as taken from the words of whoever was dictating the contents of the letter (and in these cases it was Margaret Paston).

17. The secular dating is conventional: I, 171, "xviij day of Mai"; I, 180, "the x day of May…from Haylesdon"; I, 181, "xiij day of May"; I, 182, "xx day of May." The saints who get passed over by this turn to secular dating are not otherwise noted; St Dunstan for 19 May, Ethelberht, king and martyr, for 20 May. I, 224 covers both styles, "xxiijth day of may after Trinity Sunday." It was also the feast of David of Scotland, but not for East Anglian calendars.

18. Wykes penned three letters for John II; two had secular dates (I, 232 and I, 242) and one (I, 258) in 1470 with an ecclesiastical date: "Thursday next aftere Seynt Erkenwaldes Day."

19. Looking at all the women's letters in the Stonor and Plumpton collections (including two from Queen Elizabeth Wydeville), there are 26 in the Stonor collection: 5 with ecclesiastical dates, 16 with secular dates, 4 undated, and one other. For the Plumptons the respective categories are 6, 8, 4, and 0.

20. Friar Brackely was an active figure in Paston affairs, though characterized by David Knowles as "a friar who bears an unmistakable family likeness to Chaucer's worthy limiter," *The Religious Orders in England: II, The End of the Middle Ages* (Cambridge: Cambridge University Press, 1961), p. 202. Of Brackley's Latin letters to John I, seven were undated, one with an existential date (II, 610), and three with ecclesiastical (II, 557, 608, and 609). His deathbed (April 1467) was described by John III (I, 327), who says that Brackley, when about gone, rallied to call for his confessor so he could attest, one last time, that he had acted in good faith in upholding the claim of John I to be Fastolf's heir.

21. This was conventional discourse: II, 464, the duke of Norfolk to John I (October 16, 1450), "Right Trusti and welbelouid, we grete you well…and God haue yow in his kepyng"; II, 468, earl of Oxford to John I (December 23, 1450), a letter that concludes with "as we trust yow"; II, 476, Earl of Oxford to John I (April 30, 1451), "The Trinité haue in hese kepyng."

22. Richmond, *Endings,* p. 125. Christine Carpenter, "Religion," in *Gentry Culture,* pp. 138–39: "The religion of the gentry, with few exceptions, was remorselessly orthodox and this was hardly surprising since care was taken to bring them up in orthodox belief"; Duffy, "Religious Belief," p. 331 for indications of a lack of religious zeal buy the laity, p. 336 for evidence of considerable zeal.

23. Christine Peters, *Patterns of Piety: Women, Gender, and Religion in Late Medieval and Reformation England* (Cambridge: Cambridge University Press, 2003), pp. 47–50: an examination of data from 125 parishes in Sussex indicates no patterns, no women favoring female saints in their bequests or invocations. There may have been a tendency to "save" the big-name saints for suitably important occasions (p. 98).

24. R. N. Swanson, *Church and Society,* p. 290, on the idea that "saints had to earn veneration," which posits a reciprocity that is easy to overlook or ignore.

25. On how households accommodated the strains of feasts and holidays, Kate Mertes, *The English Noble Household, 1250–1600: Good Governance and Politic Rule* (Oxford: Blackwell, 1988), pp. 152–54, and Mertes, "The Household as a Religious Community," in *People, Politics, and Community in the Later Middle Ages,* ed. Joel T. Rosenthal and Colin F. Richmond (Gloucester: Sutton, 1987), pp. 123–39; Ffiona Swabey, *Medieval Gentlewoman: Life in a Widow's Household in the Later Middle Ages* (New York: Routledge, 1999), pp. 97–131, 159 ff; Christopher Woolgar, *The Great Household in Late Medieval England* (New Haven, CT and London: Yale University Press, 1999), pp. 90–96, on how feasts and fasts determined household and table routines in the household.

26. Saints as distant figures is brought home by a caption to a Perugino painting of St John and St Lucy in the Metropolitan Museum in New York. It says the two saints are "vacant repositories whose affective content was supplied by the viewer."

27. W. W. Williamson, "Saints on Norfolk Roodscreens and Pulpits," *NA* 31 (1957), pp. 299–346. Duffy, *The Stripping of the Altars,* pp. 155–60, with a caveat on the difference between what we can see today and how things would have looked in the fifteenth century.

28. Christopher Woodforde, *The Medieval Glass of St Peter Mancroft, Norwich* (Norwich: Goose & Son, 1934), now superseded by David King, *The Medieval Stained Glass of St Peter Mancroft, Norwich,* Corpus Vitrearum Medii Aevi of Great Britain, vol. 6 (Oxford: British Academy, 2006). For St Christopher on the wall at Paston, Nikolaus Pevsner, *North-East Norfolk and Norwich* (Harmondsworth: Penguin, 1962), p. 298.

29. R. N. Swanson, *Church and Society,* pp. 260–64.

30. Duffy, *The Stripping of the Altars,* p. 181.

31. Christopher R. Cheney, *Handbook of Dates* (London: Royal Historical Society, 1955), p. 55, for the Marian festivals celebrated in England: 25 March for the Annunciation, 15 August for the Assumption, 8 December for the Conception, 3 September for the Nativity, 21 September for the

Presentation, 2 February for the Purification, and 2 July for the Visitation. Marina Warner, *Alone of All Her Sex: Myth and Cult of the Virgin Mary* (New York: Vintage Books, 1976); Jaroslav Pelikan, *Mary through the Centuries: Her Place in the History of Culture* (New Haven, CT and London: Yale University Press, 1996), p. 125, quoting Otto von Simpson, "The age was indeed the age of the Virgin." On the cult of Mary, Eileen Power in her introduction to C. C. Swinton Bland, *The Miracles of the Blessed Virgin Mary* (London: Routledge, 1928), pp. ix–xxxv; Miri Rubin, *Mother of God: A History of the Virgin Mary* (New Haven, CT: Yale University Press, 2009), pp. 285–351 for the medieval context; on local practices, Joan Greatorex, "Marian Studies and Devotion in the Benedictine Cathedral Priories in Later Medieval England," in *The Church and Mary,* ed. Robert N. Swanson, *Studies in Church History* 39 (2004), pp. 157–67, with details of which Marian feasts were celebrated at Norwich.

32. For others who dated letters by the feasts of apostles or evangelists and Jesus's friends: Matthew, used by William III, I, 407; Mary Magdelan, used by John III, I, 348 and 362; Apostle James, used by John I, I, 52; Bartholomew, used by Clement, I, 116; the Decollation of John the Baptist, used by John II, I, 301; Nativity of the Virgin, used by William II, I, 84 (and others); Conception of Our Lady, used by John III, I, 320 et al.; Agnes Plumpton (#190) for the feast of St Mark; and a Cely Letters (#121) for the feast of St Anne. Rubin, *Mother of God,* pp. 328–31 on Anne as the "favourite grandmother of late medieval Christendom."

33. On regionalism and the diffusion of the legends, Gordon H. Gerould, *Saints' Legends* (Boston: Houghton Mifflin, 1916), and William H. Hutton, *The Lives and Legends of the English Saints* (London: Wells Gardner, Darton, 1908), contrasting eastern and western saints and insular and national saints. Weinstein and Bell, *Saints and Society,* pp. 194–219, on the class origins of the saints themselves. On how new feasts might drive out old, Richard Pfaff, *New Liturgical Feasts;* the feast of the Visitation might drive the translation of St Swithin from the calendar on 2 July, or the feast of the Holy Name of Jesus replace the feast of St Sixtus.

34. John III, for St Faith (6 October) and for St Michael in Monte Tombe (16 October).

35. Kenneth Farnhill, *Guilds and the Parish Community in Late Medieval East Anglia, c. 1470–1550* (Woodbridge: York Medieval Press, 2001): In popularity of guild dedications Thomas the Apostle ranked tenth in Norwich, Thomas of Canterbury seventeenth. But as a given name Thomas ranked third, only trailing John and Richard: Virginia Davis, "The Popularity of Late Medieval Personal Names as Reflected in English Ordination Lists," in *Studies in the Personal Name,* ed. David Postles and Joel T. Rosenthal (Kalamazoo, MI: Medieval Institute Publications, 2006), p. 106.

36. David H. Farmer, "Some Saints of East Anglia," *Reading Medieval Studies* 11 (1985), pp. 31–49, for a number of local saints' cults that all went unmentioned by Margaret. For Hugh of Lincoln, Farmer, "The Cult and Canonization of St Hugh," in *St Hugh of Lincol,* ed. Henry Mayr-Harding

(Oxford: Oxford University Press, 1987), pp. 75–88. Though Hugh's feast was in the Sarum calendar (17 November), his translation (6 October) was only celebrated at Lincoln and, beyond the diocese of Lincoln, by the Carthusians. Few signs of much interest in Katherine of Alexandria, despite her general popularity; Katherine J. Lewis, *The Cult of St Katherine of Alexandria in Late Medieval England* (Woodbridge: Boydell, 2000). No mention of the local cult of St Withburga; Jeremy Griffiths, "A Mid-Fifteenth-Century Book-List and Inventory from East Dereham, Norfolk," *NA* 42 (1996), pp. 332–39.

37. For St William of Norwich, Augustus A. Jessopp and Montague Rhodes James, ed. and trans., *The Life and Miracles of St William of Norwich* (Cambridge: Cambridge University Press, 1896); Ronald C. Finucane, *Miracles and Pilgrims: Popular Beliefs in Medieval England* (Houndsmill: Palgrave Macmillan, 1995), p. 194; Norman P. Tanner, "Religious Practice," in *History of Norwich,* ed., Carole Rawcliffe and Richard Wilson (London: Hambledon and London, 2004) I, pp. 137–55, on the decline of the cult, and Ian Atherton, Eric Fernie, Christopher Harper-Bill, and Hassell Smith, eds., *Norwich Cathedral: Church, City and Diocese, 1096–1996* (London: Hambledon, 1996), p. 448 on this theme. Robert N. Swanson, "Indulgences at Norwich Cathedral Priory in the Later Middle Ages: Popular Piety in the Balance Sheet," *Historical Research* 76 (2003), pp. 18–29, for a similar tale of fading interest.

38. Jacobus de Voragine, *The Golden Legend: Readings on the Saints,* trans. William G. Ryan (2 vols., Princeton, NJ: Princeton University Press, 1993); Sherry L. Reames, *The Legenda Aurea: A Reexamination of Its Paradoxical History* (Madison, WI: University of Wisconsin Press, 1985), pp. 197–209. Caxton only published the *Legend* in 1483, after Margaret had written her will, though before her death. Thus her "a complete legende" (I, 230) was in manuscript.

39. Though Margaret's overlap of saints' days with those in the *Golden Legend* was high, she and Bokenham seem to have been ships that passed in the night. Of Bokenham's saints (i.e., those whose lives he chronicled) Margaret only used the dates of the feasts of Agnes, Agatha, Margaret, and Katherine. John III dated letters by the feasts of St Faith and Mary Magdelan, both covered by Bokenham. Mary Serjeantson, ed., *Osbern Bokenham: Legendys of Hooly Wummen.* On the popularity of the Feast of the Visitation, Mary C. Erler, "Home Visits: Margaret, Elizabeth, Margery Kempe and the Feast of the Visitation," in *Medieval Domesticity: Home, Housing, and Household in Medieval England,* ed. Maryanne Kowaleski and P. Jeremy P. Goldberg (Cambridge: Cambridge University Press, 2008), pp. 259–76.

40. The Wingfield Book of Hours is New York Public Library, Spencer Ms 3, discussed in *The Splendor of the Word: Medieval and Renaissance Illuminated Manuscripts at the New York Public Library,* ed. John J. G. Alexander et al. (New York: Harvey Miller, 2005), pp. 227–32 (with red letter days listed, p. 230). The manuscript was probably written in Bruges, 1450–60, with

English additions or insertions, 1460–70. It had been written or revised for Ann Neville, duchess of Buckingham. On the singular nature of each book of hours, John P. Harthan, *Books of Hours and their Owners* (London: Thames & Hudson, 1977): p. 9, "no two are alike," and a discussion, pp. 13–15, of the way in which "accuracy" concerning saints and their days was rarely checked, and the vagaries of scribes, as well as of patrons, were inscribed as accepted parts of the book's calendar.

41. The Ormsby Psalter lists sixteen feasts for November, the Bromholm Psalter but nine, these both being fourteenth-century books from or around Norwich: Montague Rhodes James and Sidney C. Cokerell, eds., *Two East Anglian Psalters at the Bodleian Library* (London: Roxburgh Club, 1926).

42. Bodleian Library, Rawlinson Liturgical Ms E. 3 (15799); Otto Pächt and Jonathan J. G. Alexander, *Illuminated Manuscripts in the Bodleian Library, Oxford* (Oxford: Clarendon Press, 1973), iii, no. 975; Peter Lasko and Nigel J. Morgan, *Medieval Art in East Anglia, 1300–1500* (Norwich: Thames & Hudson, 1973). Even a book of hours without fancy touches, such as British Library, Cotton Julius B vii, is noteworthy for its bold distinction between red and black letter days.

43. William George Henderson, ed., *Missale ad usum insignis ecclesiae Eboracensis,* Surtees Society 59–60 (1874).

44. All three saints (Praxedis, Apollinaris, and Germanus) are covered in the *Golden Legend.* Most calendars show a considerable variation in the saints' days noted; John Plummer, introduction and commentary, *The Hours of Catherine of Cleves* (New York: George Braziller, 1966), for Morgan Library ms. 945; John Higgitt, *The Murthly Hours: Devotion, Literacy, and Luxury in Paris, London, and the Gaelic West* (London and Toronto: University of Toronto Press, 2000), with such English saints as Weberga, Oswald, Edward King and Martyr, Guthlac, John of Beverley, Alban, the Translation of Cuthbert, etc., probably reflecting the calendar observed at Worcester (pp. 306–11). A continental calendar could differ widely; Thomas Kren, "Seven Illuminated Books of Hours Written by the Parisian Scribe Jean Dubreuil, c. 1475–1485," in *Reading Texts and Images: Essays on Medieval and Renaissance Art and Patronage in Honour of Margaret M. Manion,* ed. Bernard J. Muir (Exeter: Exeter University Press, 2002), pp. 157–200, on the Use of Le Mans and the Use of Grammont.

45. On campaigns for canonization, Nicholas Orme, "Saint Walter of Cowbeck," *Analecta Bollandiana* 108 (1990), pp. 387–93; Anne F. Sutton, "Caxton, the Cult of St Winifred, and Shrewsbury," in *The Fifteenth Century: V. Of Mice and Men: Image, Belief, and Regulation in Late Medieval England,* ed. Linda Clark (Woodbridge: Boydell, 2005), pp. 109–26. Orme, "Bishop Grandisson and Popular Religion," *Proceedings of the Devonshire Association* 124 (1992), pp. 107–18; on the costs of such a campaign (on behalf of Thomas Cantilupe), Ronald C. Finucane, *Miracles and Pilgrims,* p. 37; Julia M. Luxford, "St. Margaret of Holm: New Evidence Concerning a Norfolk Benedictine Cult," *NA* 44 (2002),

pp. 111–19; Virginia Davis, "The Rule of St Paul, the First Hermit, in Medieval England," in *Monks, Hermits, and the Ascetic Tradition,* ed. W. J. Sheils, *Studies in Church History* 22 (1985), pp. 203–14.

46. Mary Richards, "Some Fifteenth-Century Calendars for Rochester Diocese," *Archaeologia Cantiana* 102 (1985), pp. 71–85; David Thomson, "Two Lists of Fifteenth-Century Feasts in the Diocese of Hereford," *Journal of Ecclesiastical History* 34 (1983), pp. 586–90. Delaisse, "The Importance of Books of Hours," pp. 205–12, saying that distinctions between different calendars are among the most interesting characteristics of books of hours.

47. Cults of political "martyrs" as a subspecies of hagiography but never touched by the Pastons; J. C. Russell, "The Canonization of Opposition to the King in Angevin England," in *Haskins Anniversary Essays in Medieval History* (Boston, MA: Houghton Mifflin, 1929), pp. 279–90; John W. McKenna, "Popular Canonization as Political Propaganda: The Case of Archbishop Scrope," *Speculum* 45 (1970), pp. 608–23; Simon Walker, "Political Saints in Later Medieval England," in *the McFarlane Legacy: Studies in Late Medieval Politics and Society,* ed. Richard H. Britnell and Anthony J. Pollard (Stroud: Sutton, 1995), pp. 77–106; Danna Piroyansky, "Bloody Miracles of a Political Martyr: The Case of Thomas, Earl of Lancaster," in *Signs, Women, and Miracles,* ed. Kate Cooper and Jeremy Gregory, *Studies in Church History* 41 (2005), pp. 228–38.

48. David H. Farmer, "Some Saints of East Anglia," pp. 42–3: No bishop of Norwich was ever canonized, in contrast to bishops from Canterbury, York, Rochester, Worcester, Chichester, and Lincoln; R. N. Swanson, "Indulgences at Norwich Cathedral Priory in the Later Middle Ages: Popular Piety in the Balance Sheet," pp. 18–29; Richard Hart, "The Shrines and Pilgrims of Norfolk," *NA* 6 (1864), pp. 277–94. R. N. Swanson, *Church and Society,* pp. 283–88, on the surprising lack of interest in local saints.

49. Michael A. Penman, "Christian Days and Knights: The Religious Devotion and Court of David II of Scotland, 1329–71," *Historical Research* 78 (2002), pp. 249–72.

50. John Plummer, *The Hours of Catherine of Cleves,* pp. 346–50 for such feasts as those of Emertiana the Virgin (23 January), Pope Gabinus (19 February), or Bishop Valery (21 May).

51. Pevsner, *North-east Norfolk.* For Norwich, pp. 204–94; for the parish churches therein, pp. 234–55 (which includes the Methodist chapel).

52. Some saints were riding a crest of popularity in Margaret's day: Jonathan Bengston, "St George and the Formation of English Nationalism," *Journal of Medieval and Early Modern Studies* 27 (1997), pp. 317–40: In 1416 Archbishop Chichele had ordered the celebration of St George's feast, and Edward IV, with a brother named George, thought to use the saint and his legend to legitimate the house of York. On Norwich's devotion to St. George, *VCH Norfolk* II, 539.

53. The churches listed by Pevsner mostly had Norman or Plantaganet origins, and the subsequent merging of parishes may have cost us some exotic saints. James Campbell, "Norwich," in the *Atlas of Historical Towns,* ed. Mary D. Lobel, (vol. 2, London: Oxford University Press, 1975) for the earlier churches and parishes, with dedications to Vaast and Amand (indicating a Flemish presence) as well as to Cuthbert, Ethelbert, Julian, and Vedast (who lasted in London, as St Vedast Foster Lane). Norman P. Tanner, *The Church in Late Medieval Norwich,* p. 83: "No scope was offered for choosing patron saints of parish churches since no new parish churches were established in the city during the late Middle Ages," and after mid-century (fifteenth century) building was slowing down.

54. Kenneth Farnhill, *Guilds and the Parish,* p. 195.

55. The incidence of baptismal names goes, in descending order, John, William, Thomas, Richard, and Robert: Virginia Davis, "The Popularity of Late Medieval Personal Names," *Studies in the Personal Name,* pp. 103–14; Tanner, *The Church in Late Medieval Norwich,* pp. 82–84 on naming patterns in the city; Scott Smith-Bannister, *Names and Naming Patterns in England, 1538–1700* (Oxford: Clarendon Press, 1997), pp. 100, 108–9, 191–3, for material that indicates little change by the sixteenth and seventeenth centuries from the patterns of an earlier century or two.

56. David Hugh Farmer, *The Oxford Dictionary of Saints* (Oxford: Oxford University Press, 1978) lists three Henrys. A Danish hermit who died at Tynemouth in 1127 seems unlikely, as does Emperor Henry II (d. 1024). But Henry of Finland, bishop and martyr (d. 1156) had, according to William of Worcester, a chapel in his honor at the Carmelite house in Great Yarmouth, a house named in the wills of both John I and Margaret.

57. David Farmer, *The Oxford Dictionary of Saints,* talks of a Walter of Cowick. Though mostly active in Devon, a reference by William of Worcester again suggests a Norwich birthplace; an improbable patron of Paston males but a possible candidate.

58. James (James the Greater?) ranked eighth in terms of national popularity for dedications, fourteenth in Norfolk; two churches in Norwich, St James Pockthorpe and St James-in-Conisford (now in a ruined state) but no record of any Paston connections. Philip, though an apostle, was not much of a cult figure, though for whom else would Margaret's uncle Philip (Berney) had been named?

59. Duffy, *The Stripping of the Altars,* p. 371 on the domination of Katherine, Margaret, and Barbara in terms of popularity and, by extension, as the winners of the names-pool stakes.

60. For St Anne, Kathleen Ashley and Pamela Sheingorn, eds., *Interpreting Cultural Symbols;* the papers of the editors and of Gail M. Gibson are most relevant; Virginia Nixon, *Mary's Mother: Saint Anne in Late Medieval Europe* (University Park, IL: Pennsylvania State University Press, 2004); p. 115, for a reference to a poem acknowledging that Anne had lived long ago—a step toward "historicizing" the saints; Jon Brandenburg,

"St Anne and her Family: The Veneration of St Anne in Connection with Concepts of Marriage and Family in the Early Modern Period," in *Saints and She-Devils: Images of Women in the 15th and 16th Centuries* (London: Rubicon Press, 1987), pp. 101–26.

61. Though Margaret of Scotland might have been her patron saint, Margaret of Antioch (whose cult was suppressed in 1969) seems more likely for East Anglia. The feast of Margaret of Scotland was 16 November, that of her translation, 19 June; the feast of Margaret of Antioch fell on 20 July.

62. Beatrix (Viatrix) was the martyred sister of two brother-martyrs, Simplicus and Faustinus, and with virtually no indications of English devotion.

63. On naming conventions and the role of godparents: Michael J. Bennett, "Spiritual Kinship and the Baptismal Name in Traditional European Society"; Philip Niles, "Baptism and the Naming of Children in Late Medieval England"; Louis Haas, "Social Connections between Parents and Godparents in Late Medieval Yorkshire"; papers now brought together in Postles and Rosenthal, *Studies in the Personal Name,* pp. 115–45, 147–58, and 159–75, respectively. Gairdner speculates (I, 48) that the "my fader Garneyss" of Margaret's letter to John, 28 September 1443, is "perhaps her grandfather." The Garneys were lords of Gelderstone. For an Italian setting, with a strong focus on ancestry and family in the choice of names, David Herlihy, "Tuscan Names," *Renaissance Quarterly* 41 (1988), pp. 561–82.

3 Margaret Paston in Context: Things Said, Done, and Owned

1. With his particular concern for the precise language, Norman Davis talked about the question of how closely the letters mirror "real" speech: "The Language of the Pastons," pp. 120–44. Janel M. Mueller, *The Native Tongue and the Word: Developments in English Prose Style 1380–1580* (Chicago, IL: University of Chicago Press, 1984), pp. 90–94, and for a good example of Margaret moving from "indirect to direct representation" as she becomes more vivid in telling John I of the slanging match in the street (I, 129).

2. Whether it reflects rhetorical style or the circumstances of letter writing, we have fewer references to "haste" in the Stonor or Plumpton correspondence: Stonor, #113 or #130 for some uses of this throw-in tag.

3. Pritchard, "Religion and the Paston Family," p. 67. David Knowles, "The Religion of the Pastons," on their pious speech, though critical about their deeper piety. Knowles, p. 154; a letter written in 1475 is the first time Margaret heads a letter with the Holy Name of Jesus (Jhs).

4. Examples from the other letter collections; Stonor, # 216, from Thomas Betson to Elizabeth Stonor in 1478. In a letter of 31 printed lines, Betson touches many of these bases: "I beseche almighty Jhesu to preserve and

kepe to his plesour…I beseche Almyghty Jhesu send hym als virtuous helth as I wodl have myself…God knowith it…I praye God comfforte you…God knowithe it…I thannke God off all…I praye God they may do hym good to God ward…our blissid Lord preserve your good ladishipe in vertu ever. Amen."

5. Jinty Nelson, on the insecurity of the Carolingian regime: it was "not just the single crisis of 778…but, frankly, one goddamm crisis after another," p. 172 of her "Making a Difference in Eighth-Century Politics: The Daughters of Desiderius," in *After Rome's Fall: Narrators and Sources of Early Medieval History: Essays Presented to Walter Goffart,* ed. Alexander C. Murray (Toronto: University of Toronto Press, 1998), pp. 171–90.

6. The whole topic of blessings is now treated at length by Derek Rivard, *Blessing the World: Ritual and Lay Piety in Medieval Religion* (Washington, DC: Catholic University of America Press, 2009).

7. The lines quoted are at the end of the postscript. The body of the letter concluded by signing off, "Almyghty God haue yow in his kepyng."

8. Earlier in the letter he had said, "God of his hyghe mercy preserue you all vn-to his mercy and grace, and saue you from all aduersité."

9. As in the Stonor letters, some of those of the Plumptons are repetitive; #196, in 17 printed lines Henry Ardern gets in "I besech Jesu contynew and increase vnto his pleaser," and "I pray Jesu give you good speed, who haue you in his gloryour keeping," in addition to one "god-assoil" addressed to Jesus and another to "God."

10. Following the lead of John Bossy, "Christian Life in the Later Middle Ages: Prayers," *Transactions of the Royal Historical Society,* sixth series, 1 (1991), pp. 137–48.

11. These pieties precede a discussion of more worldly matters: "send me word in writing, by the bringer herof, how I shall pay my rent from henceforward and to whom."

12. For what I term the Pastons' manichean view of the universe, Joel T. Rosenthal, *Telling Tales: Sources and Narration in Late Medieval England* (University Park, IL: Pennsylvania State University Press, 2003), pp. 149–54.

13. Armburgh papers, 64 and 65; this theme is played out several more times: p. 63, "not withstanding that they were lykly men and lusty to have liven mony a yere, for theyre vntrewe labour, Godde schorted her lyfe dayes and dyede al thre with inne a while after."

14. John L. Austin, "Performative Utterances," pp. 233–52 of his *Philosophical Papers* (third ed., Oxford: Oxford University Press, 1979); John R. Searle, *Speech Acts: An Essay in the Philosophy of Language* (Cambridge: Cambridge University Press, 1969).

15. Pritchard, "Religion of the Pastons," p. 67, with various examples. Thomas F. Simmons, ed., *Lay Folks Mass Book,* EETS, o.s. 71 (1879), p. 107 for the instructions to pray for saintly intercession. Michael Clanchy, "Images of Ladies with Prayer Books: What Do They Signify," in *The Church and the Book,* ed. Robert N. Swanson, *Studies in Church*

History 38 (2004), pp. 108–22, the quote is on p. 110, dealing with how women with little Latin acquired "passive literacy." Also, Carey, "Devout Literate Laypeople," for injunctions urging "daily mass and matins, fasting and almsgiving…the invariable pious duties of the leisured class" (though it is uncertain if Margaret Paston's responsibilities would qualify as the leisured class); Andrew Taylor, "Into His Secret Chamber: Reading and Privacy in Late Medieval England," in *The Practice and Representation of Reading in England,* ed. James Raven et al. (Cambridge: Cambridge University Press, 1996), pp. 41–61.

16. An example of fairly obsequious address, I, 50: John I, in a draft letter to Lord Grey, July 15, 1454, and John III tops this regarding the "Erle of Arran" (I, 352).

17. Sarah Penketh, "Women and Books of Hours," in *Women and the Book: Assessing the Visual Evidence,* ed. Lesley Smith and Jane H. M. Taylor (London and Toronto: The British Library and the University of Toronto Press, 1996), pp. 266–81, arguing that such books created "intimate communication with the Virgin." Only one Paston reference in all of their letters seems to refer to an active presence by supernatural powers; John II to John III on the French siege of Boulogne in 1477: I, 305: "thys nyght it is seyde that ther was a vision seyne abowte the wallys…a woman wyth a mervylowse light; men deme that Owre Lady there will shewe hyre-selffe a lovere to that towne."

18. Margaret's will (I, 230) says the usual things: her soul was left to God Almighty and "to Our Lady his blessed moder" (meaning "god" means Jesus, at least here); her body was to be buried "before the ymage of Our Lady there." Her brother-in-law William II said much the same; his soul to the Lord God and "to our blessed Lady Sainte Marye Virgyne."

19. Knowles, "The Religion of the Pastons," p. 163: "our Lady's name—apart from the wills and church dedications—is found surprisingly rarely." For an odd and perhaps relevant slant on Marian devotion, the guidebook to the parish church of St Mary, Sparham, says that at Sparham 25 March was celebrated as a feast of Jesus—Dies Dominica—and 2 February as the "feast of the Presentation of Our Lord in the Temple"; that is, as feasts of Jesus rather than as Marian feasts. No reference is given in the booklet by Rev. C. L. S. Linnell, M.A. (Oxon), 1959, or in the 1976 edition (by M. J. Sayer, M.A. (Oxon)).

20. Christine Peters, *Patterns of Piety*, p. 98, on the idea that sometimes the major saints were "saved" for big purposes and lesser ones were invoked, or their churches endowed, at a lesser level. This might help explain the relative neglect of the Virgin in speech patterns in contrast to her heavy presence in the preambles of wills.

21. A joke between the brothers and a rare reference to lay comment on Church rules about daily life. Plumpton, #137 (to Sir Robert Plumpton in 1497): "I wold aduise your mastership, my lady, & all your household many from henceforth to make promise, & keepe yt, to fast the euen of St. Oswald…king & marter, yerly, and that promise truly entended to be performed."

22. The passage continues: "Involving three factors: veneration of the divine (provided by the prayers of the blessing uttered by the clergy), human behavior, condition by that venerations…and the self-interest (perceived and actual) of human life and sacred being": Derek A. Rivard, *Blessing the World*, p. 7. Also, p. 26: "The act of blessing, *barakh*, was understood as the imparting of vital power from one person to another person, thus giving another a part of the blessing of one's soul originally bestowed by God."

23. Knowles, "The Religion of the Pastons," pp. 144–45, on Agnes's imperious style. She does get some credit here: "good advice of a sort that no Paston was likely to take."

24. She continues in this vein: "euer-more desiring to here of your welfare and propserité, the which I pray God to contynw and encresce to youre hertes desire." Plumpton, #138, for blessings from the world of parent-child, top-down mode of discourse.

25. Knowles, "Religion of the Pastons," p. 145.

26. A short but pithy summation (Stonor, #91): "my ffadyr is gone to God."

27. Stonor, #100: "or ellys I must be untreue to God and to them that be dede, and fals of my promys, which God defend me fro." Perhaps more fanciful, Stonor, #262: Annys Wydeslade to Sir William Stonor in 1480, telling him she had been ill ("the ffesisicion wolle do his cunyng upon me") and was thus unable to write: "myn excuse is y have be in helle, where y had litel comfort, but as sone as y cam to Exeter then was y yn heven." In Plumpton, #31: his tenants to Sir William Plumpton in 1480, complaining of those who lived beyond their visible means: "God or some euil angel hase notice hereof," which poses the idea of a contested universe. PL III, 982: "And yff they wolle not dredde ne obey that, then they shall be quyt by Blackbern or Whyteberd, that is to sey by God or the Deuyll." Also, III, 14, when a false claim was being presented "as thow it had be trew as the godpell," or (II, 475), "as God sauf my soule at the day of Jugement."

28. No "god assoil" for casualties at the first battle of St Albans: Gairdner, I, 332–33. The peers on both sides are named and then come "other men, to the noumbre of iiijc and as many or mo hurt." Roger Dalrymple, "Reaction, Consolation and Redress in the Letters of the Paston Women," in *Early Modern Women's Letter Writing, 1450–1700,* ed. James Daybell (New York: Palgrave, 2001), pp. 16–28: p. 25 for Margaret's "emotive response" when provoked. There is a good "god assoil" in Stonor, #99: "my wyffe, zowr suster that wasse, hose sowle I beseche Jhesu have mersy upon." PL III, 142: Stephen Scrope, on his alleged mistreatment by Fastolf, "my seyd lady my moder discussed (some 5 years before), whoos soule god of hys high mercy assoile." Knowles, "Religion of the Pastons," p. 160, notes that when John II and John III addressed Margaret after Gloys's death they neglected the stock phrase but "in the next letter the usual prayer occurs, a little emphasized."

29. Fastolf got his measure of respect: II, 602, "that God on is sowle haue mercy," from John Davy, his chaplain; II, 603, "my maister, on whos

sowle Jesu haue mercy," from Geoffrey Sperling, one of the hands of the Hunterian manuscript of the "Canterbury Tales."

30. On the filiopiety of the House of York, Anne F. Sutton and Livia Visser-Fuchs, with Peter Hammond, *The Reburial of Richard, Duke of York, 21–30 July 1476* (London: for the Richard III Society, 1996).

31. Brackley's letters to John I are also rich with biblical references, and Gairdner provides the proper citations: Gairdner, I, 289, 341, 355, and 364.

32. For a biblical reference, by the escheator of Bedfordshire and Buckinghamshire to Thomas Stonor, #130: "it is reasonable a gentilman to know his pedegre and his possibilyte: seynt Poule foryete nat to write to the Romayns of what lynage he was descended. Ad Romanos xj."

33. For Fastolf's will, I, 54, I, 61; Richmond, *The Paston Family in the Fifteenth Century: Fastolf's Will* (Cambridge: Cambridge University Press, 1996), and Beadle and Richmond, *Part III,* pp. 40–191.

34. Robert N. Swanson, *Church and Society,* p. 289, pointing out that "man-made shrines" served "more as tourist attractions than as encouragements to piety."

35. Ronald C. Finucane, *Miracles and Pilgrims,* on the cults of East Anglia, including many devoted to men and women never officially canonized; David H. Farmer, "Some Saints of East Anglia" for such as Walstan, Eadnoth, and Wendreda, among others; Felix, Sigebert, Edmund, and Walstan were rood screen favorites; Duffy, "Religious Belief," pp. 316–17, on the attraction of obscure saints; Carole Rawcliffe, "Curing Bodies and Healing Souls: Pilgrimage and the Sick in Medieval East Anglia," in *Pilgrimage and the English Experience from Becket to Bunyan,* ed. Colin Morris and Peter Roberts (Cambridge: Cambridge University Press, 2002), pp. 108–40: p. 109 for a map of the major pilgrim destinations, adding Bawburgh, Great Yarmouth, and Hautbois to East Anglian sites mentioned by the Pastons. In this same volume, Eamon Duffy, "The Dynamics of Pilgrimage in Late Medieval England," pp. 166–77; most pilgrimages were local, with details of the cult of Walstan at Bawburgh, citing Capgrave's *Nova Legenda;* Richard Hart, "The Shrines and Pilgrimages of Norfolk," *NA* 6 (1884), pp. 277–94, on such sites as Winfarthings (with a relic sword), St Botolph at Foulsham, and others. For what the pilgrim encountered upon arrival, Ben Nilson, "The Medieval Experience at the Shrine," in *Pilgrimage Explored,* ed. J. Stopford (Woodbridge: York Medieval Press, 1999), pp. 95–122; Richard Marks, *Image and Devotion in Late Medieval England* (Stroud: Sutton, 2004), pp. 193–97, on the layout at Walsingham that greeted an arriving pilgrim. On focal points of veneration, Anne E. Nichols, "The East Anglian Lollards Revisited: Parochial Art in Norfolk," in *Tant D'Emprises: So Many Undertakings: Essays in Honour of Anne F. Sutton,* ed. Livia Visser-Fuchs (London: Richard III Society, The Ricardian XIII, 2002), pp. 359–70.

36. Donald J. Hall, *English Mediaeval Pilgrimage* (London: Routledge, 1965), pp. 104–29; Christopher Harper-Bill, "The Foundation and Later History of the Medieval Shrine," in *Walsingham: Pilgrimage and*

History (Walsingham: R.C. National Shrine, 1999), pp. 63–79, and Carole Rawcliffe, "Pilgrimage and the Sick in Medieval East Anglia," pp. 39–61. John C. Dickinson, *The Shrine of Our Lady at Walsingham* (Cambridge: Cambridge University Press, 1956); Finucane, *Miracles and Pilgrims,* pp. 196–97, on the sustained level of gifting at Walsingham and Bromholm, though interest in St William of Norwich trailed off. Ben Nilson, *Cathedral Shrines of Medieval England* (Woodbridge: Boydell, 1998); fifteenth-century offerings at the shrine of St William of Norwich rarely amounted to more than £1 after better days in the thirteenth and fourteenth centuries. The Lollards denounced the cult of the Holy Rood at Brohmolm, with its mechanical contrivances; Walsingham was "Falsingham," John A. F. Thomson, *The Later Lollards,* p. 126. For St Leonards, W. T. Bensky, "St Leonard's Priory, Norwich," *NA* 12 (1895), pp. 197–227; a cell of Norwich Priory with a striking image of St Leonard. For the shrines of Norwich Cathedral, Carole Rawcliffe and Richard Wilson, ed., *Medieval Norwich* (London: Hambledon and London, 2004), p. 148. For Margery Kempe as "the unpopular pilgrim" and Erasmus as the "skeptical pilgrim," John Ure, *Pilgrimage: The Great Adventure of the Middle Ages* (London: Constable, 2006). For pilgrimage and gender, Leigh Ann Craig, *Wandering Women and Holy Matrons: Women as Pilgrims, 1300–1500* (Boston, MA & Leiden: Brill, 2009).

37. For Erasmus on Walsingham, John G. Nichols, ed., Desiderius Erasmus, *Pilgrimage to St Mary of Walsingham and St Thomas of Canterbury* (London: John Murray, 1875), pp. 11–38, and on p. 19, "She [has left us] so much milk, as it is scarcely credible it should have belonged to one woman with a single child, even if the infant had taken none of it!" James Charles Wall, *Shrines of British Saints* (London: Methuen & Co., 1905); the index covers (holy) body parts to be found at the sites.

38. Margaret's son Edmund said he would accompany her: "Yf it plese yow that I may wete the seayson, as my duté is, I shalle redy to awayte vpon yow."

39. Castor, *Blood and Roses,* points out (p. 77) that Walsingham was hostile territory for the Pastons, being deep in Duchy of Lancaster holdings where their adversaries, Thomas Tuddenham and John Heydon, were well entrenched.

40. John III went on to say, regarding his still-unmarried sister who presumably would make the trip with their mother: "and let my sustyr Margery goo wyth yow to prey to them that sche may haue a good hosbond or sche com hom ayen." By this time Agnes may have been living in London with William II at Warwick's Inn near Newgate: "The place at Warwyks Inne is large and my grawntdame is agyd" as John II stated in 1474 (I, 285). On the pilgrim shrines of St Pauls, Janet Backhouse, ed., *The Medieval English Cathedral: Papers in Honour of Pamela Tudor-Craig,* Harlaxton Medieval Studies, X (Donington: Paul Watkins, 2003): the relevant papers are of Caroline M. Barron, "London and St Paul's Cathedral in the Later Middle Ages," pp. 126–49, on the shrine of St Erkenwald; Eamon Duffy,

"St Erkenward: London's Cathedral Saint and His Legend," pp. 150–67; Lucy Freeman Sandler, "The Chantry of Roger of Waltham in Old St Pauls," pp. 168–90.

41. For "how to do it" literature regarding pilgrimages, Antonia Gransden, "Letters of Recommendation from John Whethamstede for a Poor Pilgrim, 1453–55," *English Historical Review* 106 (1991), pp. 932–39; Christian K. Zacher, "Travel and Geographical Writings," in *A Manual of Writings in Middle English, 1050–1500,* ed. Albert E. Hartung (New Haven, CT: Connecticut Academy of Arts & Sciences, 1986), vol. VII.

42. A letter of about three days later is in the same vein: "Thys day seuen-nyght I trust to God to be forward to Caunterbery at the ferthest."

43. D. J. Hall, *English Medieval Pilgrimage* (London: Routledge & Kegan Paul, 1965), pp. 210–11: an unreferenced statement that the Pastons were great patrons of Bromholm and that, at the Reformation, they may have acquired a piece of the True Cross from the house's treasures. A reference to pilgrimage in Plumpton, #87: One "Byrd of Knasbrough" was to carry for them—either messages or goods—but "he went to Hales, and many other pilgrimages." Alison Hanham, *The Celys and their World* (Cambridge: Cambridge University Press, 1985), p. 90, for a pilgrimage to Compostella in 1484: "it would be delightful to have some details of Robert's journey but nothing more is related"; Wendy R. Childs, "The Perils, or Otherwise, of Maritime Pilgrimage to Santiago de Compostella in the Fifteenth Century," in Stopford, *Pilgrimage Explored,* pp. 123–43.

44. For Edward IV and Walsingham, Cora Schofield, *The Life and Reign of Edward the Fourth* (London: Longmans Green & Co, 1923), I, pp. 491–2. Charles Ross, *Richard III* (second ed., New Haven, CT: Yale University Press, 1999), p. 14. John II was told by Jakyn Hawte that the Queen planned to go on that 1469 expedition "yf God send hyr good hele." She may have been following in the king's footsteps, as Edward IV had "departyt to Walsynggame apon Fryday com vij nyght." I, 352, John II to John III, on Norfolk's resolve to bring his wife to Walsingham in thanksgiving after her confinement. Long afterwards, in 1503, the earl of Oxford told John III that he planed to go to Walsingham, "doing my pilgrimage" (II, 850).

45. Far from home but of interest: John II to the sheriff of Norfolk in March 1462: "The Kyng of Fraunce is in-to Spayne on pilgrimage with fewe fors, as thei sey; what the purpose is thei can not telle certeyn."

46. On the Calthorp family: Josiah C. Wedgwood, *History of Parliament: Biographies* (London: His Magesty's Stationery Office, 1936): entries for Sir William (1410–94), MP for Norfolk, 1445–46, and for his eldest son, Sir Philip (1463–1535), MP for Norfolk, 1491–92. Before her marriage Ann Paston Yelverton had spent time in the Calthorp household, and Calthorps were buried in the Carmelite church in Norwich.

47. Christopher Allmand, *Henry V* (Berkeley and Los Angeles, CA: University of California Press, 1992), pp. 273–93; Jeremy Catto, "Religious Change under Henry V," in *Henry V: The Practice of Kingship,*

ed. G. L. Harriss (Oxford: Oxford University Press, 1985), pp. 97–115. Edmund Clere to John I (II, 512), relating that the royal almoner was sent to Canterbury "to offer at Seint Edward" in thanksgiving because Henry VI had recovered his wits. Some miracles attributed to Henry VI took effect in East Anglia: Ronald Knox and Shane Leslie, *The Miracles of Henry VI* (Cambridge: Cambridge University Press, 1923): #96, 101, and 124. Ralph A.Griffiths, *The Reign of King Henry VI* (Berkeley and Los Angeles, CA: University of California Press, 1981), p. 257, for Margaret of Anjou and one of the king's half-brothers at Walsingham; Susan S. Morrison, *Women Pilgrims in Late Medieval England: Private Piety as Public Performance* (London: Routledge, 2000), p. 16.

48. William A. Pantin, "Instructions for a Devout and Literate Layman," pp. 398–422; Pantin suggests that the man for whom the advice book was written, or its author, may have been following advice as found in Mirk's *Festial;* Duffy, "Religious Belief," pp. 319–23; Swanson, *Religion and Devotion,* p. 98: masses were celebrated with "almost mind-boggling regularity," which meant that other business was likely to be conducted in or around the church. Stonor, #60, for an account of three horses stolen from John Elmac, "whiles he was at the chyrche at matins to haue caried hem away."

49. On Margaret's marriage portion, *Calendar of the Fine Rolls, 1471–1485,* #831, the writ of *diem clausit extremum* for Margaret, November 7, 1484. For John I's inquisition postmortem, II, 900 (October 1466). When Henry Warns (Harry Waryns) said that Margaret had no role at Paston, he was probably referring to her control of the manor, not the living: "Mastrys Margyt Pastun has non rewle here nor sell hafe" (II, 735).

50. I, 216: Margaret pointed out in 1472, "I am leke to haue but lytylle good of Mauteby yf the Dukke of Norfolke haue possession stiylle in Caster, and yf we lesse that, we lesse the fayere-este flowere of owr garland."

51. As early as 1450 Margaret was reporting to John on work being done there: "I haue sent Henry to Maultby this weke to do seche thyngys as ye commawndyd in your letter" (I, 136). Later she said that the onset winter would end the working season; "there shl nomore be made there-of this year but the gabels of the chamber and the chapel windows" (I, 144). In the flurry of letters from John's last year (1465) we have several in which he discusses the finances of Mautby (I, 72, and I, 77); in 1487 William III wrote to the bailiff there (I, 410). Some of John's accounts have survived from 36–37 Henry VI (1458–59), showing he spent 10 shillings for "glazing the chapel at Mautby," plus 3s 8d for work on Gresham church: Gairdner, I, pp. 433–34.

52. The plaque in the church at Mautby lists the vicars of the parish; Robert Iteringham became vicar in 1448, Constantine Dalby in 1453, Thomas Howys in 1460, Robert Cutler in 1465, and Thomas Heveningham in 1480. Of these men, Dalby was marginally involved in family affairs while Howys was much in their world (and various letters inform us about his final illness, his resignation, and his death: I, 131, 395, 400,

and 542). He had been parson of Blofield and Castle Combe, a Fastolf manor, and had served as a Fastolf executor: Gairdner, III, 443, on his declaration about Fastolf's final intentions. Cutler had also been vicar of Caister, and in Margaret Paston's will he is referred to regarding his mark on some swans. He told of a proverb in one of his letters (II, 652), one of the more literary allusions we find. Thomas Lyndes, whom we know from the endorsements of Margaret and John II to John I, was omitted from the list posted in the church, though he was vicar from 1465 until about 1469. He received a cash bequest in the funeral gifting of John I, and after his death his debts became a problem for John II (I, 209), who, in his own will, named Lyndes as a beneficiary of the prayers he was now subsidizing.

53. We know, from Howys's earlier activities (as in III, passim) that his heart was more in administrative than pastoral matters. Swanson, *Religion and Devotion,* p. 243.

54. Margaret continues: "and thank hym for the gret cost that he dede on me at Norwich; and if I were a grette lady he shuld vnderstand that he shuld fare the better fore me."

55. Thomas Hakon had been presented to the living at Drayton (I, 145).

56. Kate Mertes, "The Household as a Religious Community," in Rosenthal and Richmond, *People, Politics, and Community,* pp. 123–39, on the chapel and its links with family prayers and books of hours; Jeremy Catto, "Religion and the English Nobility in the Later Fourteenth Century," in *History and Imagination: Essays in Honour of H. R. Trevor-Roper,* ed. Hugh Lloyd-Jones, Valerie Pearl, and Blair Warden (London: Duckworth, 1981), pp. 43–55. The Plumptons' concern (#222 and #226) is with a chantry chapel, not a household one.

57. Henry S. Bennett, *The Pastons and their England,* pp. 205–6. Bennett accepts, as a matter of course, that such gentry folk had their own chapel, as does the old study by Edward L. Cutts, *Scenes and Characters of the Middle Ages* (London: Simpkin, 1925), pp. 208–12.

58. Christopher Woolgar, *The Great Household,* p. 178 for the chapel at Caister (most household books were "closely associated with the religious arrangements of the chapel or personal devotion"), pp. 179–80 for Fastolf's books. Also, on Fastolf's books and reading circle, Deborah Youngs, "Cultural Networks," in *Gentry Culture in Late Medieval England,* pp. 119–33. Gairdner, I, 467–90, for various inventories of Fastolf's vast accumulations; no relics, no books other than service books, and mostly concerned to list a tremendous accumulation of clothing, household furnishings, and linen. Margaret Wood, *The English Mediaeval House* (London: Phoenix House, 1968) on domestic chapels. John II saw the chapel at Caister as his, now to control: "Thomas Howes hadde a free chapel in Caster, where-of the gyfte longyth to me," writing to John II in 1469 (I, 239).

59. Even when chapel goods are included in Gairdner's documents on the Fastolf will and inventory (I, 489–91), they represent a very small

proportion of this great estate: Gairdner, I, 445–67 for Fastolf's will, pp. 467–75 for one inventory, pp. 475–90 for that of the wardrobe.

60. My emphasis on "sacrament." The bishop in the picture was Walter Lyhart, bishop since 1446. Because William I's chantry had been built in the cathedral, Lyhart and the Pastons must have had many dealings over the years.

61. There is more on this in the Plumpton Letters; Plumpton, #2 ("my new chappell"), #14 (dealing with a chantry), #50 (where Thomas Thorpe signs his letter, "your chaplain & bedman"), #178 (an incumbent defends his privileges and perquisites), #183 (on the real property of a parish church), #192 (a chantry), and #222 (on the value of land attached to a chantry), among others.

62. Margaret Aston, "Segregation in Church," in *Women in the Church*, ed. W. J. Sheils and Diana Wood, *Studies in Church History*, 27 (Oxford: Blackwell, 1990), pp. 237–94, on seating in the parish church. Andrew Brown, *Popular Piety in Late Medieval England: The Diocese of Salisbury, 1250–1500* (Oxford: Clarendon Press, 1995), p. 250: little evidence for a "detachment from parochial life" because of private or internalized prayer or family chapels.

63. When Katherine Chadderton talked of a new chapel ("my new chappell," Plumpton, #2) she told of the need for some basic books ("either salter or primmer') and then "neither gold nor siluer, but some other thing for said awter." The Stonors talked of chapel goods and heirlooms: #140, #227. Margaret's references to conversations with her sons in church may indicate that the gentry were not segregated in their seating, or that they really spoke before or after the service, or that Margaret lectured to them whenever she felt like doing so.

64. I, 355: John III to John II, "Syr Jamys is parson of Stokysby by J Bernays gyft," and then Paston adds, "I trowe he beryth hym the hyer." The Berney manor of Stokely was about six miles northwest of Great Yarmouth.

65. Daniel E.Thiery, "Plowshares and Swords: Clerical Involvement in Acts of Violence and Peacemaking in Late Medieval England, 1400–1536," *Albion* 36/2 (2004), pp. 201–22; pp. 212–13 on Gloys as a nasty character and on Margaret Paston's seemingly uncritical acceptance of his behavior. Henry S. Bennett, *The Pastons*, siding with John II and John III; Bennett's index reference to Gloys has a subheading, "overbearing way." Knowles says of him: "The priest is lost in the man of business" (p. 159), and Mertes, *the English Noble Household*, p. 46, on the "versatility" of household chaplains. It has been suggested that Gloys actually provoked that famous quarrel in the street: David Burnley, *Courtliness and Literature in Medieval England* (London: Longmans, 1998), pp. 213–14: Gloys "deliberately refused to acknowledge the offended men by removing his hat." This sounds like the opening scene of "Romeo and Juliet."

66. Davis (II, 919) considers the sermon to be Gloys's, though Blomefield attributed it to Friar Brackley; II, 919. The sermon emphasizes the need for "connyng, boldnesse, and langages" for those who would preach "the

wurd as the appostilles dede." Not very inspirational, it runs to 70 lines of spiritual commonplaces. On a sermon (II, 582) at St Paul's by "a lewd doctour of Ludgate at Pauls," as Brackley told John I. It was October 1459, the "lewd" man said that "no man schuld preyen for these lordys traytowrys," meaning the Yorkists.

67. He might have been speaking a foreign language when Roger Taverham told John I (II, 697) that he planned to turn his back on the world. "By the grace of God I shall go to Rome and in-to oder holy places to spende myn dayes of this present liff in the seruise of God." The most painful part of this decision ("grettest lamentacion") was that he would leave his friends: "I shall neuer see you no more, nor non of myn frendes."

68. The Stonors offer a few more of these "throw aways" of pious speech: Stonor, #100 ("or ellys I must be untrewe to God and to them that be dede"), or Stonor, #213 ("maister Betson at Ester was a twelmonthe was srevyn off hys goostly fadir, and that it was geven heme in penance"—for a rare reference to a sacrament).

69. Katherine French. *The Good Women of the Parish: Gender and Religion after the Black Death* (Philadelphia, PA: University of Pennsylvania Press, 2008), p. 37.

70. One of her complaints about John I was that he had, unbeknownst to her, taken possession of valuables left for safekeeping with the cathedral priory, whence John I "barre awey all, and kepyng it styll" (I, 32). For papers safely tucked away at Dale Abbey, Plumpton, #93. In a bill of complaints by John III against his uncle William II, it was charged that William "gate in-to his possession a chargere of siluer…and iij bollys of siluer that were in kepyng of Bachelere Waltere, a friere Carmelit of Norwich…which…the seid William yet with-holdith and kepith to his owne vse" (I, 387). Karen Stöber, *Late Medieval Monasteries and their Patrons: England and Wales, c. 1300–1540* (Woodbridge: Boydell, 2007), p. 23, and p. 180: "such ornamentes & juelles as ye have leffte here in thys howse for the honour of God," among the instances of using a regular house as a safe deposit box.

71. The list is small, the documents short. There were some gold chalices (I, 68), one with "calicem salutaris accipiam" engraved on it, and (I, 69) there was a pix and as osculatorium with an image of St James and a cup with an image of "Sancte Trini." The goods had been stored in John's coffer in the abbey (Norwich priory, or more probably Brohmolm).

72. The seven images listed are of John the Evangelist, John the Baptist, Denis, and James, along with two of Our Lady, and one of "owre sauyowre."

73. Jenny Stratford, *The Bedford Inventories: The Worldly Goods of John, Duke of Bedford, Regent of France (1389–1438)* (London: Society of Antiquaries, 1993); Bedford as a patron and collector, pp. 105–26, with a fragment of the True Cross and various relics listed in the inventories.

74. The catalogue is *Gothic Art for England, 1400–1547,* ed. Richard Marks and Paul Williamson (London: Victoria and Albert Museum, 2003).

75. The "not for the Pastons" items are numbers 179 and 185, respectively, in the Catalogue; the two more likely items 191 and 196; the explanation is by Marian Campbell.

76. Susan Foster, "Private Devotion," pp. 334–74; the Donne Triptych is item 213, the Bedford/Beauchamp Book of Hours, 223; the mould is 221, the window 217. To draw out the Don(ne)-Paston contrast, Ralph A. Griffiths, ed., *The Household Book (1510–51) of Sir Edward Don: An Anglo-Welsh Knight and His Circle,* Buckinghamshire Record Society 33 (Bedford: 2004). All the items displayed in the catalogue have been characterized as products of an "age of consumption."

77. On the wide interests of at least one particular lawyer, C. E. Moreton, "The 'Library' of a Late-Fifteenth-Century Lawyer," *The Library,* sixth series, 13 (1991), pp. 338–46. Of the 44 books listed, 10 were religious in nature: saints' lives, sermons and treatises, and Gregory's *Pastorale.*

78. We know the book was being circulated; it had gone from Anne to Sir John Parre, and "when he hathe doon wyth it he promysyd to delyuer it yow. I prey yow lete Portlond brynge the book hom wyth hym."

79. I, 238: the ownership is unclear: "it is the bible that the master hath."

80. Eamon Duffy, "Late Medieval Religion," in *Gothic Art for England,* p. 60.

81. Mary C. Erler, "English Vowed Women at the End of the Middle Ages," *Mediaeval Studies* 57 (1995), pp. 155–203.

4 Family Wills: Margaret Paston and the Rest

1. In proper usage of legal history, a last will governs the disposition of real property, a testament the disposition of personal goods. However, this distinction—first brought to my attention by Robin DuBoulay—has lost its edge as historians have turned so much attention to these documents and I use "will" to cover both wills and testaments.

2. John Bossy, *Christianity in the West, 1400–1700* (Oxford: Oxford University Press, 1985), pp. 170–71.

3. On the funeral procession and burial of Eleanor of Castile, John Carmi Parsons, *Eleanor of Castile: Queen and Society in Thirteenth-Century England* (New York: St Martin's Press, 1995), pp. 59–60; Elizabeth Hallum, "Introduction: The Eleanor Crosses and Royal Burial Custom," in *Eleanor of Castile, 1290–1990,* ed., David Parsons (Stamford: Paul Watkins, 1991), pp. 9–21. York and Suffolk received special treatment because "their weight had to be reduced in order that they might be taken home": James H. Wylie, *The Reign of Henry the Fifth* (Cambridge: Cambridge University Press, 1919), II, pp. 217–18. Wylie refuted suggestions that the bodies had been pickled or embalmed. For a more elaborate ceremony that was virtually contemporary with Margaret's burial, Christopher Given-Wilson, "The Exequies of Edward IV and the Royal Funeral Ceremony in Late Medieval England," *English Historical Review* 124 (2009), pp. 257–82.

4. Hannes Kleineke, "The Reburial Expenses of Sir Thomas Arundell," *The Ricardian* 11 (1998), pp. 288–96, and thanks to Caroline Barron for this reference. Katherine French, *The Good Women of the Parish,* p. 64, quoting Vanessa Harding: "a funeral was 'ane vent scripted by its central participant, or by those to whom he or she had delegated that power'." This is true in bold letters for the burial of John Paston I, as we see below, that being the only Paston burial for which we have the relevant details.

5. Sidney Painter, *William Marshal, Knight-Errant, Baron, and Regent of England* (Baltimore: Johns Hopkins University Press, 1933; reprinted, Toronto: University of Toronto Press for the Medieval Academy, 1982), pp. 275–89. Painter follows the *Histoire de Guillaume le Maréchal* on the Marshal's last days.

6. For the "good death," Philippe Ariès, *The Hour of Our Death,* trans. Helen Weaver (New York: Alfred Knopf, 1981); Duffy, *Stripping of the Altars,* chapter 9, talking about "Last Things."

7. Though Henry II was not unattended, no sons were with him. When he learned that John had deserted him, "the will to live departed": W. L. Warren, *Henry II* (Berkeley and Los Angeles, CA: University of California Press, 1973), p. 626. Warren sets the scene in terms of "an ailing lion savaged by jackals."

8. Richmond, *Endings,* pp. 78; 59–87 for a general treatment of John II, in the context of "Gentility without Means."

9. Rowena E. Archer, "Alice Chaucer, Duchess of Suffolk," in the *ODNB.*

10. For Isabel of Warwick, F. J. Furnivall, ed., *The Fifty Earliest English Wills,* EETS, o.s. 78 (1882; reprinted, 1964), pp. 116–19. Was it modesty that kept so many others from following Isabel's lead: "my Image to be made all naked, and no thing on my hede but myn here cast bakwardys, and of the gretnes and of the fascyon lyke the mesure that Thomas Porchalyn hath yn a lyst." With a focus on Alice Chaucer, Pamela King, " 'My Image to be made all Naked': Cadaver Tombs and the Commemoration of Women in Fifteenth-Century England," in *Tant D'Emprises,* pp. 294–314.

11. Though for the late medieval aristocracy the Grey Friars house in London was a popular last resting place: Charles L. Kingsford, *The Grey Friars of London: Their History* (London: British Society for Franciscan Studies 6, 1915), pp. 134–44.

12. On wills: Eber Carle Perrow, "The Last Will and Testament as a Form of Literature," *Transactions of the Wisconsin Academy of Sciences, Arts, and Letters* xvii, part 1, no. 1 (1911), pp. 682–750; Caroline A. J. Skeel, "Medieval Wills," *History* 10 (1926), pp. 300–10.

13. Gail McMurray Gibson, *The Theater of Devotion,* especially chapter 4 (pp. 67–108). The burial of John Baret of Bury in 1487 is termed "funeral theater."

14. Furnivall, *Fifty Earliest English Wills,* p. 31, from the will of John Chelmsywyk of Shropshire, 1418.

15. Karen Stöber, *Late Medieval Monasteries.*

16. For Juliet's fears about awakening amidst old family bones: "Romeo and Juliet," IV, iii, 30–54. I used this reference in a talk at the 2006 Leeds Medieval Congress; I thank Roisin Cossar and Shona Kelly Wray for inviting me to participate in a session on family wills.

17. Nigel Saul, *Death, Art, and Memory in Medieval England;* Michael Hicks on the Hungerford family: specific articles cited above. Joel T. Rosenthal, *Patriarchy and Families of Privilege in Fifteenth-Century England* (Philadelphia, PA: University of Pennsylvania Press, 1991), pp. 77–91 for the Scropes of Bolton. Also, David Lepine, "The Courtenays and Exeter Cathedral in the Later Middle Ages," *Proceedings of the Devonshire Association* 124 (1992), pp. 41–58; Jennifer C. Ward, "Fashions in Monastic Endowment: The Foundations of the Clare Family," *Journal of Ecclesiastical History* 32 (1981), pp. 427–51. For a regional approach, Peter Northeast, "Suffolk Churches in the Later Middle Ages: The Evidence of Wills," in *East Anglia's History: Studies in Honour of Norman Scarfe,* ed. Christopher Harper-Bill, Carole Rawcliffe, and Richard Wilson (Norwich: Boydell for the University of East Anglia, 2002), pp. 93–106; C. E. Moreton, "A Social Gulf? The Upper and Lesser Gentry of Later Medieval England," *Journal of Medieval History* 17 (1991), pp. 255–62. On testators' instructions, M. G. A. Vale, "Piety, Charity, and Literacy" (York: Borthwick Institute of Historical Research, 19), pp. 9–13; John Denton, "Image, Identity, and Gentility: The Woodford Experience," in *The Fifteenth Century: V. Of Mice and Men,* ed. Linda Clark (Woodbridge: Boydell, 2005), pp. 1–17.

18. Robert Kinsey, "Hedging your Bets: The Thorpe Family Chantries and the Locations of Remembrance in 14th Century England," as read at the 2008 Harlaxton Conference.

19. Skeel, "Medieval Wills," p. 10: "On the whole it is the best side of human nature that comes out in medieval wills." Against this sanguine view, H. R. Trevor-Roper, "Why must the tomb be prefabricated, the masses prepaid? It is because, in spite of all this lip-service to the family, no one really trusted anyone else, not even his sons, once his power over them was gone. In reality the family was not cultivated as such: it was a necessary alliance from which every man hoped individually to profit," in his "Up and Down in the Country: The Paston Letters," in *Historical Essays* (New York: Harper, 1961), p. 31. John III was excoriated by the prior of Bromholm in 1476 because of his dilatory approach regarding his father's tomb (I, 371): "the ille speche whyche is in the contré now of new that the tombe is not mad."

20. Elizabeth did express family concerns: prayers for "my said housbands soul and myne, our fadres and modres soules, and, for all Cristen soules."

21. Margery was the daughter of Thomas Monceaux and widow of William Lomnor and Thomas Briggs before she married into the Paston family (I, lxii).

22. This will (II, 929) is from the Norfolk Record Office Consistory Court of Norwich, Reg ix, 128a–129b.

23. II, 930: Agnes took steps to see that these prayers would be said: "if the said Sir Robert do dye within the said yeres that than myn exectuours doo fynd som other prest for the parfourmaunce of the same." The parson of Braysted [Brasted, Kent] was to be her overseer, "in trust for the weale of my soule."

24. A. B. Emden, *A Biographical Register of the University of Cambridge to A. D. 1500* (Cambridge: Cambridge University Press, 1963). William II left without taking a degree. In his will of 1496 he certainly aimed high, naming the Cardinal, the king's mother, Lord Daubney, and his own nephew Sir Edward Poynings, as executors. Davis notes that this group declined to act (I, lvii); he does not indicate who eventually undertook the obligation.

25. Margaret had been seriously ill before her final decline; John Whetley to John II on 20 May 1478: "My meastres your moder hath ben gretly diseased, and so seke that she wened to haue dyed and hath made her wyll" (II, 782). For a widow who sank into depression, Kay Lacey, "Margaret Croke (d. 1490)." In *Medieval London Widows, 1300–1500*, ed. Caroline M. Barron and Anne F. Sutton (London: Hambledon Press, 1994), pp. 143–64: Margaret had been widowed for eight months when Thomas Betson said of her, "She is a ffyn mery woman, but ye shall kow it not yit ffynd it, nor noe of yours by that I se in her."

26. Roger Virgoe, *Private Life,* p. 267, points out that this was "the last major epidemic of bubonic plague that was to hit England during the 15th century," although it is not certain that Agnes died of the plague, she already being a very old lady. Moreover, Walter had fallen ill by early July and only died on 18 or 19 August, this being a long interval of survival for a plague victim.

27. One of Margery and Richard Calle's grandchildren may have become a friar: Richmond, *Endings,* p. 122 (while Calle himself lived to at least 1496). In a will of 1510 a bequest of money and books went to a friar William Calle, as in notes made by Roger Virgoe from PRO documents.

28. Margaret to John I, perhaps in February 1454: "I pray yow if ye haue an othere sone that ye woll lete it be named Herry in remembrans of your brother Herry" (I, 151). Though Davis's dating of this letter is uncertain, he thinks that Walter was born 1455–57 and William III around 1459—with no "Herry" on the scene. Also on infant mortality: John III and Margery Brewes had a son Christopher born in 1478 and his absence from Margaret's will argues for his early death. Also, (I, 397) for Anne Yelverton's infant who died at birth. There is a brass of Anna, daughter of Sir John (III), at Oxnead, ca. 1490: Jonathan Finch, *Church Monuments in Norfolk before 1850: The Archaeology of Commemoration*, B.A.R., British Series, 317 (2000), p. 61 (and p. 32, for a sixteenth-century alabaster monument to Clement Paston at Oxnead).

29. On their dubious origins, Caroline M. Barron, "Who Were the Pastons?" *Journal of the Society of Archivists* 4 (1972), pp. 530–35. Gairdner,

II, pp. 283–5: "ancetors have been bondmen to the ancetors of the said John Pastson sithen the time that no minde is to the contrary…how their ancetors had licence to have a chaplen." Having a private or family chapel is offered as a sign of status and perhaps even of gentility.

30. Stöber, *Late Medieval Monasteries,* pp. 171–82 for the clustering of Howard burials in only a few sites, though they were patrons of 19 houses and accordingly had a very wide range of choices.

31. The tomb at the east end of the church at Paston is reputedly that of John I, moved from Bromholm at the time of the dissolution. But even if this is the case it was not a burial at Paston. Pevsner's laconic "this monument may well be what is left of John Paston's [monument]," in his *North-east Norfolk and Norwich,* p. 298. Herbert Loraine, author of the current guidebook to the church of St Margaret at Paston, is extremely circumspect about certainty regarding the monuments. Erasmus Paston (d. 1538) and his wife Mary, parents of three sons and nine daughters, were buried in the parish church at Paston: *NA* 11 (1892), p. 95. Helen Jewell, *Women in Medieval England,* p. 167: The vicar of Paston celebrated mass every Friday for the souls of William and Agnes (though neither was buried at Paston).

32. On the Carmelites, David Knowles, *The Religious Orders in England: The End of the Middle Ages* (Cambridge: Cambridge University Press, 1955), pp. 144–48, 173. For their Norwich house, *VCH Norfolk* II, pp. 431–2: William Worcester, *Itinerary,* ed. John Harvey (Oxford: Oxford University Press, 1969), pp. 235–37. Some Calthorpes were buried there, as was an Edmund Berry and his wife in the 1430s. John Weever, *Ancient Funeral Monuments* (London, 1764) and Blomefield, IV, 414. Tanner says in *The Church in Medieval Norwich,* pp. 119–25 that the Carmelites held their own for bequests and endowed prayers but did not fare so well in attracting the burials of the wealthy and powerful.

33. Judith Middleton-Stewart, *Inward Purity and Outward Splendour: Death and Remembrance in the Deanery of Dunwich, Suffolk, 1370–1540* (Norwich: Boydell, 2001); Peter Northeast, ed., *Wills of the Archdeaconry of Sudbury, 1439–1474: I. Wills from the Register "Balldwyne," part 1, 1439–1461,* Suffolk Records Society 44 (2001).

34. Clement's wife had been a Bacton, and Bacton was the village next to Paston, indicating how, at the start, local families and networks had sufficed for Paston ambitions.

35. Edgar C. Robbins, *William Paston, Justice: Founder of the Paston Family, 1378–1444* (Norwich: Jarrod & Sons, 1932).

36. Paul Binski, *Medieval Death: Ritual and Remembrance* (Ithaca, NY: Cornell University Press, 1996), p. 74.

37. Were more prayers when said by fewer people more efficacious than fewer prayers said by many? William I opened the floodgates, stipulating that the prayers were for "…et omnium quorum debitores sumus, etomnium per nos iniuriam paciencium, et eorum omnium pro quibus Deo est deprecandum, et omnium fidelium defunctorum…"

38. Davis, I, 32, for Agnes's stating that the revenue from Swainsthorpe was dedicated for this purpose; also, Blomefield, IV, 46, on William's estate. Helen Jewell, *Women in Medieval England,* p. 167: some ties were maintained, as the Vicar of Paston celebrated mass every Friday for the souls of William I and Agnes.

39. Francis Woodman, pp. 158–61, in Ian Atherton, *Norwich Cathedral,* in the chapter on "The Gothic Campaigns."

40. Though Bromholm was a famous pilgrim site because of the Holy Rood, it was not a particularly large or rich house. The prior of Bromholm held the living of Paston until the dissolution. There were 25 monks in 1298, 19 in 1349–50, 18 in 1390, and (only) 10 in 1466, so William's bequest may have been for each resident monk: *VCH Norfolk* II, pp. 359–64. On the house as a pilgrim site because of its relic: Francis Wormald, "The Rood of Bromholm," *Journal of the Warburg Institute* 1 (1937), pp. 31–45.

41. William displays a unique interest in liturgical details. His son Clement, at age 18, was to take charge of his alms-giving: "distributat manu propria in elemosinis juxta discrecionem suam inter magis paupers et debiles creatura, in honore quinque principalium vulnerum et passionis Domini Nostri Jesu Christi, et quinque gaudiorum Beate Marie Virginis et Matris eius." Gairdner, I, 52, for an agreement for prayers for the souls of William and Agnes each Friday, and for Clement on 17 June, St Botolph's Day.

42. Gairdner, II, 286: "every day iiij d. to sing and pray for his soule and myn, and al the sowles that he and I have made any goode of or be beholdyn to pray for."

43. Agnes's version does have John I as present at the end. Whether we go with the mother's memory over that of the daughter, this is an interesting discrepancy. Not having been present at the end might make John less culpable in terms of how he treated his brothers but more so in terms of not being a responsible son.

44. William II was at pains to emphasize what a light load the incumbent would have to carry: "It is butt an esy cure to kepe, for ther ar natt past xxti persons to be yerly howselyd" (I, 99).

45. In the bill of complaint that John III drew up against his uncle William II (1489) he referred to items in the latter's possession but that should have gone to the Norwich Carmelites: "to th'entent that a certeyn coost shuld have ben doon vpon the liberarye…for the sowlis of William Paston, justice, and Angnes, his wiff, which chargere and bollys the said Willaim yet with-holdith and kepith to his owne use" (I, 387).

46. Frances and Joseph Gies, *A Medieval Family: The Pastons of Fifteenth-Century England* (New York: Harper Collins, 1998), p. 317.

47. For the London Carmelites, C. M. Barron and Matthew Davies, ed., *The Religious Houses of London and Middlesex* (London: VCH and the Centre for Metropolitan History, 2007), pp. 128–32 in this newly edited version of the old *VCH, London.* The house was founded in the 1240s and in 1334 it peaked at 80 friars, making it the largest Carmelite house in Britain. At the end it had a prior and 12 friars.

48. The manuscript of John II's will, dating from 1477, is very defective. He seems to be leaving bequests to "myn vncle Edward Maudeley" and "my cousin syr William Calthorpe," figures of importance in the Paston world but not otherwise mentioned in their wills.

49. Thomas Lyndes was recommended by Margaret and John II when the living at Mautby had fallen vacant. John Daubney was well within the family's circle and ultimately a casualty of their schemes, being fatally wounded in the siege of Caister. Plate xxii in vol. II of Davis's edition shows a letter in Daubney's hand (II, 748).

50. We might see these concerns as a belated assertion of patriarchy. The will's invocation offers a roll call of saints not otherwise matched in the family: "Marye, Seint John Baptist, Seint Gorge, Seint Cristofure, and seint Barbara." Neither St Barbara nor St Christopher had feasts noted in any of Margaret's letters.

51. Entry into the church is now open on a limited basis, and a visit was made in July 2007. The church is now being converted into a stained glass museum.

52. On her favorite: "I trust to haue more joye of hym than I haue of them that bene owlder" (I, 22); this was in 1473, about when Walter would have been turning toward Oxford.

53. Walter tells one of his brothers, "I was maad baschylere … on Fryday … and I mad my fest on the Munday after" (I, 404).

54. I, 405. Among the bequests are lots of "togas," one with "manicis de mynkys" and one with "menyver." Walter must have been a style setter among his circle of young clerics, though he makes no mention of books or ecclesiastical utensils or paraphernalia.

55. The proceeding are summarized, Bennett, *The Pastons and Their England,* pp. 197–98. On John's missing will, I, 408: William III to Edmund II, telling how their father's will had been copied from the ecclesiastical register so John III could consult it in carrying out its provisions.

56. The reluctance of John I's sons to build his tomb is a familiar story (and not told here). Castor, *Blood and Roses,* pp. 250–51 and 261.

57. Blomefield, VI, 483–85. For other glimpses of John I's activity along these lines: James Gairdner, I, 433–34, for a list of John I's expenses in 36–37; Henry VI, with 10s to glaze the chapel at Mautby and a bequest to the poor of Norwich in the form of 7s for "circa reparationem murorum civitatis" to the tune of 7s.

58. David Knowles estimates a total cost of about £190: "Religion of the Pastons," p. 148: "A stupendous amount when the value of money at the time is considered." Philip Morgan thinks the costs ran about 20 percent above Knowles' estimate: "Of Worms and War, 1380–1558," in *Death in England,* ed. Peter C. Jupp and Clare Gittings (Manchester: Manchester University Press, 2000), p. 139. Thomas Stonor was buried, with a suitable feast, procession, etc., for £74 2s 5d in 1474 (Stonor, #138). A chief baron of the exchequer was buried in 1479 in a funeral that cost £13

17s 8d: Francis Steer, "A Medieval Household: The Urswick Inventory," *Essex Review* 63 (1954), pp. 4–20.

59. For the reburial of the patriarch of the House of York, Anne Sutton and Livia Visser-Fuchs with Peter Hammond, *The Reburial of Richard Duke of York* (London: Richard III Society, 1996), p. 6 for a diagram of the positioning of groups of mourners, p. 8 for the route followed by the cortège, and Plate I for a Flemish painting of the 1460s depicting a royal funeral procession.

60. For maps that show the villages at which a royal cortege came to rest, Anne Sutton and Livia Visser-Fuchs, with R. A. Griffiths, ed., *The Royal Funerals of the House of York at Windsor* (London: Richard III Society, 2005), p. 23 for the route of Edward IV's cortege, p. 59 for that of Princess Mary and Queen Elizabeth Woodville. Kleineke, "Reburial Expenses" also has a route map for the long procession.

61. Though we know nothing of the subsequent fate of Margery Paston Calle, Richard remained a trusted employee. It seem unlikely that Margery was reduced to the level of her brother's worries when he said that now Calle "shold neuer haue my good wyll for to make my sustyr to sell kandyll and mustard in Framlyngham" (I, 332). For an ironic note, in the inventory of what are probably John II's goods (I, 259) are "a peyre quernes to grynd wyth mustard."

62. *ODNB*, entry for "The Paston Family." In an extreme example of distancing one London widow reverted to the use of her maiden name after his husband's death: Robert A. Wood, "Poor Widows, c. 1393–1415," in *Medieval London Widows,* ed. Caroline M. Barron, pp. 55–67. The widow who followed this line of behavior did so after burying her second husband (p. 59).

63. Rosenthal, *Telling Tales,* pp. 144–47.

64. On the link between the de la Poles of East Anglia and duchess Alice at Ewelme in Oxfordshire, John A. Goodall, "The Architecture of Ancestry at the Collegiate Church of St. Andrews, Wingfield, Suffolk," in *Family and Dynasty in Late Medieval England: Proceedings of the 1997 Harlaxton Conference,* Harlaxton Medieval Studies ix, ed. Richard Eales and Shaun Tyas (Donington: Shaun Tyas, 2003), pp. 157–71. On the idea of the monuments at Wingfield as models for de la Pole projects at Ewelme, King, "'My Image to be Made All Naked'."

65. Margaret makes references to the Duchess who is usually on the other side in the partisan struggles of fifteenth-century East Anglia, I, 188, I, 196, etc. In 1462 she told John I that the Duchess was unpopular (I, 168), while in 1469 she thought the Duchess, now at Ewelme, might intervene on behalf of the Pastons. Chaucer-Paston links antedated Margaret's arrival, for in 1427 William Paston had bought Gresham from Thomas Chaucer, Alice's father: Mary-Jo Arn, "Thomas Chaucer and William Paston Take Care of Business: HLS Deed 349," *Studies in the Age of Chaucer* 24 (2002), pp. 237–67.

66. Pevsner says "it is a pity the aisle hasn't survived; for it was the monument commanded by Margaret Paston, daughter of John Mautby, widow of John Paston... The specification for the monument exists, but not alas the monument," *North-east Norfolk,* p. 155.

67. On the escutcheons chosen by Alice Chaucer for her tomb, G. Lamburn, "The Arms in the Chaucer Tomb at Ewelme," *Oxoniensia* 5 (1940), pp. 78–93. For the Countess of Warwick's escutcheons, *Fifty Earliest English Wills,* pp. 116–17; the Black Prince left comparable instructions: Teresa G. Frisch, *Gothic Art, 1140–c. 1450: Sources and Documents* (New York: Prentice Hall, 1971; reprinted, Toronto: University of Toronto Press and the Medieval Academy, 1987), pp. 114–15. For an elaborate gloss of virtually every provision in Margaret's will: Dawson Turner, "The Will of Margaret Paston," *NA* 3 (1852), pp. 157–72. Her genealogy, based on Harleian mss 1552, f. 173 (p. 159), explains her choice of the escutcheons; her paternal grandmother was a daughter of Richard Beauchamp of Bletsoe—and thus a legitimate if thin claim to aristocratic ancestry.

68. In her invocation Margaret commends her soul to God Almighty, Our Lady "his blessed moder," to St Michael and St John the Baptist, and to "alle seintes." Gairdner (Introductory volume, p. cccliii) was most impressed by Margaret's piety and he spoke of "how strongly she felt the claims of the poor, the sick, and the needy, as well as those of hospitals, friars, anchorites, and parish churches."

69. I read this bequest to mean the transmission of books already in Margaret's ownership. Caroline Barron reads it to mean that she left money for their purchase, so they could be given to the church. Prof. Barron is probably correct. On such bequests, Fiona Kisby, "Books in London Parish Churches before 1670: Some Preliminary Observations," in *The Church and Learning in Late Medieval Society,* ed. Caroline M. Barron and Jenny Stratford, Harlaxton Medieval Studies XI (Donington: Shaun Tyas, 2002), pp. 305–26; Stacey Gee, "Parochial Libraries in Pre-Reformation England," in *Learning and Literacy in Medieval England and Abroad,* ed. Sarah Rees-Jones (Turnhout: Brepols, 2003), pp. 199–222.

70. For Mautby parish church in the fourteenth century, Aelred Watkin, *Archdeaconry of Norfolk: Inventory of Church Goods 1368, temp. Edward III,* Norfolk Record Society xix, parts 1 and 2 (1947), p. 45: the church had a martyrology, two antiphonals (one with a psalter), two missals, and six pairs of vestments. For other churches named by Margaret, Redham, p. 40, Sparham, p. 71, and St Michael Coslany, pp. 5–6.

71. The manors-villages or the churches at Reedham, Matelask, Bessingham, and Freton (Fritton) are almost unmentioned in the Letters; small cash cows at best, well away from the centers of Paston activity and conflict. By way of contrast John's correspondence with Margaret showed his interest in keeping up the Mautby property, as discussed above. Turner, "The Will of Margaret Paston," pp. 163–65, explaining the basis of her links with each village.

72. The inquisition post mortem taken on John I (II, 900) spells out the property Margaret brought upon her marriage. Gairdner, III, 417 and Blomefield, VI, 482–83, on the Mautby dowry settlement.

73. Chaucer-Paston business at Gresham is mentioned in Martin M. Crow and Clair C. Olson, eds., *Chaucer Life-Records* (Austin, TX and London: University of Texas Press, 1966), p. 543.

74. Richmond, *Endings,* pp. 123–25, for a very critical assessment of Margaret's charity as illustrated in her will, one he characterizes "austere,… [with] no sense of a wider religious world." I strongly disagree; though each sum was small, as was the custom, there are a huge number of both institutional and individual recipients of her bequests.

75. Margaret's relations with the prior of Norwich were such that she and Agnes could run to him in midday for his support in the great slanging match between Gloys and Wymondham in 1448 (I, 129). The family felt free to go directly to the bishop (Walter Lyhart in 1469) when they sought to have him dissolve the union between Margery Paston and Richard Calle (I, 203).

76. For the friars of Yarmouth, *VCH Norfolk* II, pp. 435–37. All the friaries in the town, including that of the Austins across the water in Little Yarmouth, remained popular to the end as judged by the flow of testamentary benefactions. An Elizabeth de Clere of Ormesby was buried there in 1492, and prayers were said there for a John Fastolf, doctor of divinity and a suggestive name.

77. On Norwich's rich ration of anchorites, presumably of both sexes, Anne Warren, *Anchorites and their Patrons in Medieval England* (Berkeley, CA: University of California Press, 1985) and Tanner, *The Church in Late Medieval Norwich,* pp. 198–204: 18 percent of the lay wills from Norwich named at least one anchorite or hermit. Rotha M. Clay, *The Hermits and Anchorites of England* (London: Methuen, 1914): the hermit at the Magdelan gate presided over the lepers who also assembled there. Turner, "The Will of Margaret Paston," p. 168: one of the anchoresses whom Margaret remembered was Catherine Mann, the recipient of 20s per annum for life from the city. Carol Hill, "Julian and Her Sisters: Female Piety in Late Medieval Norwich," in *The Fifteenth Century VI,* ed., Linda Clark (Woodbridge: Boydell, 2006), pp. 165–87.

78. *VCH Norfolk* II, pp. 442–50 for the hospitals of Norwich; Carole Rawcliffe, *The Hospitals of Medieval Norwich* (Norwich: University of East Anglia, 1995) and Rawcliffe, *Medicine for the Soul: The Life, Death, and Resurrection of an English Medieval Hospital* (Stroud: Sutton, 1999). For Margaret's quarrel with Selot, master of the hospital, Rawcliffe, *The Hospitals,* p. 104; in a letter of September 1465 (I, 192): "the demenyng and parcialté of Master John Salatt," as Margaret reports to John I in September 1465.

79. *VCH Norfolk* II, p. 449 on the lazar houses at the five gates. The largest was at the St Mary Magdelan gate, with others by the Austin's gate, Westwick, Needham, by Fybridge on Magdelan gate, and Newport at

St Giles Gate. For Chapel in the Fields, Carole Rawcliffe and Richard Wilson, *Medieval Norwich,* pp. 115–18: p. 118, "Until its dissolution in January, 1544, the college expressed the religious spirit of the city far more than did the cathedral." It was from the Chapel that John I and Margaret bought the living of St Peter Hungate and turned it into "their church."

80. On the popularity of women's religious institutions: Marilyn Oliva, *The Convent and the Community in Late Medieval England: Female Monasteries in the Diocese of Norwich, 1350–1540* (Woodbridge: Boydell, 1998).

81. On bequests for church bells: Judith Middleton-Steward, "Time and the Testator, 1370–1540," in *The Use and Abuse of Time in Christian History,* ed. Robert N. Swanton, *Studies in Church History* 37 (2002), pp. 133–44; R. Hindry Mason, *The History of Norfolk* (London: Wertheimer, Lea, & Co., 1894), pp. 589–602 on the bells of Norfolk churches; A. G. G. Thurlow, "Church Bells of Norwich," *NA* 28 (1945), pp. 241–84.

82. Maureen Jurkowski, ed., *Income Tax Assessments of Norwich, 1472 and 1498,* Norfolk Record Society 71 (2007); the always-poor parish of St Peter Hungate in 1472 was evaluated at 25s 8½d (of which Margaret Paston was assessed at 4s on a holding of 40s). For comparison, the large and wealthy (and nearby) parish of St Peter Mancroft was assessed at £7 2s 8d.

83. St Peter Hungate just staggered along over the centuries. By 1904 (and probably well before) it was "in such a condition that Divine Service could no longer be celebrated there" and it was transferred to the city of Norwich as a museum of architectural and ecclesiastical remnants: *Guide to the St Peter Hungate Museum* (Norwich: Norwich Museum Commission, 1955) and Geoffrey Graham and Rachel M. R. Young, *The Church of St Peter Hungate* (Norwich: Norwich Museum Commission, 1965). In the valor of 1535 it was the fourth poorest of the city's churches; Turner, "The Will of Margaret Paston," p. 167, on Margaret's tie to the church.

84. Margaret always had trouble letting go. While other children in the family came of age at 18 (as William I had stipulated for Clement in 1444) or at 21, those of Margery and Richard Calle only received their bequests at age 24. Margaret's executors are a puzzle. She named John III, and we have his working notes on the margins of her will indicating the payments made in fulfillment of her wishes (I, 230). His three coexecutors are mysterious figures. There is no other mention of Thomas Drentall or Walter Lymyngton in the letters, and but one to Simon Gerard, that coming in a letter of about 1500 from John III to Richard Croft and indicating that Gerard must have been a lawyer and a local man of affairs. John III says, "I prey yow take the warrant to Symond Gerrard and prey hym in my name to send for the bayly of the hundred and to casue hym to geve warnyng to theym that be empanellid to kepe ther day at Thettford."

85. Among the ranks and categories of the unmentioned, Colin Richmond notes the absence of fraternities or guilds in any of the Paston wills (though Agnes was a lay sister of the Carmelites); Richmond, *Endings,*

pp. 124–5. Also, though Margaret focuses on Mautby parish church in much detail, she makes no mention of ancestors actually buried there.

86. Katherine French, *The Good Women,* p. 37, on "the material culture of piety," and—following Martha Howell's judgment (with apologies to Kit French for lifting from her scholarly digging)—on the way women thought of the property they transmitted in their wills more as cultural and social capital than as economic capital: p. 42, and p. 46, for "gifts that adorn the liturgy."

87. Caroline M. Barron, "Johanna Hill (d. 1441) and Johanna Sturdy (d. c. 1460), Bell-Founders," in *Medieval London Widows, 1300–1500,* ed. Caroline M. Barron and Anne F. Sutton (London: Hambledon Press, 1994), pp. 99–112: the quote is on p. 108.

88. Kay Lacey, "Margaret Croke (d. 1491)," in *Medieval London Widows,* pp. 143, 157–58.

5   What Did Margaret See?

1. For the later history of the family, George Edward Cokayne ("G.E.C."), ed., *The Complete Peerage,* XII, part ii (under Yarmouth) (12 vols. in 13, London: St Catherine's Press, 1910–1959): Robert Paston, son and heir of Sir William of Oxnead and first baronet Paston, succeeded his father as second baronet in 1641 and was created Viscount Yarmouth in 1673 and Earl of Yarmouth in 1679. He was followed by his son and heir, William (1654–1732). The second earl survived his loyalty to James II, having been treasurer of that king's household, and he eventually became (in 1719) vice admiral of Norfolk. Like his father he was a fellow of the Royal Society, and in the footsteps of his distant ancestor John I he too spent time in prison (in his case, it was in the Tower in 1690 and 1691, facing charges of high treason). His management of his affairs and fortune was so bad that by the end it was just a tale of "vast debts…[and he] cannot be perswaded to take any method of putting his affairs into a better posture," as a contemporary summed it up. His son Charles had predeceased him and had died (in 1718) without male heirs. R. W. Ketton-Cremer has a chapter on "The End of the Pastons" in his *Norfolk Portraits* (Norwich: Faber & Faber, 1944).

2. The letters directly relating to the Pastons (rather than to Fastolf) are now collected in the first part of Beadle and Richmond, *Part III,* including letters that wound up in such places as The Morgan Library in New York and the Houghton Library of Harvard. On the letters, Davis, I, xxiv–xxxv; David A. Stoker, "'Innumerable Letters of Good Consequence in History': The Discovery and First Publication of the Paston Letters," *The Library,* sixth series, 17 (1995), pp. 107–55.

3. John III bought "Paston house" in St Etheldred parish from William Yelverton in 1474, and in 1487 he moved to The Music House in King Street or perhaps to the Elm Hill home that burned in 1507. The site of

the Music House was occupied by the Strangers Club at one time; Ernest A Kent, "Isaac's House or the Music House," *NA* 29 (1945), pp. 31–38; K. N. Marshall, *The Pastons, 1378–1732* (Norwich: Jarold, 1957); R. W. Ketton-Cremer, *Catalogue of a Loan Exhibition: The Pastons, May–August 1953* (Norwich: Norwich Castle Museum, 1953), Introduction. In 1599 Erasmus Paston moved the family from Caister to Oxnead and Caister had to be sold in 1659 to pay a debt of £6500 that Sir William Paston owed to William Crowe, a London moneylender: Colin Tooke, *Caister: 2000 Years of a Village* (Caister, 2000). When Sir Edward Coke married Lady Paston he bought what had been one of the Paston houses in Hungate, Norwich: Kent, p. 36.

4. Entries in Emden's biographical dictionaries of Oxford and Cambridge have been mentioned above. Because they sat in Parliament, there are entries for John I, John II, and William II in Josiah C. Wedgwood, *History of Parliament: II, Biographies,* pp. 665–67.

5. On the guild of St George: Ken Farnhill, *Guilds and the Parish Community in Late Medieval East Anglia, c. 1470–1550* (Woodbridge: York Medieval Press, 2001); Ben R. McRee, "After 1452: The Evolution of the Gild of St George in the Wake of Yelverton's Mediation," *NA* 45/1 (2006), pp. 26–40; Mary Grace, ed., *Records of the Gild of St George in Norwich, 1389–1547: A Transcript with an Introduction,* Norfolk Record Society 9 (1937). Grace alludes to Paston membership in the guild but offers no documentation in support of this statement.

6. Anthony Goodman, *Margery Kempe and her World* (London: Longman, 2002) pursues a similar line of thinking; what did Margery Kempe see when entering churches and other sites still standing?

7. Ffiona Swabey, *Medieval Gentlewoman,* pp. 97–132, for table attendance at meals. Marıan Dale and V. Redstone, *Household Book of Alice de Bryene* (Suffolk: Suffolk Institute of Archaeology and Natural History, 1931); Woolgar, *The Great Household,* pp. 87–89.

8. Looking at Margaret's letters that indicate where she was when she wrote: 25 were penned at Norwich, 4 at Caister, 2 at Oxnead, 4 at Hellesdon, and 1 each at Geldiston, Thetford, and Sustead. Her first dated letter from Mautby was written on 28 January 1475, and from then on all seven dated letters emanated from her residence there.

9. Richard Marks and Paul Williamson, ed., *Gothic Art for England, 1400–1547* (London: Victoria and Albert Museum, 2003). This being the catalogue of a major exhibition; particularly relevant are chapters by Geoff Egan, Marian Campbell, Susan Foster, Paul Williamson, and Paul Binski. For items likely to have been found in a household like that of the Pastons, Peter Lasko and N. J. Morgan, *Medieval Art in East Anglia, 1300–1520* (Norwich: Jarold, 1973); the catalogue of a 1973 exhibition at Norwich Castle Museum.

10. Just for comparison, we can look at the will of a northern widow, Elizabeth Sywardby (d. 1468). Her books include a missal valued at £4, a psalter, an English version of St Brigitte's revelations (valued at 46s 8d),

a life of Christ "in lingua maternal," a mystery of the passion of Our Lord in English, a Life of Christ, and various vestments, images, and lesser items: James Raine, ed., *Testamenta Eboracensia iv,* Surtees Society 53 (1869), pp. 161–68.

11. We know of 43 depictions of St Christopher in Norfolk churches, out of 186 for all of England. Ernest W. Tristram. *English Wall Painting of the Fourteenth Century* (London: Routledge & Kegan Paul, 1955), pp. 62–63 and 233–34 for Paston, p. 174 for Fritton; John Salmon, "St Christopher in English Medieval Art and Life," *JBAA* n.s. 41 (1936), pp. 76–115, noting that Christopher's popularity as a subject of wall painting did not translate into many church dedications; N. H. Brindley, "Notes on the Mural Painting of St Christopher in English Churches," *Antiquaries Journal* 4 (1924), pp. 227–41.

12. Monica Bardswell, "Recent Discoveries at Paston," *NA* 22 (1926), pp. 190–93; the Christopher figure is 12 feet in height, and there also is a badly faded three living-three dead, plus what might have been a last judgment: E. Carleton Williams, "Mural Painting of the 3 Living and 3 Dead," *JBAA,* third series, 7 (1942), pp. 31–39, with about 30 English examples. *VCH Norfolk* II, pp. 529–53 for a general survey of religious painting, pp. 530–35 for the cathedral, pp. 539–40 on St Michael at Plea in Norwich.

13. On the destruction of the Lady Chapel, Francis Woodman, in Ian Atherton, ed., *Norwich Cathedral,* pp. 158–61; the chapel's outline can be detected in the grass; it measures 36 feet by 72 feet. On the fate of the Norman Tower, the clocher, and the bells, Paul Catermole, in *Norwich Cathedral,* pp. 502–3; an ironic twist is that the lead from the bells was bought for £200 by Clement Paston of Oxnead around 1750. Colin Richmond doubts that the chantry for William I was ever built, John I having taken so much money from the family treasure that not enough remained for the project. I think this unlikely, as subsequent complaints by Agnes are about John's duplicitous conduct, while no one laments the absence of a memorial to William (as they later were to do for John I), and we are told several times that the revenues from the manor of Swainsthorpe were designated for prayers for William.

14. A. E. Nichols, *The Early Art of Norfolk: A Subject List of Extant and Lost Art* (Kalamazoo, MI: Medieval Institute Publications, Western Michigan University, 2004), p. 114, where the only material listed for Mautby is the statue of the Virgin before which Margaret asked to be buried (on the assumption that it is the same statue). Samuel R. Howard, *Mautby Remembrance* (Hemsby, Norfolk: Desne Publishing, 1996), p. 116: "The chapel at Mautby Hall was demolished in 1979, although it had been disused for that purpose for three centuries (at least). It was formerly opened and consecrated for worship for Margaret Paston's use in her old age...For the past hundred years it has been used in connection with the farm as a cow house. It had no repairs carried out." Though this is local lore, it is hard to imagine that Pevsner,

among others, would have failed to notice an historical cow barn with fifteenth-century connections.

15. Claude J. W. Messent, *The Round Towers to English Parish Churches* (Norfolk: Fletcher & Son, 1958); Jack Sterry, *Round Tower Churches: Hidden Treasures of North Norfolk* (Norwich: Crown, 2003). On the temptation to assign improbably early dates to the round towers, Stephen Heywood, "Architecture in Norfolk," in *A Festival of Norfolk Archaeology,* ed. Sue Margeson (Norfolk: Norfolk and Norwich Archaeological Society, 1996), pp. 72–85. Also, Dorothy Shreeve and Lyn Stilgoe, *The Round Tower Churches of Norfolk* (Norwich: Canterbury Press, 2001).

16. For lugubrious details of nineteenth-century restoration, J. Charles Cox, *Norfolk* (London: G. Allen & Co, 1911). The parish church at Matlask was restored in 1878, its tower in 1903; Gresham was "badly restored" in 1856 and its much-vaunted round tower in 1886; Sparham in 1889. Also, H. Munro Cautley, *Norfolk Churches* (Ipswich: N. Adlard, 1949). For more sad tales of this sort: Montague Rhodes James, *Norfolk and Suffolk* (London: J. M. Dent, 1930), p. 10, treating the "many sins" of restoration, the three most heinous being the addition of organ chambers, the introduction of varnished pitch pine, and the use of "cathedral glass" to fill in windows in place of the old "clear glazing." Kathleen Kameric, *Popular Piety and Art in the Late Middle Ages: Image Worship and Idolatry in England, 1350–1500* (New York: Palgrave, 2002), pp. 70–84 on what has been lost because of zealous restoration.

17. Nichols, *Early Art,* pp. 184–88; other depictions of St Edmund are in Norwich Cathedral and at Sparham, as well as at Carrow Priory (which was also remembered by Margaret in her will).

18. Sterry, *Round Tower Churches,* pp. 40–42; Nikolaus Pevsner, *North-east Norfolk and Norwich,* p. 88: an arch on "simple (early Norman) imposts," among the few features of interest. Pevsner accepts the tower as Anglo-Saxon and Sterry says it may be mid-tenth century.

19. Sterry, *Round Tower Churches,* pp. 38–39: "eight corbel heads… could be portraits of those who built the church, they could be medieval characters, or could represent different moods." Two are depicted, p. 39.

20. Ann E. Nichols, *Seeable Signs: The Iconography of the Seven Sacraments, 1350–1544* (Woodbridge: Boydell, 1994); the Gresham font (#126) is thought to be c. 1500, a "golden age" for such pieces. It probably owes its preservation to having been plastered over, and its eighth side shows the baptism of Christ. H. S. Squirrel, "The Seven Sacrament Fonts of Norfolk," *NA* 25 (1934), pp. 83–94; there are 23 such fonts in Norfolk, 14 in Suffolk. Squirrel talks of the near "perfect preservation" of the Gresham font, and of an artist who must have been a "sensitive and very human personality." Duffy, *Stripping of the Altars,* Plate 123 for the Gresham font.

21. On the Paston manor house at Gresham, Pevsner, *North-east Norfolk,* p. 155; Ketton-Cremer, *Catalogue,* p. 4; "the scanty ruins of their square fortified house still surrounded by its moat, exist in a dense wood." This

wood happens to be in the midst of a large agricultural field and the site has not been excavated.

22. Philip Nelson, *Ancient Painted Glass in England, 1170–1500* (London: Methuen, 1913), p. 154, for a depiction of St Anthony with a bell and one of St Leonard, from the church of St Mary, Sparham. Blomefield, VII, 255–62; Peter Mautby asked for buried at Sparham in 1438 (or 1428, according to the church's guidebook).

23. Duffy, *Stripping of the Altars,* p. 304; the screen is depicted, p. 114; Pevsner, *North-east Norfolk,* p. 319, for the scrolls. Pevsner suggests that some bench ends (though not the benches) are of the fifteenth century. W. W. Williamson, "Saints on Norfolk Rood Screens and Pulpits," *NA* 31 (1959), pp. 299–346; Simon Cotton, "Medieval Roodscreens in Norfolk: Their Construction and Painting Dates," *NA* 40 (1987), pp. 44–55. The quotations on the scrolls are from Job 10:19 and 14, and the "Church Tours" guidebook talks of this as an indication of the "morbid obsession with death" that characterizes medieval society.

24. The 1962 edition of Pevsner's *North-east Norfolk* has the virtue of antedating the fire and therefore of describing the church as it might have looked in Margaret's day. She had gone to Reedham (in November 1452) to see her uncle Philip, he being "so seke sith that I come to Redham that I wld he shuyld never an askapid it, nor not is leke to do but if he have redy help" (I, 144). The current guidebook to the church says Margaret gave 8s 4d at some point to help with the construction of the tower; no reference to this is in any of the extant letters. A brass of 1502 to Alyce Yelverton and a monument of the 1580s to Henry Berney do suggest links with Margaret's family: Blomefield, XI, 121–23.

25. The current guidebook for the church says that after the fire there was a debate about moving the church closer to the center of the current village. However, it was decided to rebuild where it had been "resorted to for prayer by countless numbers of people with the same purpose for 1300 years." The medival font, lost in the fire, has been replaced by a font from the "redundant" Norwich church of St Miles Coslany.

26. Pevsner, *North-east Norfolk,* pp. 260–61, the entry being for "St Andrew's Hall," p. 260: "The only English friar's church which has come down to our day so complete—in spite of what Norwich did to it (and had to do) to use it as a public hall." For excavations of the site, Percy A. Nash, "The Sackfriars and Blackfriars Conventual Buildings in the Parish of St Andrew and St Peter Hungate, Norwich," *NA* 22 (1926), pp. 370–82.

27. Carole Rawcliffe, *Medicine for the Soul* is now the definitive study. Margaret's bequest was made despite her quarrel with Master John Selot over what she perceived as his partisanship—hostile to the Paston interests in town. The Hospital was a popular recipient of benefactions: Rawcliffe, chapter 4 ("Paupers and Provisions").

28. Atherton, *Norwich Cathedral,* passim. So much building was being carried out through the entire course of the century that I will not try to pinpoint each project. Virtually every aspect of the cathedral was

undergoing changes, additions, or restorations. For more on what Margaret might have seen, Arthur B. Whittingham, *The Stalls of Norwich Cathedral* (Norwich: Norwich Cathedral Chapter, 1961); Whittingham, "The Erpingham Retable or Reredos in Norwich Cathedral," *NA* 39 (1985), pp. 202–6, dating it around 1475, or just in time to catch Margaret's gaze, assuming she came back to Norwich after moving to Mautby; Veronica Sekules, "Religious Politics and the Cloister Bosses of Norwich Cathedral," *JBAA* 159 (2006), pp. 284–306; Martial Rose and Julie Hedgecoe, *Stories in Stone: The Medieval Roof Carvings of Norwich* (London: Herbert Press, 1997).

29. J. Philip McAlear, "The Façade of Norwich Cathedral: The Nineteenth Century Restoration," *NA* 41 (1993), pp. 381–409.

30. Pevsner, *North-east Norfolk,* pp. 248–49, noting some bits of "original glass" in the east window of the north aisle, though original may only meant from c. 1500. Nichols, *Early Art,* notes some small bits of embroidery and sculpture for St Michael but hardly a major find.

31. The quote on the church's ruinous condition is from the 1968 guidebook to St Peter when it was being used as a museum of ecclesiastical bits and pieces. The 1968 guidebook by Rachel M. A. Young for the City of Norwich Museums replaced a 1958 version, and both depict the interior with the display cases that marked St Peter's use at the time. Because it is no longer a consecrated church, Pevsner's treatment (*North-east Norfolk,* p. 262) is in his "public buildings" section. He does single out the roof with its hammerbeams and arched braces—features of the Paston building scheme—as being of exceptional interest.

32. David King has prepared a detailed treatment of these, though as yet his notes are unpublished. King discusses the bits of heraldic glass with the arms of John II and John III, though probably these date from the early sixteenth century. For an earlier survey of the interior, George King, "Ancient Stained Glass in the Church of St Peter Hungate, Norwich," *NA* 16 (1907), pp. 205–18; G. V. Barnard, "St Peter Hungate," *Archaeological Journal* 106 (1949), pp. 79–111.

33. Though this great window has been dealt with many times over the years, it now has the publication it deserves: David King, *The Medieval Stained Glass of St Peter Mancroft, Norwich,* Corpus Vitrearum Medii Aevi: Great Britain, vol. 5 (London: British Academy, 2006).

34. David King's extensive notes on the church, with particular emphasis on its glass, are as yet unpublished. I thank him for his generosity in sharing his elaborate and learned notes, as I do Carole Hill and Carole Rawcliffe who helped arrange my "guided visit" of a church now being made accessible (at a fee) to the public as a glass museum.

35. On Margaret's social circles, Colin Richmond, "Elizabeth Clere: Friend of the Pastons," in *Medieval Women,* ed. Joyce Wogan-Brown et al., pp. 251–73. Perhaps Margaret, like her mother-in-law Agnes, had outlived most of her friends (Richmond, III, p. 115). That none of them figure in her will may be a sign of her isolated and melancholy last years,

though it is unsafe to draw conclusions from what is not covered in a will. On social ties in the world of Margaret Paston, Philippa Maddern, "'Best Trusted Friends': Concepts and Practices of Friendship among the Fifteenth-Century Norfolk Gentry," in *England in the Fifteenth Century: Proceedings of the 1992 Harlaxton Symposium,* ed. Nicholas Rogers (Stamford: Paul Watkins, 1994), pp. 100–17.

36. Though Walter may have been leaning toward the law after taking his BA (II, 734): "May be bachelor at soch tyme as shal lyke yow, and then to go to lawe. I kan think it to his preferring," as his tutor, Edmund Alyard, wrote to Margaret in March 1479.

37. J. C. Wedgwood, *History of Parliament,* II, p. 666.

38. C. L. Kingsford, *English Historical Literature* (Oxford: Clarendon, 1913), p. 206. Other voices, other views: Laurie A. Fink, *Women's Writing in English: Medieval England* (London: Longmans, 1999), p. 194: "Margaret would hardly be anyone's candidate for mother of the year," as a counterbalance to the more poetic "Delightful Dame Margaret! Her gentle wraith seems to haunt the meads of Mautby and the ruins of her Caister Home," William A. Dutt, *The Norfolk Broads,* fourth ed. (London: Methuen, 1931), p. 190.

BIBLIOGRAPHY

Alexander, Jonathan J. G. et al., ed. *The Splendor of the Word: Medieval and Renaissance Illuminated Manuscripts at the New York Public Library.* New York: Harvey Miller Publishers, 2005.

Anderson, Mary D. *Imagery of British Churches.* London: John Murray, 1955.

Archer, Rowena A. "Piety in Question: Noblewomen and Religion in the Later Middle Ages." In *Women and Religion in Medieval England,* ed. Diana Wood. Oxford: Oxbow, 2003. Pp. 118–40.

————. "Alice, Duchess of Suffolk." In *ODNB* 54434, January 2008.

Ariès, Philippe. *The Hour of Our Death,* trans. Helen Weaver. New York: Alfred Knopf, 1981.

Arn, Mary-Jo. "Thomas Chaucer and William Paston Talk of Business: Harvard Law School Deed 349." *Studies in the Age of Chaucer* 24 (2002): 237–67.

Arnold, John H. and Katherine Lewis, ed. *A Companion to "The Book of Margery Kempe."* Woodbridge: D. S. Brewer, 2004.

Ashley, Kathleen and Pamela Sheingorn, ed. *Interpreting Cultural Symbols: Saint Anne in Late Medieval Society.* Athens, GA: University of Georgia Press, 1990.

Aston, Margaret. "Devotional Literacy." In her *Lollards and Reformers: Images and Literacy in Late Medieval Religion.* London: Hambledon Press, 1984, paper iv.

————. "Segregation in Church." In *Women in the Church.* Ed. W. J. Shiels and Diana Wood. *Studies in Church History* 27 (Oxford, 1990). Pp. 237–94.

Atherton, Ian, Eric Fernie, Christopher Harper-Bill, and Hassell Smith, ed. *Norwich Cathedral: Church, City, and Diocese, 1096–1996.* London: Hambledon Press, 1996.

Austin, J. L. *Philosophical Papers.* 3rd ed., Oxford: Oxford University Press, 1979.

Backhouse, Janet, ed. *The Medieval English Cathedral: Papers in Honour of Pamela Tudor-Craig: Harlaxton Medieval Studies X* (Donington: Shaun Tyas, 2003).

Barnard, G. V. "St. Peter Hungate." *Archaeological Journal* 106 (1949): 79–112.

Barron, Caroline M. "Who Were the Pastons?" *Journal of the Society of Archivists* 4 (1972): 530–35.

————. "London and St Paul's Cathedral in the Later Middle Ages." In Backhouse. *The Medieval English Cathedral.* Pp. 126–49.

Barron, Caroline M. and Anne F. Sutton, ed. *Medieval London Widows, 1300–1500.* London: Hambledon, 1994.

Barron, Caroline M. and Matthew Davies, ed. *The Religious Houses of London and Middlesex*. London: Centre for Metropolitan History, 2007.

Beadle, Richard and Colin Richmond, ed. *Paston Letters and Papers of the 15th Century, Part III*. Early English Text Society, ss 22. Oxford, 2005.

Bengston, Jonathan. "St George and the Formation of English Nationalism." *Journal of Medieval and Early Modern Studies* 27 (1997): 317–40.

Bennett, Henry Stanley. *The Pastons and Their England: Studies in an Age of Transition*. 1st ed., Cambridge: Cambridge University Press, 1922: 2nd ed., 1968.

Bennett, Michael J. "Spiritual Kinship and the Baptismal Name in Traditional European Society." In *Studies in the Personal Name*. Ed. David Postles and Joel T. Rosenthal. Kalamazoo, MI: Medieval Institute Publications, Western Michigan University, 2006. Pp. 15–45.

Bensky, W. T. "St Leonard's Priory, Norwich." *NA* 12 (1985): 197–227.

Binski, Paul. *Medieval Death: Ritual and Representation*. Ithaca, NY: Cornell University Press, 1996.

Blain, Virginia, Patricia Clements, and Isobel Grundy. *The Feminist Companion to Literature in English: Women Writers from the Middle Ages to the Present*. New Haven, CT: Yale University Press, 1990.

Blomefield, Francis (and Charles Parkin). *An Essay towards The Topography of the County of Norfolk*. 11 vols., London, 1805–10.

Bossy, John. *Christianity in the West, 1400–1700*. Oxford: Oxford University Press, 1985.

———. "Christian Life in the Later Middle Ages: Prayers." *Transactions of the Royal Historical Society*, 6th series, 1 (1991): 137–48.

Brandenburg, Jon. "St Anne and Her Family: The Veneration of St Anne in Connection with the Concepts of Marriage and Family in the Early Modern Period." In *Saints and She-Devils: Images of Women in the Fifteenth and Sixteenth Centuries*. Ed. Lene Dresen Coenders et al. London: Rubicon Press, 1987. Pp. 101–26.

Brindley, N. H. "Notes on the Mural Paintings of St. Christopher in English Churches." *Antiquaries Journal* 4 (1924): 227–41.

Brown, Andrew D. *Popular Piety in Late Medieval England: The Diocese of Salisbury, 1250–1550*. Oxford: Clarendon Press, 1995.

———. *Church and Society in England, 1000–1500*. New York: Palgrave-Macmillan, 2003.

Bryan, Jennifer. *Looking Inward: Devotional Reading and Private Self in Late Medieval England*. Philadelphia, PA: University of Pennsylvania Press, 2008.

Burnley, J. David. *Courtliness and Literature in Medieval England*. London: Longmans, 1998.

Campbell, James. "Norwich." In *The Atlas of Historic Towns: Maps and Plans of Towns and Cities in the British Isles II*. Ed. Mary D. Lobell. London: Oxford University Press, 1975.

Carey, Hilary M. "Devout Literate Laypeople and the Pursuit of the Mixed Life in Late Medieval England." *Journal of Religious History* 14 (1987): 361–81.

Carpenter, Christine. "Religion of the Gentry in Fifteenth Century England." In *England in the Fifteenth Century: Proceedings of the 1986 Harlaxton Symposium*. Ed. Daniel Williams. Woodbridge: Boydell Press, 1987. Pp. 53–74.

————, ed. *Kingsford's Stonor Letters and Papers, 1290–1483*. Cambridge: Cambridge University Press, 1996.

————, ed. *The Armburgh Papers: The Brokholes Inheritance in Warwickshire, Herefordshire, and Essex, c. 1417–c. 1453*. Woodbridge: Boydell, 1998.

————. "Religion." In *Gentry Culture in Late Medieval England*. Ed. Raluca Radulescu and Alison Truelove. Manchester: Manchester University Press, 2005. Pp. 134–50.

Castor, Helen. *Blood and Roses: The Paston Family in the Fifteenth Century*. London: Faber and Faber, 2004.

————. John Paston I. *ODNB*.

————. John Paston II. *ODNB*.

Catermole, Paul. "The Bells." In *Norwich Cathedral*. Ed. Ian Atherton et al. Pp. 494–504.

Catto, Jeremy. "Religion and the English Nobility in the Later Fourteenth Century." In *History and Imagination: Essays in Honour of H. R. Trevor-Roper*. Ed. Hugh Lloyd-Jones, Valerie Pearl, and Blair Warden. London: Duckworth, 1981. Pp. 43–55.

————. "Religious Change Under Henry V." In *Henry V: The Practice of Kingship*. Ed. Gerald L. Harriss. Oxford: Oxford University Press, 1985. Pp. 97–115.

Cautley, H. Munro. *Norfolk Churches*. Ipswich: N. Allard, 1949.

Cheney, Christopher R. *Handbook of Dates for Students of English History*. London: Royal Historical Society, 1955.

Cherewatuk, Karen and Ulrike Wiethaus, ed. *Dear Sister: Medieval Women and the Epistolary Genre*. Philadelphia, PA: University of Pennsylvania Press, 1993.

Childs, Wendy. "The Perils or Otherwise, of Maritime Pilgrimage to Santiago de Compostela." In *Pilgrimage Explored*. Ed. John Stopford. Woodbridge: York Medieval Press, 1999. Pp. 123–43.

Clay, Rotha M. *The Hermits and Anchorites of England*. London: Methuen, 1914.

Cokayne, George E. and Vicary Gibbs, ed. *The Complete Peerage*. 12 vols. In 13, London: St Catherine's Press, 1910–59.

Colledge, Edmund and James Walsh, ed. *A Book of Showings to the Anchoress Julian of Norwich*. Toronto: Pontifical Institute of Medieval Studies, 1978.

Collton, Simon. "Mediaeval Roodscreens in Norfolk: The Construction and Painting Dates." *NA* 40 (1987), 44–55.

Compton, C. H. "Notes on the Church of St Michael Coslany, Norwich." *Journal of the British Archeological Association*, 42 (1886): 395–99.

Cox, John Charles. *Norfolk*. In "County Churches" series: 2nd ed., London, G. Allen and Co., 1911.

Craig, Leigh Ann. *Wandering Women and Holy Mothers: Women as Pilgrims in the Later Middle Ages*. Leiden: Bill, 2009.

Crow, Martin M. and Clair C. Olsen, ed. *Chaucer Life Records*. Austin, TX: University of Texas Press, 1966.

Cullum, Patricia and P. J. P. Goldberg. "How Margaret Blackburn Taught Her Daughters: Reading Devotional Instruction in a Book of Hours." In *Texts and Contexts in Late Medieval Britain: Essays for Felicity Riddy.* Ed. Jocelyn Wogan-Brown, et al. Turnhout, Brill, 2000. Pp. 217–36.

———. "Gendering Charity in Medieval Hagiography." In *Gender and Holiness: Men, Women, and Saints in Late Medieval Europe.* Ed. Samantha J. E. Riches and Sarah Salih. London: Routledge, 2002. Pp. 135–51.

Cutts, Edward L. *Scenes and Characters of the Middle Ages.* London: Simpkin, 1925.

Dalrymple, Roger. "Reaction, Consolation, and Redress in the Letters of the Paston Women." In *Early Modern Women's Letter Writing.* Ed. James Daybell. New York: Palgrave, 2001. Pp. 16–28.

Davis, Norman. "The Text of Margaret Paston's Letters." *Medium Aevum* 18 (1949): 12–28.

———. "A Scribal Problem in the Paston Letters." *English and Germanic Studies* 4 (1951–52): 31–64.

———. "The Language of the Pastons." *Proceedings of the British Academy* 40 (1955): 120–44.

———. "The Litera Troili and English Letters." *Review of English Studies,* n.s. 16 (1964): 233–44.

———. "Style and Stereotype in Early English Letters." *Leeds Studies in English,* n.s. 1 (1967): 7–17.

———, ed. *The Paston Letters and Papers of the Fifteenth Century.* 2 vols., Oxford: Oxford University Press, 1971–76.

———. "Margaret Paston's Use of 'Do'." *Neuphilologische Mitteilungen* 73 (1972): 55–62.

Davis, Virginia. "The Rule of St Paul, the First Hermit in Medieval England." In *Monks, Hermits, and the Ascetic Tradition.* Ed. Wm J. Sheils. Studies in Church History 22 (1985): 203–14.

———. "The Popularity of Late Medieval Personal Names as Reflected in English Ordination Lists." In *Studies in the Personal Name.* Ed. Postles and Rosenthal. Pp. 103–14.

Daybell, James, ed. *Early Modern Women's Letter Writing, 1450–1700.* New York: Palgrave, 2001.

Delaisse, L. M. J. "The Importance of the Book of Hours for the History of the Medieval Book." In *Gatherings in Honor of Dorothy E. Miner.* Ed. Ursula E. McKracken, Lilian M. C. Randall, and R. H. Randall Jr. Baltimore, Walters Art Gallery, 1974. Pp. 203–25.

Delany, Sheila, trans. *A Legend of Holy Women: Osbern Bokenham: Legends of Holy Women.* Notre Dame, IN: University of Notre Dame Press, 1992.

———. *Impolitic Bodies: Poetry, Saints, and Society in Fifteenth Century England: The Works of Osbern Bokenham.* New York: Oxford University Press, 1993.

Denton, Jon. "Image, Identity, and Gentility: The Woodford Experience." In *The Fifteenth Century: Of Mice and Men.* Ed. Linda Clark. Woodbridge: Boydell, 2005. Pp. 1–17.

D'Evelyn, Charlotte and Frances A. Foster. "Saints' Legends." In *A Manual of the Writings in Middle English, 1050–1500, vol. II.* Ed. J. Burke Severs. New

Haven, CT: Connecticut Academy of Arts and Sciences, 1970. Pp. 410–57, 553–635.

Dewick, E. S. "On a Manuscript Psalter Formerly Belonging to the Abbey of Bury St Edmunds." *Archaeologia* 54/2 (1895): 399–416.

Dickinson, J. C. *The Shrine of Our Lady of Walsingham.* Cambridge: Cambridge University Press, 1956.

Doyle, A. I. "The Work of a Late-Fifteenth Century English Scribe: William Ebesham." *Bulletin of the John Rylands Library* 39 (1956–57): 298–325.

Duffy, Eamon. *The Stripping of the Altars: Traditional Religion in England, 1400–1580.* New Haven, CT and London: Yale University Press, 1992.

———. "St Erkenwald: London's Cathedral Saint and His Legend." In *The Medieval English Cathedral.* Ed. Janet Backhouse. Pp. 150–67.

———. "The Dynamics of Pilgrimage in Late Medieval England." In *Pilgrimage and the English Experience from Becket to Bunyan.* Ed. Colin Morris and Peter Roberts. Cambridge: Cambridge University Press, 2002. Pp. 166–77.

———. "Late Medieval Religion." In *Gothic Art for England, 1400–1547.* Ed. Richard Marks and Paul Williamson. London: Victoria and Albert Museum, 2003. Pp. 56–67.

———. "Religious Belief." In *A Social History of England, 1200–1500.* Ed. Rosemary Horrox and W. Mark Ormrod. Cambridge: Cambridge University Press, 2006. Pp. 293–339.

———. *Marking the Hours: English People and their Prayers.* New Haven, CT and London: Yale University Press, 2006.

———. "The Book of Hours and Lay Piety in the Later Middle Ages." In *Elite and Popular Religion.* Ed. Kate Cooper and Jeremy Gregory. Studies in Church History 42 (2006). Pp. 140–61.

Dutt, William A. *The Norfolk Broads.* 4th ed., London: Methuen, 1932.

Emden, Alfred B. *A Biographical Dictionary of the University of Oxford to A.D. 1500.* 3 vols., Oxford: Oxford University Press, 1957–59.

———. *A Biographical Register of the University of Cambridge to A.D. 1500.* Cambridge, Cambridge University Press, 1963.

Erler, Mary C. "English Vowed Women at the End of the Middle Ages." *Mediaeval Studies* 57 (1995), 155–202.

———. *Women, Reading, and Piety in Late Medieval England.* Cambridge: Cambridge University Press, 2003.

Erasmus, Desiderius. *Pilgrimage to St Mary of Walsingham and St Thomas of Canterbury,* trans. John Gough Nichols. London: John Murray, 1875.

Farmer, David H. *Oxford Dictionary of Saints.* Oxford: Oxford University Press, 1978.

———. "Some Saints of East Anglia." *Reading Medieval Studies* 11 (1985), 31–49.

———. "The Cult and Canonization of St Hugh. In *St Hugh of Lincoln.* Ed. Henry Mayr-Harting. Oxford: Oxford University Press, 1987. Pp. 75–88.

Farnhill, Ken. *Guilds and the Parish Community in Late Medieval East Anglia, c. 1470–1550.* Woodbridge: Boydell, for the York Medieval Press, 2001.

Finch, Jonathan. *Church Monuments in Norfolk before 1850: The Archaeology of Commemoration*. British Archaeological Reports, British Series, 317 (2000).

———. "The Churches." In Carole Rawcliffe and Richard Wilson, ed. *Medieval Norwich*, Pp. 49–72.

Finke, Laurie A. *Women's Writing in English: Medieval England*. London: Longman, 1999. Pp. 187–97.

Finucane, Ronald C. *Miracles and Pilgrimage: Popular Belief in Medieval England*. New York: St. Martin's Press, 1995.

Fleming, Peter. "Charity, Faith, and the Gentry of Kent, 1422–1529." In *Property and Politics: Essays in Later Medieval English History*. Ed. Tony Pollard. Gloucester: Sutton, 1984. Pp. 36–58.

Foss, Edward. *The Judges of England, vol iv*. London: John Murray, 1870.

French, Katherine. *The People of the Parish: Community Life in a Late Medieval English Diocese*. Philadelphia, PA: University of Pennsylvania Press, 2001.

———. *The Good Women of the Parish: Gender and Religion after the Black Death*. Philadelphia, PA: University of Pennsylvania Press, 2008.

Frisch, Teresa G. *Gothic Art, 1140—c. 1450: Sources and Documents*. Englewood Cliffs, NJ: Prentice Hall, 1987; reprinted, Medieval Academy Reprints, Toronto: University of Toronto Press, 1987.

Furnivall, F. J., ed. *The Fifty Earliest English Wills*. EETS, o.s. 78 (1882).

Gairdner, James, ed. *The Paston Letters, 1422–1509 A.D.* 3 vols., Westminster: Constable, 1895.

Gee, Stacy. "Parochial Libraries in Pre-Reformation England." In *Learning and Literacy in Medieval England and Abroad*. Ed. Sarah Rees-Jones. Turnhout: Brepols, 2003. Pp. 199–222.

Gerould, Gordon H. *Saints' Legends*. Boston, MA: Houghton Mifflin, 1916.

Gibbons, Rachel. "The Piety of Isabeau of Bavaria, Queen of France (1385–1422)." In *Courts, Counties, and the Capital in the Later Middle Ages*. Ed. Diana E. S. Dunn. New York: St Martin's Press, 1996. Pp. 205–24.

Gibson, Gail McMurray. *The Theater of Devotion: East Anglian Drama and Society in the Later Middle Ages*. Chicago, IL: University of Chicago Press, 1989.

———. "Saint Anne and the Religion of Childbed: Some East Anglian Texts and Talismans." In *Interpreting Cultural Symbols*. Ed. Ashley and Sheingorn. Pp. 95–110.

Gies, Frances and Joseph Gies. *A Medieval Family: The Pastons of Fifteenth-Century England*. New York: Harper Collins, 1998.

Gill, Miriam. "Female Piety and Impiety: Selected Images of Women in Wall Paintings in England after 1300." In *Gender and Holiness*. Ed. Riches and Salih. Pp. 101–20.

Given-Wilson, Christopher. "The Exequies of Edward IV and the Royal Funeral Ceremony in Late Medieval England." *English Historical Review* 124 (2009), 257–82.

Goodall, John A. "The Architecture of Ancestry at the Collegiate Church of St Andrew, Wingfield, Suffolk." In *Family and Dynasty in Late Medieval England: Proceedings of the 1997 Harlaxton Conference*. Ed. Richard Eales and Shaun Tyas. Harlaxton Medieval Studies, ix (Donington: Shaun Tyas, 2003). Pp. 157–71.

Goodman, Tony. "The Piety of John Brunham's Daughter of Lynn." In *Medieval Women*. Ed. Derek Baker. Studies in Church History, Subsidia I (1978). Pp. 347–58.

———. *Margery Kempe and Her World*. London: Longmans, 2002.

Grace, Mary, ed. *Records of the Gild of St. George in Norwich, 1389–1547*. Norfolk Records Society 9 (1937).

Graham, Geoffrey and Rachel M. R. Young. *The Church of St Peter Hungate*. Norwich: Norwich Museum Commission, 1965.

Gransden, Antonia. "Letters of Recommendation from John Whethamstede for a Poor Pilgrim." *EHR* 106 (1991), 932–39.

Greatorex, Joan. "Marian Studies and Devotions in the Benedictine Cathedrals Priories in Later Medieval England." In *The Church and Mary*. Ed. Robert N. Swanson. Studies in Church History 39 (2004). Pp. 157–67.

Griffiths, Jeremy. "A Mid-Fifteenth Century Book List and Inventory from East Dereham, Norfolk." *NA* 42 (1987): 332–39.

Griffiths, Ralph A. *The Reign of King Henry VI*. Berkeley and Los Angeles, CA: University of California Press, 1981; 2nd ed. Stroud: Sutton, 2004.

Haas, Louis. "Social Connections between Parents and Godparents in Late Medieval Yorkshire." In *Studies in the Person Name*. Ed. Postles and Rosenthal. Pp. 159–75.

Hall, D. J. *English Medieval Pilgrimage*. London: Routledge and Kegan Paul, 1965.

Hallum, Elizabeth. "Introduction: The Eleanor Crosses and Royal Burial Custom." In *Eleanor of Castile,1250–1990*. Ed. David Parsons. Stamford: Paul Watkins, 1991. Pp. 9–21.

Hanham, Alison, ed. *The Cely Letters, 1472–1488*. EETS 273 (1975).

———. *The Celys and Their World: An English Merchant Family of the Fifteenth Century*. Cambridge: Cambridge University Press, 1985.

Hanson, Elaine. "Margaret Paston." In *An Encyclopedia of British Women Writers*. Ed. Paul and June Schlueter. New Brunswick, NJ: Rutgers University Press, 1988. Pp. 505–6.

Harper, John. *The Forms and Orders of the Western Liturgy from the Tenth to the Eighteenth Centuries: A Historical Introduction and Guide for Students and Musicians*. Oxford: Oxford University Press, 1991.

Harper-Bill, Christopher. "The Foundation and Later History of the Medieval Shrine." In *Walsingham: Pilgrimage and History*. Walsingham: Roman Catholic National Shrine, 1999. Pp. 63–79.

Harper-Bill, Christopher and Carole Rawcliffe. "The Religious Houses." In *Medieval Norwich*. Ed. Rawcliffe and Wilson. Pp. 73–119.

Harthan, John. *Books of Hours and their Owners*. London: Thames & Hudson, 1977.

Heath, Sidney. *In the Steps of the Pilgrims*. London: Rich & Cowan, 1953.

Henderson, W. G., ed. *Missale ad usum insignis ecclesiae Eboracensis*. Surtees Society 59–60 (1874).

Henisch, Bridget A. *The Medieval Calendar Year*. University Park, PA: Pennsylvania State University Press, 1999.

Heywod, Stephen. "Architecture in Norfolk, I." *A Festival of Norfolk Archaeology*. Ed. Sue Margeson. Norfolk and Norwich Archaeological Society, 1998. Pp. 72–85.

Hicks, Michael. "Piety and Lineage in the Wars of the Roses: The Hungerford Experience." In *Kings and Nobles in the Later Middle Ages*." Ed. Ralph A. Griffiths and James Sherborne. New York, St Martin's Press, 1986. Pp. 80–108.

———. "The Piety of Margaret Lady Hungerford (d. 1478)." *Journal of Ecclesiastical History* 38 (1987): 19–38.

———. "Four Studies in Conventional Piety." *Southern History* 13 (1991): 1–21.

Higgitt, John. *The Murthly Hours: Devotion, Literacy and Luxury in Paris, London, and the Gaelic West*. London and Toronto: University of Toronto Press and The British Library, 2000.

Hill, Carole. "Julian and Her Sisters: Female Piety in Late Medieval Norwich." In *The Fifteenth Century, vi*. Ed. Linda Clark. Woodbridge: Boydell, 2006. Pp. 165–87.

Horobin, Simon. "Politics, Patronage and Piety in the Work of Osbern Bokenham." *Speculum* 82 (2008): 932–49.

Howard, Samuel R. *Mautby Remembered*. Hemsby, Norfolk: Deane Publishing, 1996.

Howards, F. R. B. "The Grey Friars Cloister, Great Yarmouth." *JBAA* ns 31 (1925): 107–9.

Hughes, Jonathan. *The Religious Life of Richard III: Piety and Prayers in the North of England*. Stroud: Sutton Publishing, 1997.

Hurt, Richard. "The Shrines and Pilgrims of Norfolk." *NA* 6 (1864), 277–94.

Hutton, William H. *The Lives and Legends of the English Saints*. 2nd ed., London: Wells, Garnder, Darton, & Co., 1908.

Jack, Ian. "The Ecclesiastical Patronage Exercised by a Baronial Family in the Late Middle Ages." *Journal of Religious History* 3 (1965): 275–90.

Jacobus de Voragine (Jacques of Lorraine). *The Golden Legend: Readings of the Saints,* trans. William G. Ryan. 2 vols., Princeton, NJ: Princeton University Press, 1993.

Jambeck, Karen K. "Patterns of Women's Literary Patronage: England, 1200- ca 1475." In *The Cultural Patronage of Medieval Women*. Ed. June Hall McCash. Athens, GA: University of Georgia Press, 1996. Pp. 228–48.

James, Montague Rhodes. *Suffolk and Norfolk*. London: J. M. Dent, 1930.

James, Montague Rhodes and Sidney C. Cockerell, ed. *Two East Anglian Psalters at the Bodleian Library*. London: Roxburgh Club, 1926.

Janson, Katherine. *The Making of the Magdalen: Preaching and Popular Devotion in the Later Middle Ages*. Princeton, NJ: Princeton University Press, 2000.

Jessopp, Augustus A. and Montague Rhodes James, ed. and trans. *The Life and Miracles of St William of Norwich*. Cambridge: Cambridge University Press, 1896.

Jewell, Helen. *Women in Medieval England*. Manchester: Manchester University Press, 1996.

Kamerick, Kathleen. *Popular Piety and Art in the Late Middle Ages, 1350–1500.* New York: Palgrave, 2002.

Kelton-Cremer, R. W. *Catalogue of a Loan Exhibition: The Pastons, May–August, 1953.* Norwich: Norwich Castle Museum, 1953.

Kent, Ernest A. "Isaac's House of the Music House." *NA* 29 (1945): 31–38.

King, David. *The Medieval Stained Glass of St. Peter Mancroft, Norwich.* Corpus Vitrearum Medii Aevi Great Britain, vol. 6. London: British Academy, 2006.

King, George. "Ancient Stained Glass in the Church of St. Peter Hungate, Norwich." *NA* 16 (1907): 205–18.

King, Pamela. "'My Image to be Made All Naked': Cadaver Tombs and Commemoration of Women in Fifteenth-Century England." In *Tant D'Emprises—So Many Undertakings: Essays in Honour of Anne F. Sutton.* Ed. Livia Visser-Fuchs. The Ricardian, xiii (2003): 294–314.

Kinsey, Robert. "Hedging their Bets: The Thorpe Family Chantries and the Location of Commemoration in Fourteenth Century England." Paper read at the 2008 Harlaxton Conference.

Kingsford, Charles L. *English Historical Literature in the Fifteenth Century.* Oxford: Clarendon Press, 1913.

———. *The Grey Friars of London: Their History.* London: British Society for Franciscan Studies, 6 (1915).

Kirby, Joan, ed. *The Plumpton Letters and Papers.* Camden Society, 5th series, 8 (1990).

Kisbey, Fiona. "Books in London Parish Churches before 1670: Some Preliminary Observations." In *The Church and Learning in Late Medieval Society.* Ed. Caroline M. Barron and Jenny Stratford. Harlaxton Medieval Studies XI. Donington: Shaun Tyas, 2002. Pp. 305–26.

Kleineke, Hannes. "The Reburial Expenses of Sir Thomas Arundell." *The Ricardian* 11 (1998), 288–96.

Knowles, David. "The Religion of the Pastons." *Downside Review* 42 (1924), 143–63.

———. *The Religious Orders in England: II. The End of the Middle Ages.* Cambridge: Cambridge University Press, 1961.

Knowles, David and R. Neville Hadcock. *Medieval Religious Houses: England and Wales.* London: Longman, 1971.

Knox, Ronald and Shane Leslie, ed. *The Miracles of Henry VI.* Cambridge: Cambridge University Press, 1923.

Kren, Thomas. "Seven Illuminated Books of Hours Written by the Parisian Scribe Jean Dubreuil, c. 1475–1485." In *Reading Texts and Images: Essays in Medieval and Renaissance Art and Patronage in Honour of Margaret M. Manion.* Ed. Bernard J. Muir. Exeter: Exeter University Press, 2002. Pp. 157–200.

Krug, Rebecca. *Reading Families: Women's Literate Practice in Late Medieval England.* Ithaca, NY: Cornell University Press, 2002.

Lacy, Kay. "Margaret Croke (d. 1491)." In *Medieval London Widows.* Ed. Barron and Sutton. Pp. 143–64.

Lambourn, G. "The Arms in the Chaucer Tomb at Ewelme." *Oxoniensia* 5 (1940): 78–93.

Lasko, Peter and Nigel J. Morgan. *Medieval Art in East Anglia, 1300–1500.* Norwich: Jarold & Son, 1973.

Legg, J. Wickham. *The Sarum Missal, edited from Three Early Manuscripts.* Oxford: Clarendon Press, 1916: reprinted, 1966.

Lepine, David. "The Courteneys and Exeter Cathedral in the Later Middle Ages." *Proceedings of the Devonshire Association* 124 (1992): 41–58.

Lester, G. A. *Sir John Paston's `Grete Boke.'* Cambridge: D. S. Brewer. 1984.

Lewis, Katherine J. *The Cult of St Katherine of Alexandria in Late Medieval England.* Woodbridge: Boydell, 2000.

Leyser, Henrietta. *Medieval Women: A Social History of Women in England, 450–1500.* London: St Martin's Press, 1996.

Linnell, C. L. S. *Guidebook to St Mary's Parish Church, Sparham* (1959).

———. *Norfolk Church Dedications.* Borthwick Institute of Historical Research, St Anthony's Hall Publication 21: York, 1962.

Loraine, Herbert. *St Margaret's Church, Paston.* (Paston, Norfolk: n.d.).

Luxford, Julia M. "St Margaret of Holm: New Evidence Concerning a Norfolk Benedictine Cult" *NA* 44 (2002): 111–19.

Maddern, Phillipa. "Order and Disorder." In *Medieval Norwich.* Ed. Rawcliffe and Wilson. Pp. 189–212.

Marks, Richard. *Image and Devotion in Late Medieval England.* Stroud: Sutton, 2004.

Marks, Richard and Paul Williamson, ed. *Gothic Art for England, 1400–1547.* London: Victoria and Albert Museum, 2003.

Marshall, K. N. *The Pastons, 1378–1732.* Norwich: Jarold, 1957.

Mason, Emma. "The Role of the English Parishioner, 1100–1500." *Journal of Ecclesiastical History* 27 (1976): 17–29.

Mason, R. Hindry. *The History of Norfolk from Original Records.* London, Wertheimer, Lea, and Co., 1894.

McAlear, J. Philip. "The Façade of Norwich Cathedral: The Nineteenth Century Restoration." *NA* 41 (1993)" 381–409.

McAvoy, Liz, ed. *A Companion to Julian of Norwich.* Cambridge: D. S. Brewer: 2008.

McFarlane, Kenneth Bruce. *Lancastrian Kings and Lollard Knights.* Oxford: Oxford University Press, 1972.

McKenna, John W. "Popular Canonization as Political Propaganda: The Case of Archbishop Scrope." *Speculum* 45 (1970): 608–23.

McRee, Ben R. "Traditional Belief and Practice." In *A Companion to Tudor Britain.* Ed. Robert Tittler and Norman Jones. Oxford: Blackwell, 2004. Pp. 207–20.

———. "After 1452: The Evolution of the Gild of St George in the Wake of Yelvertons' Mediation." *NA* 45/1 (2006): 26–40.

McSheffrey, Shannon. *Gendered Heresy: Women and Men in Lollard Communities.* Philadelphia, PA: University of Pennsylvania Press, 1995.

Meale, Carole, ed. *Women and Literature in Britain, 1150–1500.* 2nd ed., Cambridge: Cambridge University Press, 1996.

———. "'alle the bokes that I haue of latyn, Englisch, and frensch': Laywomen and their Books in Late Medieval England." In *Women and Literature in Britain, 1150–1500.* Ed. Carol Meale. Cambridge: Cambridge University Press, 1993. Pp. 128–58.

Mertes, Kate. "The Household as a Religious Community." In *People, Politics, and Community in the Later Middle Ages.* Ed. Colin Richmond and Joel T. Rosenthal. Gloucester: Alan Sutton, 1987. Pp. 123–39.

———. *The English Noble Household, 1250–1600: Good Governance and Politic Rule.* Oxford: Basil Blackwell, 1988.

Messent, Claude J. W. *The Round Towers to English Parish Churches.* Norwich: Fletcher and Son, 1958.

Middleton-Steward, Judith. *Inward Purity and Outward Splendour: Death and Remembrance in the Deanery of Dunwich, Suffolk, 1370–1547.* Woodbridge: Boydell and the University of East Anglia Centre of East Anglian Studies, 2001.

———. "Time and the Testator, 1370–1540." In *The Use and Abuse of Time in Christian History.* Ed. Robert N. Swanton. Studies in Church History 37 (2002). Pp. 133–44.

Moore, Samuel. "Patrons of Letters in Norfolk and Suffolk, c. 1450." *Publications of the Modern Language Association,* 27 (1912): 188–207; 28 (1913): 79–105.

Moreton, C. E. "The 'Library' of a Late-Fifteenth Century Lawyer." *The Library,* 6th series, 13 (1991): 338–46.

———. "A Social Gulf? The Upper and Lesser Gentry of Late Medieval England." *Journal of Medieval History* 17 (1991): 255–62.

Morgan, Philip. "Of Worms and War, 1380–1558." In *Death in England: An Illustrated History.* Ed. Peter C. fJupp and Clare Gittings. Manchester: Manchester University Press, 1999.

Morrison, Susan S. *Women Pilgrims in Late Medieval England: Private Piety as Public Performance.* London and New York: Routledge, 2000.

Mueller, Janel M. *The Native Tongue and the Word: Developments in English Prose Style, 1380–1580.* Chicago, IL: University of Chicago Press, 1984.

Myers, Michael B. "A Fictional-Truth Self: Margery Kempe and the Social Reality of the Merchant Elite of King's Lynn." *Albion* 31 (1999): 377–94.

Nash, Percy A. "The Sackfriars and Blackfriars Conventual Buildings in the Parish of St Andrew and St Peter Hungate." *NA* 22 (1926): 370–82.

Nelson, Jinty L. "Making a Difference in Eighth-Century Politics: The Daughters of Desiderius." In *After Rome's Fall: Narrators and Sources of Early Medieval History: Essays Presented to Walter Goffart.* Ed. Alexander C. Murray. Toronto: University of Toronto Press, 1998. Pp. 171–90.

Nelson, Philip. *Ancient Painted Glass in England, 1170–1500.* London: Methuen & Co., 1913.

Nichols, Ann E. *Seeable Signs: The Iconography of the Seven Sacraments, 1350–1544.* Woodbridge: Boydell, 1994.

Nichols, Ann E. *The Early Art of Norfolk: A Subject List of Extant and Lost Art*. Kalamazoo, MI: Medieval Institute Publications, Western Michigan University, 2002.

———. "The East Anglian Lollards Revisited: Parochial Art in Norfolk." In *Tant D'Emprises* (see Pamela King). Pp. 359–70.

Niles, Philip. "Baptism and the Naming of Children in Late Medieval England." In *Postles and Rosenthal*. Studies in the Personal Name. Pp. 147–58.

Nilson, Ben. *The Cathedral Shrines of Medieval England*. Woodbridge: Boydell, 1998.

———. "The Medieval Experience at the Shrine." In *Pilgrimage Explored*. Ed. John Stopford. Woodbridge: Boydell, for the University of York Centre for Medieval Studies, 1999. Pp. 95–122.

Nixon, Virginia. *Mary's Mother: St Anne in Late Medieval Europe*. University Park, PA: Pennsylvania State University Press, 2004.

Noble, Elizabeth. *The World of the Stonors: A Gentry Society*. Woodbridge: Boydell, 2009.

Northeast, Peter, ed. *Wills of the Archdeaconry of Suffolk, 1439–1474: Wills from the Register, `Baldwyne', Part I: 1439–1461*. Suffolk Record Society 44 (2001).

———. "Suffolk Churches in the Later Middle Ages: The Evidence of Wills." In *East Anglia's History: Studies in Honour of Norman Scarfe*. Ed. Christopher Harper-Bill, Carole Rawcliffe, and Richard G. Wilson. Norwich: Boydell for the University of East Anglia Centre of East Anglian Studies. Pp. 93–106.

Norwich Museum Committee. *Guide to the St Peter Hungate Museum*. Norwich, 1955.

Oliva, Marilyn. *The Convent Community in Late Medieval England: Female Monasteries in the Diocese of Norwich, 1350–1540*. Woodbridge: Boydell Press, 1998.

O'Mara, V. M. "Female Scribal Ability and Scribal Activity in Late Medieval England: the Evidence?" *Leeds Studies in English*, n.s. 27 (1996): 87–130.

Orme, Nicholas. "St Walter of Cowbeck," *Analecta Bollandiana* 108 (1990): 387–93.

———. "St Breage: A Medieval Virgin Saint of Cornwall." *Analecta Bollandiana* 111 (1992): 341–52.

———. "Bishop Grandisson and Popular Religion." *Proceedings of the Devonshire Association* 124 (1992): 107–18.

Ormrod, W. Mark. "The Personal Religion of Edward III." *Speculum* 64 (1989): 849–77.

Oxford Dictionary of National Biography, ed. H. C. G. Matthew and Brian Harrison. Online Version Edited by Lawrence Goldman. Oxford: Oxford University Press, 2004.

Pächt, Otto and Jonathan J. G. Alexander. *Illuminated Manuscripts in the Bodleian Library*. Oxford: Clarendon Press, 1966.

Painter, Sidney. *William Marshal, Knight Errant, Baron, Regent of England*. Baltimore: Johns Hopkins University Press, 1933: reprinted, Toronto: University of Toronto Press for Medieval Academy Reprints, 1982.

Palmer, Charles. "Remarks on the Monastery of the Dominican Friars at Great Yarmouth." *NA* 3 (1852): 377–93.

Pantin, William A. *The English Church in the Fourteenth Century.* Notre Dame, IN: Notre Dame University Press, 1963; Reprinted, Toronto: University of Toronto Press, for the Medieval Academy of America, 1980.

———. "Instructions for a Devout and Literate Layman." In *Medieval Language and Literature: Essays Presented to R. W. Hunt.* Ed. Jonathan J. G. Alexander and Margaret Gibson. Oxford: Clarendon Press, 1976. Pp. 398–422.

Parker, Jane. "Lynn and the Making of a Mystic." In *A Companion to 'The Book of Margery Kempe.* Ed. John H. Arnold and Katherine J. Lewis. Cambridge: D. S. Brewer, 2004. Pp. 55–73.

Parsons, John Carmi. *Eleanor of Castile: Queen and Society in Thirteenth Century England.* New York: St. Martin's Press, 1995.

Pelikan, Jaroslav. *Mary through the Centuries: Her Place in the History of Culture.* New Haven, CT: Yale University Press, 1996.

Penketh, Sandra. "Women and Books of Hours." In *Women and the Book: Assessing the Visual Evidence.* Ed. Lesley Smith and Jane H. M. Taylor. London and Toronto: British Library and University of Toronto Press, 1996. Pp. 266–81.

Penman, Michael A. "Christian Days and Knights: The Religious Devotion and Court of David II of Scotland, 1329–71." *Historical Research* 78 (2002): 249–72.

Perrow, Eber Carle. "The Last Will and Testament as a Form of Literature." *Transactions of the Wisconsin Academy of Sciences, Arts, and Letters,* 17, part 1, #1 (1911). Pp. 682–750.

Peters, Christine. *Patterns of Piety: Women, Gender, and Religion in Late Medieval and Reformation England.* Cambridge: Cambridge University Press, 2003.

Pevsner, Nikolas. *The Buildings of England: North-East Norfolk and Norwich.* Harmondsworth: Penguin Publishing, 1962.

Pfaff, Richard. *New Liturgical Feasts in Later Medieval England.* Oxford: Oxford University Press, 1970.

———. "Why Do Medieval Psalters Have Calendars?" In (his) *Liturgical Calendars, Saints and Services in Medieval England.* Aldershot: Ashgate, 1998, paper vi.

Phillips, Kim M. "Desiring Virgins: Martyrs and Femininity in Late Medieval England." In *Youth in the Middle Ages.* Ed. P. J. Goldberg and Felicity Riddy. Woodbridge: Boydell, 2004. Pp. 45–59.

Phythian-Adams, Charles. "Ceremony and the Citizen: The Communal Year at Coventry, 1450–1650." In *The English Medieval Town: A Reader in English Urban History, 1200–1540.* Ed. Richard Holt and Gervase Rosser. London: Longmans, 1990. Pp. 238–64.

Piroyansky, Dannal. "Bloody Miracles of a Political Martyr: The Case of Thomas, Earl of Lancaster." In *Signs, Women, and Miracles.* Ed. Kate Cooper and Jeremy Gregory. Studies in Church History 41 (2005). Pp. 228–38.

Plummer, John. *The Hours of Catherine of Cleves.* New York: George Braziller, 1966.

Poos, Lawrence. "Social History and the Book of Hours." In *The Book of Hours in Medieval Art and Life*. Ed. Roger S. Wieck. London: George Braziller, in Association with the Walters Art Gallery, Baltimore, 1988. Pp. 32–40.

Possell, Rayn. "Margery Kempe: An Exemplar of Late Medieval Piety." *Catholic Historical Review* 89 (2003): 1–29.

Postles, David and Joel T. Rosenthal, ed. *Studies in the Personal Name in Later Medieval England and Wales*. Kalamazoo, MI: Medieval Institute Publications, Western Michigan University, 2006.

Powell, Sue. "The Transmission and Circulation of the *Lay Folks Catechism*." In *Late Medieval Religious Texts and Their Transmission: Essays in Honour of A. I. Doyle*. Ed. A. J. Minnis. Woodbridge: D. S. Brewer, 1994. Pp. 67–84.

Power, Eileen. "Introduction" to C. C. Swinton Bland. *The Miracles of the Blessed Virgin Mary by Johannes Herolt*. London: Routledge, 1928.

Powicke, F. Maurice. *The Reformation in England*. Oxford: Oxford University Press, 1941.

Pritchard, Gillian. "Religion and the Paston Family." In *Daily Life in the Late Middle Ages*. Ed. Richard H. Britnell. Stroud: Sutton, 1998. Pp. 65–82.

Raine, James, ed. *Testamenta Eboracensia: A Selection of Wills from the Registry at York, vol. iv*. Surtees Society, 53 (1869).

Rawcliffe, Carole. *The Hospitals of Medieval Norwich*. Norwich: University of East Anglia, 1995.

———. *Medicine for the Soul: The Life, Death, and Resurrection of an English Medieval Hospital: St. Giles's Norwich, c. 1249–1550*. Stroud: Sutton, 1999.

———. "Curing Bodies and Healing Souls: Pilgrimage and the Sick in Medieval East Anglia." In *Pilgrimage and the English Experience from Becket to Bunyon*. Ed. Colin Morris and Peter Roberts. Cambridge: Cambridge University Press, 2002. Pp. 108–40.

———. "Pilgrimage and the Sick in Medieval East Anglia." (See) Harper-Bill. *Walsingham*. Pp. 39–61.

Rawcliffe, Carole and Richard Wilson, ed. *Medieval Norwich*. London: Hambledon, 2004.

Reames, Sherry L. *The Legenda Aurea: A Reexamination of Its Paradoxical History*. Madison, WI: University of Wisconsin Press, 1985.

Redstone, V. and Marian Dale, ed. *The Household Book of Alice de Byrene*. Suffolk Institute of Archaeology and Natural History, 1932.

Reinburg, Virginia. "Hearing Lay People's Prayers." In *Culture and Identity in Early Modern Europe, 1500–1800: Essays in Honor of Natalie Zeman Davis*. Ed. Barbara B. Diefendorf and Carla Hesse. Ann Arbor, MI: University of Michigan Press, 1993. Pp. 19–39.

Richards, Mary. "Some Fifteenth Century Calendars for Rochester Diocese." *Archaeologia Cantiana* 102 (1985): 71–85.

Richmond, Colin F. "Religion and the Fifteenth Century English Gentleman." In *The Church, Politics, and Patronage*. Ed. R. B. Dobson. Gloucester: Alan Sutton, 1984. Pp. 198–208.

———. *The Paston Family in the Fifteenth Century: The First Phase*. Cambridge: Cambridge University Press, 1990.

————. "The English Gentry and Religion, c. 1500." In *Religion, Belief, and Ecclesiastical Careers*. Ed. Christopher Harper-Bill. Woodbridge: Boydell, 1991. Pp. 121–50.

————. "Religion." In *Fifteenth Century Attitudes: Perceptions of Society in Late Medieval England*. Ed. Rosemary Horrox. Cambridge: Cambridge University Press,1994. Pp. 183–201.

————. *The Paston Family in the Fifteenth Century: Fastolf's Will*. Cambridge: Cambridge University Press, 1996.

————. *The Paston Family in the Fifteenth Century: Endings*. Manchester: Manchester University Press, 2000.

————. "William Paston I." *ODNB*.

————. "Elizabeth Clere: Friend of the Pastons." In *Medieval Women: Texts and Contexts in Late Medieval Britain: Essays for Felicity Riddy*. Ed. Jocelyn Wogan-Brown. Turnhout: Brepols, 2000. Pp. 251–73.

Richmond, Colin F. and Roger Virgoe. "The Paston Family." *ODNB*.

Riddy, Felicity. "Women Talking abut the Things of God: A Late Medieval Sub-Cult." In *Women and Literature*. Ed. Carol Meale. Pp. 104–27.

————. "Mother Knows Best: Reading Social Change in a Courtesy Text." *Speculum* 71 (1996): 66–86.

Rivard, Derek A. *Blessing the World: Ritual and Lay Piety in Medieval Religion*. Washington, DC: Catholic University of America Press, 2009.

Robbins, Edgar C. *William Paston, Founder of the Paston Family, 1378–1444*. Norwich: Jarrod and Sons Ltd, 1932.

Rose, Martial and Julie Hedgecoe. *Stories in Stone: Medieval Roof Carvings of Norwich*. (London: Herbert Press, 1997).

Rosenthal, Joel T. *The Purchase of Paradise*. London: Routledge & Kegan Paul, 1972.

————. "Aristocratic Cultural Patronage and Book Bequests, 1350–1500." *Bulletin of the John Rylands University Library* 68 (1982): 599–611.

————. *Patriarchy and Families of Privilege in Fifteenth Century England*. Philadelphia, PA: University of Pennsylvania Press, 1991.

————. "Local Girls Do It Better." In *Traditions and Transformation in Late Medieval England*. Ed. Douglas Biggs, Sharon Michalove, and A. Compton Reeves. Leiden: Brill, 2002. Pp. 1–20.

————. *Telling Tales: Sources and Narration in Late Medieval England*. University Park, PA: Pennsylvania State University Press, 2003.

————. *Late Medieval England (1377–1485): A Bibliography of Historical Scholarship, 1900–1999*. Kalamazoo, MI: Medieval Institute Publications, Western Michigan University, 2003.

————. "The Paston Letters." In *Oxford Encyclopedia of British Literature*. Ed. David S. Kastan. Oxford: Oxford University Press: 2006. Vol. IV. Pp. 184–87.

————. "Margaret Paston: Matriarch of the Paston Family." Dereham, Nofolk: Larks Press, 2009.

Ross, Charles. *Richard III*. 2nd ed., New Haven, CT: Yale University Press, 1999.

Rubin, Miri. *Mother of God: A History of the Virgin Mary.* New Haven, CT: Yale University Press, 2009.

Russell, Josiah Cox. "The Canonization of Opposition to the Kings in Angevin England." In *Haskins Anniversary Essays.* Boston, MA: Houghton Mifflin Publishing Co., 1929. Pp. 279–90.

Saenger, Paul. "Books of Hours and the Reading Habits of the Later Middle Ages." In *The Culture of Print: Power and the Uses of Print in Early Modern Europe.* Ed. Roger Chartier. Cambridge: Polity Press, 1989. Pp. 141–73.

Sage, Lorna. *Cambridge Guide to Women's Writing in English.* Cambridge: Cambridge University Press, 1999.

Salih, Sarah. "Margaret Paston." In *Cambridge Guide to Women's Writing.* Ed. Lorna Sage. Cambridge: Cambridge University Press. Pp. 529–30.

———. *Versions of Virginity in Late Medieval England.* Woodbridge: D. S. Brewer, 2001.

Salmon, John. "St. Christopher in English Medieval Art and Life." *JBAA,* n.s. 41 (1936): 76–115.

Sandler, Lucy Freeman. "The Chantry of Roger of Waltham in Old St Paul's Cathedral." In *The Medieval Cathedral.* Ed. Janet Backhouse. Pp. 168–90.

Sargent, Steven D. "Saints' Cults and Naming Patterns." *Catholic Historical Review* 76 (1990): 673–96.

Saul, Nigel. "The Religious Sympathies of the Gentry in Gloucestershire, 1200–1500." *Transactions of the Bristol and Gloucestershire Archaeological Society* 98 (1980): 99–112.

———. *Knights and Esquires: The Gloucestershire Gentry in the Fourteenth Century.* Oxford: Clarendon Press, 1981.

———. *Death, Art, and Memory in Medieval England: The Cobham Family and Their Monuments, 1300–1500.* Oxford: Oxford University Press, 2001.

Saunders, O. F. *A History of English Art in the Middle Ages.* Oxford, Clarendon Press, 1932.

Sayer, M. J. *Guidebook to Sparham Parish Church.* Sparham, Norfolk, 1976.

Scahill, J. *Middle English Saints' Legends: Annotated Bibliography of Old and Middle English, vii.* Woodbridge: D. S. Brewer, 2005.

Scarisbrick, J. J. *The Reformation and the English People.* Oxford: Blackwell, 1982.

Schluster, Paul and June Schluster, ed. *An Encyclopedia of British Women Writers.* Revised and Expanded: Rutgers, NJ: Rutgers University Press, 1988.

Schofield, Cora. *The Life and Reign of Edward the Fourth.* 2 vols. London: Longmans Green & Co., 1923.

Searle, John R. *Speech Acts: An Essay in the Philosophy of Language.* Cambridge: Cambridge University Press, 1969.

Sekula, Veronica. "Religious Politics and the Cloister Bosses of Norwich Cathedral." *JBAA* 159 (2006): 284–306.

Serjeantson, Mary, ed. *Legendys of Hooly Wummen,* E.E.T.S., os 206 (Oxford, 1938).

Shreeve, Dorothy and Lyn Stilgoe. *The Round Tower Churches of Norfolk.* Norwich: Canterbury Press, 2001.

Simmons, Thomas F., ed. *Lay Folks Mass Book.* EETS, o.s. 71 (1879).

Skeel, Caroline A. J. "Medieval Wills." *History* 10 (1926): 300–310.

Smith, H. Maynard. *Pre-Reformation England.* London: Macmillan, 1938.

Smith, Kathryn A. *Art, Identity and Devotion in Fourteenth Century England: Three Women and their Books of Hours.* London and Toronto, for the British Library, 2003.

Smith, Sidonie. *A Poetics of Women's Autobiography, Marginality, and the Fictions of Self-Representation.* Bloomington, IN: Indiana University Press, 1987.

Smith-Bannister, Scott. *Names and Naming Patterns in England, 1538–1700.* Oxford: Oxford University Press, 1997.

Squirrel, H. S. "The Seven Sacrament Fonts of Norfolk." *NA* 25 (1935): 83–94.

Staley, Lynn. *Margery Kempe's Dissenting Fictions.* University Park, PA: Pennsylvania State University Press, 1994.

Steer, Francis. "A Medieval Household: The Urswick Inventory." *Essex Review* 63 (1956): 4–20.

Sterry, Jack. *Round Tower Church: Hidden Treasures of North Norfolk.* Norwich: Crown, 2003.

Stöber, Karen. *Late Medieval Monasteries and Their Patrons: England and Wales, c. 1300–1540.* Woodbridge: Boydell, 2007.

Stoker, Davis. "Innumerable Letters of Good consequence in History: The Discovery and First Publication of the Paston Letters." *The Library,* 6th series, 17 (1995): 107–55.

Stokes, Charity Scott. *Women's Books of Hours in Medieval England: Selected Texts.* Cambridge: D. S. Brewer, 2006.

Stratford, Jenny. *The Bedford Inventories: The Worldly Goods of John, Duke of Bedford, Regent of France (1389–1435).* London: Society of Antiquaries, 1993.

Sutton, Anne F. "Caxton, the Cult of St Winifred, and Shrewsbury." In *The Fifteenth Century, V: Of Mice and Men: Image, Belief, and Regulation in Late Medieval England.* Ed. Linda Clark. Woodbridge: Boydell, 2005. Pp. 109–26.

Sutton, Anne F. and Livia Visser-Fuchs, with Peter Hammond. *The Reburial of Richard, Duke of York, 21–30 July, 1476.* London: Richard III Society (1996).

Sutton, Anne F. and Livia Visser-Fuchs. *Richard II's Books: Ideals and Reality in the Life and Library of a Medieval Prince.* Stroud: Sutton, 1997.

Sutton, Anne F. with Livia Visser-Fuchs and R. A. Griffiths, ed. *The Royal Funerals of the House of York at Windsor.* London: Richard III Society, 2005.

Swabey, ffiona. *Medieval Gentlewoman: Life in a Widow's Household in the Later Middle Ages.* New York: Routledge, 1999.

Swanson, Robert N. *Church and Society in Late Medieval England.* Oxford: Blackwell, 1989.

———. *Religion and Devotion in Europe, c. 1215–c. 1515.* Cambridge: Cambridge University Press, 1995.

———. "Indulgences at Norwich Cathedral Priory in the Later Middle Ages: Popular Piety in the Balance Sheet." *Historical Research* 76 (2003): 18–29.

Tanner, Norman P., ed. *Heresy Trials in the Diocese of Norwich, 1428–31.* Camden Society, 4th series, 20 (1977).

———. *The Church in Late Medieval Norwich, 1370–1532.* Toronto: Pontifical Institute of Medieval Studies, 1984.

Tanner, Norman P., ed. "The Reformation and Regionalism: Further Reflections on the Church in Late Medieval Norwich." In *Towns and Townspeople in the Fifteenth Century*. Ed. John A. F. Thomson. Gloucester: Sutton, 1988. Pp. 129–49.

———. "Religious Practice." In *Medieval Norwich*. Ed. Carole Rawcliffe and Richard Wilson. Pp. 137–55.

Tarvers, Josephine K. "In a Woman's Hand? The Question of a Medieval Woman's Holography Letters." *Postscript: Publications of the Philological Association of the Carolinas* 13 (1998): 89–100.

Taylor, Andrew. "Into his Secret chamber: Reading and Privacy in Late Medieval England." In *The Practice and Representation of Reading in England*. Ed. James Raven, Helen Small, and Naomi Tadman. Cambridge: Cambridge University Press, 1996. Pp. 41–61.

Thiery, Daniel E. "Plowshares and Swords: Clerical Involvement in Acts of Violence and Peacemaking in Late Medieval England, 1400–1536." *Albion* 36/2 (2004): 201–22.

Thomson, David. "Two Lists of Fifteenth Century Feasts in the Diocese of Hereford." *Journal of Ecclesiastical History* 34 (1983): 586–90.

Thomson, John A. F. *Later Lollards*. Oxford: Oxford University Press, 1965.

———. "Piety and Charity in Late Medieval London." *Journal of Ecclesiastical History* 16 (1965): 147–95.

Thurlow, A. G. G. "Church Bells of Norwich." *NA* 28 (1945): 241–84.

Todd, Janet. *British Women Writers: A Critical Reference Guide*. New York: Continuum, 1989.

Tooke, Colin. *Caister: 2000 Years of a Village*. Caister, Norfolk: 2000.

Trevor-Roper, Hugh R. "Up and Down in the Country: The Paston Letters." In *Historical Essays*. New York, Harper, 1957. Pp. 30–34.

Tristram, E. W. *English Wall Painting of the Fourteenth Century*. Ed. Eileen Tristram. London: Routledge & Kegan Paul, 1955.

Truelove, Alison. "Commanding Communication: The Fifteenth Century Letters of the Stonor Women." In *Early Modern Women's Letter Writing*. Ed. James Daybell. Pp. 42–58.

Turner, Dawson. "The Will of Margaret Paston." *NA* 3 (1852): 157–72.

Ure, John. *Pilgrimage: The Great Adventure of the Middle Ages*. London: Constable, 2006.

Vale, Malcolm G. A. *Piety, Charity, and Literacy*. Borthwick Institute of Historical Research, 19. York, 1976.

VCH, London, I., ed. William Page. London: Constable, 1909.

VCH, Norfolk, II., ed. William Page. London: Archibald Constable, 1906.

Virgoe, Roger. *Private Life in the Fifteenth Century: Illustrated Letters of the Paston Family*. London: Macmillan, 1989.

Walker, Simon. "Political Saints in Late Medieval England." In *The McFarlane Legacy: Studies in Late Medieval Politics and Society*. Ed. Richard H. Britnell and Anthony J. Pollard. Stroud: Sutton, 1995. Pp. 77–106.

———. "Between Church and Crown: Master Richard Andrews, King's Clerk." *Speculum* 74 (1999): 956–91.

Walker, Sue Sheridan, ed. *Wife and Widow in Medieval England.* Ann Arbor, MI: University of Michigan Press, 1993.

Wall, James Charles. *Shrines of British Saints.* London: Methuen and Co., 1905.

Walsham, Alexandra. "Jewels for Gentlewomen: Religious Books as Artifacts in Late Medieval and Early Modern England." In *The Church and the Book.* Ed., Robert N. Swanton. Studies in Church History 38 (2004). Pp. 123–42.

Ward, Jennifer. "Fashions in Monastic Endowment: The Foundations of the Clare Family." *Journal of Ecclesiastical History* 32 (1981): 427–51.

———. *English Noblewomen in the Later Middle Ages.* London: Longman, 1992.

Ward, Rachel. "The Chantry Certificates of Norfolk." *NA* (1997): 287–99.

Warner, Marina. *Alone of All Her Sex: Myth and Cult of the Virgin Mary.* New York: Vintage Books, 1976.

Warren, Anne. *Anchorites and their Patrons in Medieval England.* Berkeley, CA: University of California Press, 1985.

Warren, Wilfrid L. *Henry II.* Berkeley, CA and Los Angeles: University of California Press, 1973.

Watkin, Aelred, ed. *Archaeology of Norfolk: Inventory of Church Goods, temp. Edward III.* Norfolk Record Society, xix, parts 1 and 2 (1947).

Watson, Nicholas and Jacqueline Jenkins, ed. *The Writings of Julian of Norwich.* University Park, PA: Pennsylvania State University Press, 2006.

Watt, Diane. "'No Writing for Writing's Sake': The Language of Service and Household Rhetoric in the Letters of the Paston Women." In *Dear Sister.* Ed. Karen Cherewatuk and Ulrike Wiethaus. Pp. 122–38.

———. *The Paston Women: Selected Letters Translated from the Middle English.* Cambridge: D. S. Brewer, 2004.

Wedgwood, Josiah C. *History of Parliament: Vol. II, Biographies.* London: His Majesty's Stationery Office, 1936.

Weever, John. *Ancient Funeral Monuments.* London, 1764: reprinted, Amsterdam: Theatrum Obris Terrarum, 1979.

Weinstein, Donald and Rudolph M. Bell. *Saints and Society: The Two Worlds of Western Christendom, 1000–1700.* Chicago, IL: University of Chicago Press, 1982.

Whittingham, Arthur B. *The Stalls of Norwich Cathedral.* Norwich: Norwich Cathedral Chapter, 1961.

———. "The Erpingham Retable or Reredos in Norwich Cathedral." *NA* 39 (1985): 202–6.

Whittock, Marty. *The Pastons in Medieval Britain.* Oxford: Heinemann, 1993.

Wieck, Roger S. *Time Sanctified: The Book of Hours in Medieval Art and Life,* with Essays by Lawrence R. Poos et al. New York: George Braziller in association with the Walters Art Gallery,1988.

———. *Painted Prayers: The Book of Hours in Medieval and Renaissance Art.* New York: George Braziller in association with the Morgan Library, 1997.

———. William M. Voelkle, and K. Michelle Hearne. Ed. *The Hours of Henry VIII: A Renaissance Masterpiece by Jean Payet.* New York: George Braziller in Association with the Pierpont Morgan Library, 2000.

Williamson, W. W. "Saints on Norfolk Rood-Screens and Pulpits." *NA* 31 (1957), 299–346.

Windeatt, Barry A., trans. *The Book of Margery Kempe*. Harmondsworth: Penguin, 1985.

Winsted, Karen A. *John Capgrave's Fifteenth Century*. Philadelphia, PA: University of Pennsylvania Press, 2007.

Wilson, Janet. "Communities of Dissent: The Secular and Ecclesiastical Communities in Margery Kempe's *Book*." In *Medieval Women in Their Communities*. Ed. Diane Watt. Toronto: University of Toronto Press, 1997. Pp. 155–85.

Wood, Margaret. *The English Medieval House*. London: Phoenix House, 1968.

Wood, Robert. "Poor Widows, c. 1393–1415." In *Medieval London Widows*. Ed. Caroline Barron. Pp. 55–70.

Woodforde, Christopher. *The Medieval Glass of St Peter Mancroft, Norwich*. Norwich: Goose & Son Ltd, 1934.

Woodman, Francis. "The Gothic Campaign." In *Norwich Cathedral*. Ed. Atherton. Pp. 158–96.

Woods, Marjorie C. "Shared Books, Primers, Psalters: Adult Acquisition of Literacy." In *New trends in Feminine Spirituality: The Holy Women of Liège and Their Impact*. Ed. Juliette Dor, Lesley Johnson, and Jocelyn Wogan-Brown. Turnhold: Brepols. Pp. 177–93.

Woolgar, Christopher. *The Great Household in Late Medieval England*. New Haven, CT and London: Yale University Press, 1999.

Worcester, William of. *Itinerary* (Ed. John Harvey). Oxford: Oxford University Press, 1969.

Wormald, Francis. "The Rood of Bromholm." *Journal of the Warburg Institute* 1 (1937): 31–45.

Wylie, James H. *The Reign of Henry the Fifth, Vol. II*. Cambridge: Cambridge University Press, 1919: reprinted, New York: Greenwood, 1968.

Youngs, Deborah. "Cultural Networks." In *Gentry Culture in Late Medieval England*. Ed. Raluca Radulescu and Alison Truelove. Manchester: Manchester University Press, 2005. Pp. 119–33.

———. *Humphrey Newton (1466–1536): An Early Tudor Gentleman*. Woodbridge: Boydell, 2008.

Zacker, Christian K. "Travel and Geographical Writing." In *A Manual of Writings in Middle English, 1050–1500*. Ed. Albert E. Hartung. Connecticut Academy of Arts and Sciences, vi. New Haven, CT, 1986.

Manuscripts

British Library, Add Ch 17253
   Cotton Julius B vii
Norfolk Record Office, Norwich: Wills of the Consistory Court
Bodleian Library, Oxford University: Rawlinson Liturgical MS E 3 (15799)
New York Public Library: Wingfield Book of Hours, Spenser Ms 3

INDEX

Page numbers in **bold** denote figures and tables.